DISCOVER THE HORROR

One Man's 50-Year Quest for Monsters, Maniacs, and the Meaning of it All

JON KITLEY

Kitley's Krypt - Chicago, IL

Copyright © 2019
Cover design by Dave Voigt
Back cover and interior layout by John Pata

No part of this book may be reproduced or transmitted in any form or by any means, electronic or mechanical, including photocopying or recording, or by any information storage and retrieval system, without permission in writing from the publisher.

The views and opinions expressed here are solely that of the author and not necessarily that of the publisher.

Some film titles discussed in this book might not mention the year of their release, and if you're that worried about that sort of thing, just look them up on IMDB!

ISBN-13: 978-0-9911279-1-7

*"And What Good Is a Life
That Leaves Nothing Behind
Not a Thought or a Dream
That Might Echo in Time"*

"What Is Eternal" by Trans-Siberian Orchestra

Dedication

Dawn
None of this would have been possible had it not been for you.
Love you, always and forever.

Nick
I'm more than proud of the man you're becoming
and so glad you are following your dreams.

Contents

Acknowledgements — 11

Foreword — 13

Introduction — 17

Chapter 1 — Growing Up on Horror — 21

Chapter 2 — Finding the Path — 25

Chapter 3 — Frankenstein and Me — 33

Chapter 4 — Becoming a Cinematic Archeologist — 39

Chapter 5 — Sharks Come Cruisin' — 45

Chapter 6 — Working in the Film Business — 49

Chapter 7 — The Bride of Kitley — 57

Chapter 8 — You Can't Serve Two Masters — 61

Chapter 9 — Fango, Weaver, and a Man Called Stone — 67

Chapter 10 — The Birth of the Krypt — 71

Chapter 11 — They Came from the Krypt! — 81

Chapter 12 — New Eyes — 85

Chapter 13 — You Can Never Have Too Many Reference Books — 93

Chapter 14 — The Curse of the Critics — 101

Chapter 15 — What Is Your Favorite? — 107

Chapter 16 — The Drive-In Experience — 137

Chapter 17 — The Day of the Turkey — 145

Chapter 18 — And the Oscar Doesn't Go To... Wait? What? No Shit!?!? — 149

Chapter 19 — Psycho-Babble — 155

Chapter 20 — This is Halloween — 165

Chapter 21 — Science Fiction Isn't Really a Genre — 175

Chapter 22 — Tales from the Road — 179

Chapter 23 — Becoming a Dealer — 215

Chapter 24 — Further Adventures from the Kryptic World Tour — 233

Chapter 25 — Epilogue — 265

Acknowledgements

"The labyrinth is a primordial symbol. It can mean so many things, culturally, depending on where you find it. But the main thing for me is that, unlike a maze, a labyrinth is actually a constant transit... It's about finding, not losing, your way."

Guillermo del Toro

There have been so many people that have guided me through this labyrinth called life, as well as with this book. They have helped me, given me support over the years, and are probably (or at least partially) responsible for keeping me up until the wee hours of the morning talking about movies. Because of these amazing people, I have definitely found my way.

First and foremost, if I had never met Aaron Christensen back in 2005, you probably wouldn't be reading this book right now. To say he's inspired me in so many ways would be the greatest understatement in history. He continually shows me the kind of person I hope to be someday, when I finally decide to grow up. I am deeply honored and privileged to consider him a friend.

My longtime friend Jon Stone introduced me to the cinematic world of Paul Naschy, and it would take an entire other book to explain what his friendship has meant to me. From corresponding and trading VHS tapes all those years ago to those early conventions where we traveled miles and miles to meet our horror heroes, and the many, *many* late-night conversations about movies, life, and everything else… For all this and more, I will be forever thankful. Stone is not only my brother in horror, but one of the greatest friends a person could have.

Special thanks to Ken Johnson. Even though he still thinks *Flash Gordon* is one the greatest movies ever made, this book wouldn't be half as good without his editing skills and the courage to ask me at times just what the hell I was trying to say! I treasure those many hours of talking movies with him over the years, and am forever grateful that he introduced me to Jockomos Pizza!

To John Pata for laying out this book and making it, and me, look so damn good! You're an incredible friend… even if you still spell your first name wrong.

To Dave Voigt, one of the most talented artists I know, for designing the amazing cover of this book.

To Nathan Hanneman and Aaron Crowell and *HorrorHound* magazine for giving me an outlet for my ranting.

To Billy and Vanessa and the whole *Evilspeak* magazine family for letting me continue to sing the praises of Paul Naschy and his work.

To those that continue to inspire me, pushing me even harder just to catch up with them: Scott Bradley, Jason Coffman, Troy Howarth, Dave Kosanke, Leon Marcello, Bryan Martinez, Adam Rockoff, Gavin Schmitt, Tom Sueyres, and Will Wilson.

To my artist friends that have opened my eyes to a whole new world of appreciation through your talented works: Steve Bejma, Matt "Putrid" Carr, Don England, Chris Kuchta, Mark Maddox, Colin Rogers, and Aaron Stockwell.

To the rest of my convention family, you are the reason that I keep coming back to the shows: Bob, Nicole, and Duke (my book cover model!), Gregg and Jill, Mariano and Coralina, Rachel and Rhea, Hoby Abernathy, Ron Adams, Justin Allison, Reggie and Gigi Bannister, John Borowski, Neil Calderone, Dave Canfield, Craig Clark, Barry Crawford, Rafael Diaz, Jerry Downing, Nina England, Rob and Phyllis Floyd, Scott and Lori Ford, Brian Fukala, Damien and Jenn Glonek, Matt Harding, Kevin Hart, Jeff Hartz, Barry Kaufman, Jay Kay, Mike and Mia Kerz, Greg Ketter, Dan Kiggins, Brian Kirst, Ken and Pam Kish, David Kostman, Lori Kuchta, Erik Martin, Monster Mark McConnaughey, Maximillian Meehan, Phil Meenan, Craig Merritt, Ryan Olson, Eric and Linda Ott, Jeff Owens, James Schmeichel, Alan Tromp, Coye Vega, AJ Wagar, Joe Wallace, and Ryan Oestreich and Will Morris of Chicago's Music Box Theatre. I'm sure there are others that I have missed and for that, I am deeply sorry. I'll make up for it in the next one!

Foreword

There is inarguably a dividing line in my fright fan genesis that can be labeled "Before Kitley" and "After Kitley." In August 2005, feeling a renewed interest in the genre, I decided it was time to take myself to a legitimate horror convention, especially since there was a newish one in our own backyard called Flashback Weekend. I donned my favorite Godzilla t-shirt (gifted to me by my supportive and understanding femalien) and made my way out to the suburb of Rosemont, IL.

My initial experience was one of feeling overwhelmed by the immersive atmosphere and enthusiastic crowds. Like many other aficionados who enjoyed their passions in isolation, I was convinced that no other person in the world loved horror movies with the same ardor that I did. Suddenly, I was elbow-to-elbow with like-minded folks, proving that such was not the case. It was equal parts thrilling and alarming as I milled through the aisles, barely daring to get too close to the various dealers for fear of getting snagged in some time-sucking wormhole that would find me spending hours leafing through film posters and video boxes and subsequently missing the rest of the show.

Suddenly, I heard a voice call out, "Hey, where'd you get that shirt?"

I turned to find the owner of this inquiring mind and found it belonged to a tall bald gentleman standing behind a table covered with... horror reference books. Being a child of the '60s and '70s, these tomes had been my gateway to the genre, and I was floored to see not only a few that I recognized from the library shelves of my youth, but dozens of others that I had never heard of before, covering an array of iconic figures and films. As I gaped, his smile grew wider and wider, realizing here was a fellow soul who truly appreciated the treasures before him. Whereas others might have said, "Hey, you've got a lot of books," I instead exclaimed, "Holy crap, that's William Castle's autobiography! And Ed Naha's *Horrors: From Screen to Scream*! You've got the Film Classics Library fotonovel of *Frankenstein*! I used to read that over and over as a kid!"

I stared blankly at him a few seconds longer, feeling like a man lost in the desert who had somehow wandered into a 7-Eleven giving away free Slurpees, and then stuck out my hand. He shook it and said, "Hi. I'm Jon Kitley."

Life ain't been the same since.

Whenever I find myself talking to anyone about my so-called career within this beloved genre, it's impossible not to mention Jon Kitley somewhere along the way. I wouldn't be the fan I am today were it not for him, and it's no exaggeration to say that most of the opportunities that have presented themselves over the past fifteen years have been a direct result of my association with the Keeper of the Krypt.

It was he who helped shape my first Dr. AC book, *HORROR 101*, which opened a lot of doors, and it was he who recommended me to the crew at *HorrorHound* magazine, where I subsequently spent five years cranking out articles, interviews, and film festival coverage, as well as serving as copy editor and hosting a number of Q&A panels at their HorrorHound Weekend conventions.

It was he who introduced me to the perverse joy of watching Turkeys the day after Thanksgiving, the underrated charms of Paul Naschy, and any number of "What do you mean you've never seen _____?" gems. It was he who got me to wear a Halloween costume after a 20-year hiatus – being a professional actor, I had always been able to use the "Hey, I get dressed up as other people every day" excuse with everyone else, but Kitley was adamant that no one walked through his door without making an effort. (Trust me, you want to walk through that door – the culinary wizardry of his wife Dawn and son Nick is expressly next-level.)

It was he who laughed loudest at my efforts to draw a "woolly lamb" during a round of Horror Pictionary (vainly attempting to convey 2006's Kiwi horror/comedy *Black Sheep* to my unfortunate teammate) and it was he who tirelessly worked alongside me, sifting through endless digital frame grabs as we sought the perfect images to enliven the pages of my second book, *Hidden Horror*, for which he also served as publisher, launching the Kitley's Krypt imprint for physical media in the process. It was he who lured me to convention after convention, sometimes working behind his table, sometimes simply keeping it as the center of my weekend-long orbit amidst the freaks and the faithful and the fellow fiends. And it was he who first convinced me to test my mettle at the Music Box Theatre's 24-hour horror marathons, which ultimately led to my co-hosting a couple of them.

In return, I convinced him to join MySpace and Netflix. I think I got the better end of the deal.

Over the past decade and a half, we have been collaborators and confidantes, as well as a gentle spur and critical eye/ear. We have pushed one another to do better, dig deeper, and continue expanding our own knowledge in order to share it with others. Perhaps most importantly, we have been "that guy," the one you can call up any hour of the day or night and, with barely a word of "Hey, how are ya," launch into an hours-long discussion about movies we have seen recently or some convention or film festival from which we have just returned. You know, "that guy" who cares about this stuff as much as you do. Yes, we've had frequent discussions about Real Life Stuff, but we also understand the value of having someone with whom you can take a vacation from Real Life Stuff and dive together into the deep end of the pool. Someone who already knows who Michael Ripper is, who happily ribs you when you mention *The Cabinet of Dr. Caligari* ("Did that come out in 1919 or 1920?"), who rattles off any number of Italian directors as though they were frequently ordered items on a Sicilian menu, and who intimately understands the difference between Baragon and Barugon.

Now, to be fair, I have yet to personally meet anyone who knows as much about the horror genre as Kitley. He's forgotten more than I will ever learn. So when I say we're both in the deep end of the pool, I mean I'm still using my floaties and he's coaching me from the deck because he's already done his 400 laps for the day. Jon reads at least 1-2 reference books a month and has seen all the A, B, C, D, and Z-list flicks multiple times. He lives and breathes horror, with a boundless enthusiasm that never seems to wane. He started his website over twenty years ago, plugging away and providing content out of pure passion, just on the off-chance that someone might stumble across it and find it worthwhile. (This is where my pushing MySpace and later Facebook came in, because I was insistent that his efforts find a wider and appreciative audience. Needless to say, it didn't take long.)

I'll never be able to repay Jon for all he's given, but if there's anything I'm most proud of, it's being the chap who has continually held the mirror up, reassuring him that what he is putting out into the world is valid, useful, necessary, welcomed, and worthwhile. That even if nobody else wanted to read his ramblings (which is obviously NOT the case – hello, Rondo Award), I sure as hell did and he'd better keep cranking them out!

For those of you lucky enough to already know my favorite blood brother and respected mentor, this book provides a fantastic opportunity to become better acquainted and read a few stories you may not have heard before (and/or be reminded of some you'd forgotten). If you're meeting him for the first time, I can assure you that life is about to get very interesting and infinitely rewarding.

Hit the lights, pass the popcorn, and down in front! Here come the previews....

Aaron "Dr. AC" Christensen
Chicago, IL

Introduction

"Welcome to my house. I'm delighted you could come. I'm certain you will find your stay here most illuminating. Think of me as your unseen host, and believe that during your stay here I shall be with you in spirit. May you find the answer that you seek. It is here, I promise you. And now, auf Wiedersehen."

Emeric Belasco, *The Legend of Hell House* (1973)

So, just how does one grow up to be a horror fanatic?

Actually... let me rephrase that, since one definition of the word "fanatic" means "a person with an extreme and uncritical enthusiasm," and I definitely wouldn't call myself uncritical of the horror genre. (I prefer to refer to myself as a student of the genre. I'll explain what I mean by that a little later – for now let's get back to my original question.)

What happens in a person's life that turns them into an individual so obsessed with horror movies that they spend the rest of their life watching them, reading about them, writing about them, and talking about them to any captive audience they can find? Is it one's childhood and upbringing? The social environment in which they grow up? Or maybe just simple genetics? Almost sounds like some scientific experiment, or a bet made between two old rich guys, doesn't it? In reality, there could be a variety of reasons that would require a lifetime's worth of study to even attempt to come close to any sort of conclusion. However, I will attempt to give some insight as to what may have done it for this particular horror fan.

Within these pages, I offer no definitive reasoning that explains my particular taste or fascination with these films. Nor am I trying to give detailed accounts of what I think might have happened in my life that could have led up to why I chose this path. Those answers could be here, but you'll have to see for yourself. Just like in the movies, even the simplest story can be interpreted in many different ways, which I've always considered one of the beauties of film. It is up to the person experiencing it to make their own decisions on what they think really happened and, more importantly, what it means to them. Same goes with this book and my story. While this may sound like a confession, like right before I tell you where the bodies are hidden, it's not. One of my goals with this book is to give a glimpse into the mind of a person who became not just a fan of horror films, but a student of the genre.

Please do not view that last statement as representative of some sort of elitism. Nothing could be further from the truth. Whatever your range of fandom is, that's perfectly fine. It is all about individualism... whatever works for you and however far you wish to take it. This is not a race, but a journey, and one that each of us can take as far as we wish and at our own pace. Some may like to partake every now and then, while others march onward, eagerly making their way down that long and twisting road. We shouldn't question or judge another fan just because they might not be on the same path as you, or as far along as you are. I think a lot of fans these days need to be reminded of that little lesson. In fact, all of us probably do at some point in time.

Now, what do I mean by the term "student" and how is that different from being a fan? I consider a fan someone that likes film in general, or maybe takes a step further by enjoying a particular genre. An enthusiastic observer, shall we say. Sure, you might collect some of the movies and maybe some posters, but that's about it. And, once again, I affirm that if you're content with that level of involvement, that is just fine by me.

Students of the genre, however, take it beyond that point. Not content with just watching the movies, they want to know more about them. More about the production, the actors and crew involved, how and why the film was made, learning and exploring down to the smallest of details. And it doesn't stop there either. We go even further by finding out what other films the director might have made or what other rubber-suited creatures the effects people created. We want to know the film's place within the genre specifically and its place in film history in general. To me, a student of the genre is on a never-ending quest, one where we will always be searching and discovering new things about a film, person, subgenre, etc. One of the best parts about following or *enrolling* upon this path is that you will never come to the point where you are even close to being finished. Yet another reason I just love the genre.

My other goal with this book, particularly the beginning, is to show that as a fan of creature features and monster movies, you are not alone. You may be sitting at home, surrounded by movie memorabilia and monster toys, and feel that you're alone in this world because of your particular taste in films. I'm here to tell you that you're not. When you consider that the second feature film ever made was a horror movie (*Le Manoir du Diable*, 1896), well, let us just say that they've been around for a while. This means so too have the fans. You are not alone in your obsession. There are plenty of us out there, now more than ever. You just need to find your tribe. Seek them out by going to conventions and film festivals and zombie walks... or reach out via the Internet to various message boards and online communities. Make those connections, build those friendships, and share your passions. (It not only justifies what you're doing, but also makes it a lot more fun.)

Lastly, within this book you will read the stories of my experiences, from the places I've visited to the fellow fans and celebrities that I've met, all because of the genre. Some of these kindred spirits I've known for close to 30 years. A few I consider some of my closest friends. Along the way, you will also read a lot of my opinions about these movies and the people that make them. And to make sure you read that correctly… these are my OPINIONS. The only thing I can claim over any other fan is that I've been doing this a very long time. It doesn't mean I know everything or have seen everything. Not even close. Nor does it mean that my opinion about a movie is worth more than someone's who just started watching fright flicks last year. You cannot have a wrong opinion.

To clarify: Yes, you can have an *uninformed* opinion, but not a wrong one. For example, if you have only seen two Italian giallo films and said the subgenre as a whole was boring, then that would be an uninformed opinion. But if you watched one and didn't like that particular film, it is just your personal taste. You can't be wrong with that. Granted, that can change over time, which I'll get into later, but it is still your opinion. So don't let anyone tell you that you are wrong… but be open to other people's thoughts as well.

The reason I bring this up is because I have met some fans over the years that were embarrassed about what they liked, or maybe that they hadn't seen all the Argento and Bava movies and felt intimidated talking with more experienced aficionados. For younger fans, I am envious of you because you still have such sights to witness for the first time. Enjoy those first steps, no matter when you are taking them, and never be afraid of what you have or haven't seen. If you get looked down on by other fans, then they are just too insecure about their own knowledge, and have forgotten what it was like when they started out. Once again, this is not a race, but a journey.

So when you read one of my opinions, or theories, just remember it is my own. You might agree with me, you might not, and that is perfectly okay. If and when you ever see me at a convention, I invite you to come up to me and start a conversation about it. Or drop me a line on Facebook. Let's have that dialogue. That is one of the greatest things about being a horror fan… the community.

But in the meantime… for the next few hundred pages, you're just going to have to listen to me.

So let's get started!

Jon Kitley
April 2019

1

Growing Up on Horror

"Deep into that darkness peering, long I stood there, wondering, fearing, doubting, dreaming dreams no mortal ever dared to dream before."

"The Raven" by Edgar Allan Poe

Like all good stories, let's start at the beginning. I was born in August, 1965, in Philip, South Dakota, the same year that saw the release of classics like Amicus' *Dr. Terror's House of Horrors*, Mario Caiano's *Nightmare Castle*, Mario Bava's *Planet of the Vampires*, and even William Grefe's *Sting of Death*! Pretty good output that year, huh? Granted, it would be over 20 years before I would see or even learn of these fantastic titles. I was the youngest of seven children (apparently there was not a lot to do out there in the Dakotas back then). I once jokingly told my mother that it seems that it took them seven tries to finally get it right. She replied, "No. After you, we gave up."

We moved away from Philip when I was only two years old, so the only images I have in my head of that time are from photos that I've seen, such as me pushing our pet raccoon Mickey around in my sister's baby doll carriage. (Yes, we had a pet raccoon.) Philip wasn't – and still isn't – a big city, so I don't think I missed much. We then moved to Eaton Rapids, Michigan, "The ONLY Eaton Rapids on the Planet," as stated right on the city limits sign at one point. (Pretty impressive, huh? I always thought so too.) Located in the lower part of the state, i.e. the middle of the palm if you're showing someone your right hand, like all good people from Michigan do, Eaton Rapids had a population of about 4,500 people. (As of this writing, they are up to around 5,200.)

Eaton Rapids was one of those stereotypical small towns from the movies, where everyone seemed to know everyone else. And being the youngest of the Kitley clan, by the time I got to school, my siblings had already set the stage for me, for better or for worse. It was the kind of town where the main street that runs through the middle of it is called… you guessed it, Main Street. The name of the elementary school, which was located on King Street, was called… wait for it… King Street School! It was about 30 miles to the nearest "bigger" town, either Jackson or Lansing, where you could find all those luxuries of the big city, like a McDonalds. (Trust me, a trip to Mickey D's was a pretty big deal back then. Oh, how times have changed.)

I had a fairly normal childhood, other than my parents being divorced, though that is somewhat normal these days. My father was overseas in Vietnam, not in the military, but building airports for the U.S. government. So while I remember him not being around, I'm not sure why. He may have been working overseas, or my parents may have already separated, or a combination of the two. I do remember my father being a very handy kind of guy and could build (and had built) just about anything. One summer, he added a small front porch to our house with cement steps going up to the front door. On the first step, he had all seven of us kids put our handprints in the cement. Years later, after we had moved out, I heard that they had torn the house down to make room for a parking lot for the church nearby and the first thought that went through my mind was, "If only I could have saved that front step." I do remember him taking my older brother Bill and me to the Jackson County Fair where I won a stuffed Snoopy doll that I kept for years. There are a few memories of when he would come to town to visit on occasion, but these were very few and far between. He was already re-married to his new wife, Ann, by this time and they would take Bill and me to lunch. I do remember ordering onion rings and pulling the onion out and just eating the fried coating. He wasn't too pleased when I did that. Sadly, there are not too many other memories of him from my childhood.

So, for the most part, I didn't really have a father figure as a young kid. That said, most of my friends that I hung around with didn't seem to spend a lot of time with their fathers either. Fathers seemed to work all the time, so usually weren't around. It never really dawned on me that I was missing something – hard to miss something that wasn't there – and I kept myself occupied like any youngster would.

In 1975, the year I turned 10, my father decided that it would be better that my brother Bill and I live with him and Ann, so they took our mother to court for custody. I'm not sure how long the actual process took, having been pretty much kept in the dark about the whole thing, other than the one day we had to go to court. (Even then we only waited outside the actual courtroom during the session.)

My father's stated reason for starting the custody proceedings was that he believed he could provide a better life for us. Most of my siblings were still living at home with our mother, who was unemployed and living on welfare and child support. I don't remember wanting for much or going to bed hungry. Sure, we didn't have any money, but growing up that way, I didn't know any different. Sometime after my father passed away, Ann told me that it was just too expensive to continue with the child support, and that my father thought it would just be easier to raise my brother and me under his roof. From what my mother had told me, she rarely got any financial support and that he had only gotten custody of us to get back at her for some reason.

When my father won the court decision, most of my siblings turned their back on him and it would be many years before those wounds healed. (He didn't meet his first grandchild for nearly a decade.) While he never let on, I think that deeply affected him. Over the years, there were countless times when my brethren were in trouble and would need some help (meaning money) and they would turn to him. He always would help too, despite the hatred and ill will shown him over the years, even knowing that shortly after that check cleared, it would be radio silence once again. For that alone, I could never hate my father. (Sure, I might not know the whole story, but I know what I know and I saw what I saw.) Even when there were plenty of things that we didn't agree on, I always knew he was doing what he thought was best. Of course, this is something you realize more and more once you become a parent yourself. Thankfully for my dad, he was able to mend those relationships with most of my siblings before he died.

It's really hard, as a kid, or even as an adult, to know what the truth was behind all of this. Whatever the reasons, I don't think it could change my feelings towards my father. While I do suspect that he wasn't entirely honest regarding his true motivations, I don't think he ever intended to hurt his children. I'll never really know.

On August 10th, 1975, nine days before my tenth birthday, my father came to pick up my brother and me to start our new lives in Illinois. After we had loaded the few belongings we were taking into the trunk of the car, we went inside to say goodbye to our mom, who had not come outside the whole time. She was desperately trying not to cry. Seeing her at that moment, trying to hold it together, it made me feel like crying myself. I remember her telling me not to cry, that everything was going to be okay. It's a memory that is etched in my brain like it happened yesterday.

I never did cry that day. As we drove away, leaving the town I grew up in, waving to all our friends that had gathered outside our house to say goodbye, my little nine-year-old brain had learned that crying was bad. That crying was a result of emotional pain caused by loss, sadness, or whatever, and it was bad. This also taught me that having an emotional connection with someone meant that when you had to leave, it was going to hurt.

In that instant, I figured out that the only way to not get hurt when that connection is severed was to not have an emotional connection with anybody.

Now, I'm not trying to say that I changed into a little sociopath, or a mini-Hannibal, but it was the start of having an emotional disconnect from people. The fact that my father and stepmother weren't the most outwardly affectionate people who didn't really hug or "bond" simply confirmed my newfound path of emotional isolation.

The apartment that we first moved into was right across the street from where my dad worked. I went to a new school for 5th grade and really tried hard to make some new friends. It was tough and I had very little success. In Michigan, I was used to knowing everyone at school because I grew up with all of them. This was so different and I didn't know how to handle it. To make things worse, the following summer we moved again to the other side of town, this time into a house. Sure, I got my own room, but I had to start over at a completely new school, with completely new kids, and it was even tougher that year since I didn't fit into any of the traditional *Breakfast Club* categories.

I was like this for many years, and still am, to a point. But thanks to my wife Dawn and the many great connections that I've created over the years, I've slowly come out of that little loner shell that I once made my home. I now have more enduring friendships than I ever thought possible, enough that I consider many of them my "family" and love them like they were my blood. But old habits die hard, and I know that old thought process is still running in my brain somewhere, that it's so much easier to simply flip that emotional switch than dealing with the loss of something, even as simple as a friendship.

I didn't realize it at the time and it took many years of self-analysis to understand that it all stemmed from that moment my mother told me, "Don't cry." (Years later, I found out that she had spent the next few weeks herself crying for days on end.)

I am not a religious person by any means, and I don't really believe in ghosts or messages from the dead, as much as I'd like to. I know that what I'm going to tell you next is going to sound like something from the ending of one of those Lifetime movies, but it honestly happened.

My mother passed away in May of 2016. It was a tough loss, but she had not been doing well her last year and was in a lot of pain. At her funeral, the pastor, who I had never met before, said something during her eulogy that hit me like a ton of bricks. He was speaking about grieving, and how hard it is sometimes for men to show their grief because we're taught to be strong and tough. Then he looked up from his bible and simply said:

"It's okay to cry."

It was as if my mother was sending a message to me, trying to undo something that accidently happened 40 years ago. Sure, I know it was probably just a coincidence, and that this was likely a speech the pastor had given many times over the years. But that day, it sure hit me hard. I still wonder at the odds of that particular phrase being said, at this particular funeral, and I'm grateful for the impact that it had on me.

2

Finding the Path

"It is true, we shall be monsters, cut off from all the world; but on that account we shall be more attached to one another."

The Creature, *Frankenstein; or The Modern Prometheus* by Mary Shelley

All kids go through something traumatic in their lives at some point, some harder than others, and each of them deals with it in very different ways. For me, the horror genre became my escape, my safe place. At first, it was just to get away from people, to leave the real world for 90 minutes at a time. But, over time, I discovered a kinship with the creatures and monsters from these movies because none of us could have that connection with "normal" people. Like them, I felt I was on the outside, never being able to fit in, and often misunderstood. As a result, they became my friends and companions. Ones that would never judge me, and more importantly, ones that would never leave. Even though I hadn't yet become obsessed with horror movies, sitting in front of the TV Saturday afternoons, I started to realize how misunderstood these creatures were... just like me.

At that time in my life, monsters and such hadn't become a big part just yet, but the signs were there. Going to Jackson or Lansing to a movie theater was a rarity, maybe two or three times that I can remember, usually seeing kid movies, like something from Disney. I think in my first ten years, I probably saw maybe five movies on the big screen. Kind of strange looking back on it. Later on, when I had the opportunity to go to the theater on a regular basis, I think it was exactly at the right time for those films to make an impact on me.

While we might not have had a movie theater in town, one thing we did have in Eaton Rapids was TV. I spent many hours of my youth in front of our huge console television watching it. A lot of it. Back then, we only had three TV channels. That's right... three channels. Those were the three big networks, NBC, CBS, and ABC. Actually, it was more like two and a half channels, since ABC was always a bit iffy coming in clear enough to watch some days. This was also the time before remote controls. Wait, let me correct that. We did have remote controls. They were called "little brothers." Since I was the youngest, I was assigned to stand beside the TV as my older brother told me to switch to channel 6… then to 10… then to see what was on channel 8… then back to 6. This could go on for what seemed like hours. I can't even imagine how long I would have been standing there if we had the hundreds of channels that we do now!

Another thing that I didn't have as a child, when it came to my introduction to the horror genre, was a mentor. Over the years, talking to different fans, I always hear stories of how others were introduced to different movies and monsters. It would be a parent, an aunt or uncle, a grandparent, or even a neighbor, someone that would be a guide or companion on their young journey. Honestly, I'm forever envious of that, since I didn't have one. I was on my own, for better or for worse. (Trust me, I made sure that I was that person for my own son… but, let's not jump ahead.)

Cartoons only played on Saturday mornings back then, decades before whole channels were dedicated to them, so kids made it a ritual to get up early on Saturday to sit in front of the TV. It really was a way of life. One of the shows that I loved was called *Groovie Goolies* (1970), an offshoot of *Sabrina the Teenage Witch*, which in itself was a spin-off from *The Archies* (a cartoon version of the famous comic book series). The *Goolies* themselves were cartoon variations of Dracula, Frankenstein, and the Wolfman, now called Drac, Frankie, and Wolfie. While Drac seemed to be closest to the original source, Frankie didn't seem to be too smart, and Wolfie was sort of a surfer dude, riding around on either his skateboard or in his Wolf Mobile, a car that looked like a giant skull. There was also a mummy, a giant hand, witches, skeletons, and a bunch of other monstrous misfits. It was sort of a young adult/monster version of the TV series *Laugh in*, with plenty of silly jokes and bubble-gum rock songs thrown in for good measure. I just loved it. It only ran for about two years, with episodes running multiple times during the same season, but I didn't care. It is still one of those shows that, when watched today, immediately takes me back to that time and always puts a smile on my face.

Of course, you couldn't have grown up in that era and not have been watching *The Munsters* and *The Addams Family* (both 1964-66). Granted by the time I was watching them, they had already ended their initial run and were being played over and over in reruns. Both were staples for any growing monster kid, and I watched them religiously. (I confess I am more in the *Addams Family* camp than *The Munsters*; Herman and Co. just seemed silly, whereas I can still find humor with the Addams to this day.)

One movie I was always on the lookout for was *Mad Monster Party?* (1967) from Rankin & Bass, the geniuses that brought us all those stop-animation

Christmas classics like *Rudolph the Red-Nosed Reindeer* (1964) and *Santa Claus Is Comin' to Town* (1970). *Mad Monster Party?* was a veritable "Who's Who" of the monster world, featuring Dracula, Frankenstein and his Bride, the Wolfman, Dr. Jekyll and Mr. Hyde, the Hunchback, and all the rest of the famous monster gang. There was even Baron Frankenstein, the scientist who was throwing this mad party, voiced by none other than the father of all monsters, Boris Karloff. It was made for kids, so it was cheesy, silly, and a lot of fun. I can still watch it as an adult and instantly become that six-year-old sitting in front of the TV once again.

Growing up in the early '70s was the perfect time for any up-and-coming horror fan, with tons of TV shows and made-for-TV movies with a horror theme. Best (or worst, depending on your tastes), the stories didn't always have a typical Hollywood happy ending. Sometimes the bad guys won!

One of the earliest memories I have of watching a horror-themed program, though not produced especially for kids, was for a new series called *Ghost Story*. Produced by William Castle, it was hosted each week by a man named Winston Essex (played wonderfully by Sebastian Cabot) who lived in a huge mansion called Mansfield House and would introduce a haunting tale each week. These may not have been the scariest of stories, but for a seven-year-old kid, they made quite an impact. The pilot episode for the series, "The New House," aired back in March of 1972; the series began its official run a few months later in September.

"The Dead We Leave Behind" was one of three specific *Ghost Story* episodes that stayed embedded in my psyche over the years. Jason Robards plays a forest ranger with an unhappy wife (Stella Stevens) who just sits and watches TV all day. Bored of living in the middle of nowhere, she is always causing him grief. During one of their many fights, she is accidently killed. In a panic, he buries her body in the floor of his tool shed. When a man turns up looking for her, it is revealed that the stranger was her lover. The ranger kills him as well, and buries him in the tool shed. That night, the TV turns on all by itself and shows what is happening inside the shed, with fingers slowly working their way up from the dirt. (This was a great example of scare tactics, getting under your skin by what they DIDN'T show you.) The image of fingers worming through the soil is something that has stayed in my brain for decades, immediately bringing back those childhood chills that it gave me all those years ago.

"House of Evil" featured a very young Jodie Foster as a child who cannot speak, but who can somehow hear her visiting Grandpa talk to her in her head. There is some bad blood between Grandpa (Melvyn Douglas) and his son in-law whom he blames for the death of his daughter. Grandpa wants to do away with this family and take his granddaughter with him. Under his guidance, the little girl learns how to make little dolls out of cookies, not realizing they are little voodoo effigies of her family! While not as frightening as the Robards story, it still made a lasting impression.

"Dark Vengeance" has Martin Sheen playing a construction worker who finds a suitcase buried at a worksite. He brings it home and finds a little wooden horse that fits perfectly inside, next to a piece of a broken mirror. His wife, played by '70s regular Kim Darby, doesn't seem to like it for some reason. When he tries to put it back into the suitcase... it doesn't fit. Somehow it has gotten larger. As the story plays out, Darby continues to have more and more nightmares about the horse, with the horse getting a little bigger each time and moving around by itself. The way the nightmares are presented and that they focus on a little wooden horse may not make it sound scary. But for me, at that age, it made a big impact.

Unfortunately, *Ghost Story* only lasted one season, whereupon they changed the name to *Circle of Fear* and dropped Cabot as the host. While some of the tales don't hold up too well by today's standards, they still have some sort of magical hold on me. Thankfully, Warner Archives released the complete series on DVD a few years back, so now I can travel back to my horror roots and wallow in childhood fears anytime I want!

Around that same time, *Kolchak: The Night Stalker* (1974-75) was on TV as well and it quickly became one of my favorites. Carl Kolchak (Darren McGavin) was a bumbling newspaper reporter that would stumble upon a strange story every week, involving numerous corpses and some kind of nasty creature. He was regularly in trouble with his boss, threatened by the police, and never, ever getting any credit for what he was doing. Watching him fight a different kind of monster each week – from vampires to ghostly motorcycle riders to swamp creatures – was something I could never get enough of. While the show featured many monsters horror fans expected to see, such as vampires, werewolves, and mummies (often with different, more contemporary spins on them), it also incorporated fantastic new creatures as well. As Kolchak, McGavin never took things too seriously, but always got the job done. Since he was joking around more than being scared, it made it easier for us kids in the audience to breathe a little easier. Plus, even as he was up to his neck in the serious monster stuff, no one would ever believe him. This was something that really resonated with every little kid with an active imagination routinely dismissed by the adults.

Rod Serling's *Night Gallery* (1969-73) provided my first introductions to the works of H.P. Lovecraft and Edgar Allan Poe, though at the time I had no clue who they were. While numerous episodes were more cheeky and fun than scary, every now and then, there would be one that would send the chills down the spine. "Green Fingers" is about an eccentric old lady (played by Elsa Lanchester, who I later learned played the title character from *The*

Bride of Frankenstein!!!) who loves her garden so much that she refuses to sell her house and move, creating conflict with the head of the construction company (Cameron Mitchell) who plans to demolish it to make room for a new building. The old woman claims that *anything* she plants into the ground will grow… and proves it in a cheesy yet chilling way.

At the end of November in 1973, there was a two-night (!) television event that had a profound effect on me. The film was daringly called *Frankenstein: The True Story* (which, when you consider the novel is an entirely fictitious construct… well, there you go). I remember anxiously sitting in front of our giant console television, watching the old-but-new tale of Dr. Frankenstein, who wants to uncover the mysteries of life after witnessing death firsthand. He later meets up with the mysterious Dr. Clerval, who seems to be just the right person to help him unlock those doors. There is one scene where Clerval drops his bag and a bloody severed arm falls halfway out, as if reaching out. This disembodied limb proceeds to figure prominently in two other scenes that I still remember in great detail. While explaining his experiments to the young Frankenstein, Clerval shows off a large tank of water in which floats an arm. When he takes the arm out, it grabs Frankenstein's arm, whereupon Clerval laughs and shouts, "It knows you!" Later, the arm meets its grisly fate after some acid is poured on it; watching it being eaten away onscreen was like nothing I had ever seen before in all of my eight years on this planet!

Another memorable viewing experience was watching the pilot episode for *The World Beyond* (1978), one that, to my knowledge, has never been officially released on VHS, DVD, Blu-ray or any other format, which is a damn shame. Directed by Noel Black and starring Granville Van Dusen, JoBeth Williams, and Barnard Hughes, the story concerns a man who has died briefly in the emergency room but was brought back from death. After that experience, he seems to be drawn to an island from some strange reason, seeing strange visions. On his way there, he meets up with a young woman going to the same island to see her brother. Once they arrive, they find the brother missing and other strange things going on, including a bizarre creature terrorizing the small island: a mud monster (aka golem).

This was one of those types of movie experiences that stays with you forever. Even though I have now seen the movie a few times in my older adult life, I can still remember sitting on the floor watching it with my two nieces. The mud monster terrified them, so much so that they refused to go into their unfinished basement because they were sure the slimy creature was waiting to grab them from just under the stairs when they came down. Even after they had grown up, they would still rush up and down the stairs, with that childhood fear still resonating in their brain! (Of course, I'm sure it didn't help that I would keep reminding them about it.)

Then there was the first time I watched the original 1958 version of *The Blob*. Wait... let me clarify that statement: the first time I watched *parts* of *The Blob*. Not sure why, but anytime the titular terror showed up on screen, I quickly turned the TV off. A few minutes later, when my nerves settled a bit, I would turn it back on. But the second that gooey glob came on screen, off the TV would go. It just scared the crap out of me! The last part I remember seeing that evening was when Steve McQueen goes back to the doctor's office and looks through the window to see the doc getting attacked. That was it for me – the TV never went back on that night. I'm not sure why it bothered me so much, though I think it was the fear of being eaten alive, which really went into overdrive after seeing *Jaws*. (More on that famous shark movie later.)

Sometime around 6th grade, I started to really get into Godzilla and other *kaiju* movies, not that I knew that term at that point. I had watched a few of these when I was younger, but my interests were piqued once again, wanting to see more and more of them. (This kind of all-consuming desire to see the entirety of a franchise or of a director's output was something that grew even stronger as I got older.) Unfortunately, the only way to see these films was to hopefully catch them on some Saturday or Sunday afternoon screening on TV. In the hopes of doing so, I went through the *TV Guide* each week to make notes and plans to discover some new (or old) rare treasures.

What is this "TV Guide" of which I speak? Well, this might be hard for younger audiences to understand, but this was a time before Netflix, YouTube, cable, or even video stores, when there was only regular broadcast television when it came to "home entertainment." If you were lucky, you might have HBO, which added another possibility for finding some rare title. But for the most part, it was the *TV Guide*, a weekly publication that listed what programs were going to be on that week and when. Movie fans young and old would impatiently wait each week, and once it arrived, we would sit down and go through each and every page, searching for a screening of some rare horror movie that we had seen mentioned in one of our books or magazines, or really just anything that looked interesting. (If a movie was deemed a "Thriller," that was usually a good indication it was worth checking out.)

There were also no VCRs (or DVRs) at this time, so if we did find something, and we weren't lucky enough to have it playing sometime during the weekend, we would have to either try and stay up late to see it, or set our alarm clock for the middle of the night. Of course, this had to be done in secret because there was no way our parents would approve of such behavior, especially on a school night, let alone understand our passion for wanting to do this. If we were successful, without getting caught, it was a pleasure unlike any other, one beyond "normal" folks' understanding. Granted, there were times that we ended up falling asleep during the movie anyway, but it never stopped us from trying.

Of course, today, all we need to do is jump on the computer and within minutes we can be watching a movie that we learned about mere moments ago. Just that quick. It boggles the mind to think how far we've come in a few decades, where technology has advanced to the point of giving us instant access to movies that once were thought to be rare, or even lost. The downside to this era of instant gratification is that the thrill of the hunt is now gone. There were titles that we'd search for years just to be able to SEE, let alone actually own a copy. Once we finally did have that chance, the experience was highly memorable, even if the movie wasn't. The fact that you were finally able to watch it was half the excitement! Now, with everything available at one's fingertips, it almost seems like overload. With so many titles coming at you these days, some really good ones can slip through your fingertips and get lost in the vast abyss of available viewing choices.

One final childhood monster memory, one that doesn't involve the boob tube. In my 6th grade art class, one of the projects was for each of us to design our own custom pin-back button that we could wear. We were given a sheet of paper with four circles drawn on them. Our assignment was to draw and color four different designs that we'd like for our button, and then we'd get to choose which one we liked the best. Well, I decided that I would draw four different monsters: Godzilla, Invisible Man, Dracula, and of course, Frankenstein. Well, my art teacher told me that if I could draw these characters over again, he would make buttons of all four of my designs instead of just the one! I guess he liked my monster designs so much that he wanted a set for himself. I really wish I knew where those were today. Not that they were great, but it would be fun to have them as a little artifact from this budding young horror nerd's early days.

So those are a few of the little stepping stones that created a path for me to follow, one I've been traveling ever since. These programs, TV shows, and movies really helped me through my childhood. Sure, it might have been just a way to escape from reality. I know that's how I have always considered it… as an escape. Later on in life, I began to think deeper about that statement. Instead of these programs about monsters being an escape from reality, maybe, like so many other kids, I was trying to create my *own* reality, one where I felt strangely safe amidst the shivers.

with Frankenstein

3

Frankenstein and Me

*"Some people find Jesus. I found Frankenstein.
The reason I'm alive and articulate and semi-sane is monsters."*

Guillermo del Toro

Out of all the monsters from the genre, even with the popular modern-day ones like Freddy Krueger, Jason Voorhees, and Michael Myers, the old classic characters from Universal still are as popular today as they ever were. Maybe it is because for us older fans, characters like the Wolf Man, the Mummy, Dracula, and the rest were the ones we were first introduced to. If you are a younger fan that grew up with Freddy and Jason, you still knew who Frankenstein and the Creature from the Black Lagoon were, even if you hadn't seen the movies yet, because they were already part of the horror culture.

With these original movie monsters, everyone has their favorite. Some like the Invisible Man or the Mummy. Personally, for many different reasons, it is the poor misunderstood creature from James Whale's *Frankenstein* that has always had my allegiance. I always thought his origin, the whole process of how he came into being, was fascinating. What little kid could not help but be entranced by all of that mad science going on? The bubbling jars of mysterious liquids, with smoke oozing from the top. The cracking and popping sounds of electrical currents being generated by large machines covered with gauges and levers, all taking place in some dark and secluded laboratory hidden away from normal society. I know my wanting a chemistry set when I was a kid was inspired, at least in part, by these movies. Granted, we only saw what the filmmakers wanted us to see, their own creative vision, even if that meant completely changing the story and meaning from the original source material, putting their own personal spin on the story.

But what if the original 1931 film's storyline had followed Mary Shelley's novel instead of that of Peggy Webling's and John Balderston's stage play? If the creature was intelligent, well-read, trying to figure why his creator abandoned him at birth, as opposed to being the lumbering child-like being from the film adaptation, would it have made the same kind of impact? Would children have felt as strong of a kinship with the creature? Karloff had always maintained that children were never scared of the monster because they understood the character he was portraying, stating, "Over the years thousands of children wrote, expressing compassion for the great, weird creature who was so abused by its sadistic keeper that it could only respond to violence with violence. Those children saw beyond the makeup and really understood."

More importantly, would it still have been a "famous monster," used over and over again throughout countless films over the years? I know there is no real definitive answer to this, but it is an interesting question to ponder. What exactly is it about this film and character that made its appeal strong, resonating throughout society over all these years? (Needless to say, there are many opinions on this subject.)

No matter what has changed over the two centuries since the original novel was written, something still remained, sewn deep within the context, underneath the scars and pale skin of this incredible tale. The more you explore, watching the movies, reading the original story, learning about all its different interpretations, a bond begins to form. Being a horror fan, you start to understand why we relate to this poor creature. As I got older and learned more about the genre, I discovered quite a bit more about this character, as well as myself.

It all began on that (naturally) dark and stormy night on June 18th, 1816 in Geneva, Switzerland, when the young Mary (18 years old at the time!) created one of the longest lasting and popular characters in the horror genre. A character that is so much more than the lumbering monstrosity the name inherently conjures. Along with her future husband Percy Shelley, their friend and fellow poet Lord Byron, his personal physician John Polidori, and Mary's step-sister Claire Clairmont, the group spent the evening entertaining themselves by reading German ghost stories. As the night carried on, a challenge was put forth: they would each write their own chilling tale. It would take a few days for Mary to give birth to her story, but once it did come to life, like the character in the story, there was no stopping it. *Frankenstein, or The Modern Prometheus* was first published (anonymously) in March of 1818 to little praise or acknowledgement. Before long, however, the story achieved a lasting popularity which has not diminished over 200 years later.

Granted, the story that most film fans are familiar with is not exactly the same story that Shelley wrote, but one that, like the creature itself, has been stitched together from different sources. In fact, the Universal film that we all know and love was based more on the stage play by Peggy Webling, who had adapted the novel in 1927. Her version changed the name of Victor

Frankenstein to Henry, as well as adding the scenes with the young girl drowning and the creature being entranced by the sunlight. Webling's take was later re-written and adapted for the American stage by John Balderston, and it was this version that was thrown around, torn apart, and sewn back together by several different people to finally form the 1931 film version.

But beyond its origin and evolution, what is the story actually about? Over the years, I've read many fascinating theories. There are some that say the story came from Mary Shelley's personal life and loss. The fact that her own mother died a very short time after Mary's birth might lead one to draw a conclusion of her having some abandonment issues, or at least a resulting sense of loss. Then there are the themes of morality. In the movies, we always see and hear mad scientists dabbling in things that are not meant for man. Jeff Goldblum's famous quote as Dr. Malcolm in *Jurassic Park* (1993), "Your scientists were so preoccupied with whether or not they could that they didn't stop to think if they *should*," could be taken right from Shelley's novel, where Victor is solely concerned about creating life and doesn't think about if he should or what comes next. In fact, once he does succeed, he abandons it.

What of Victor's actions? Being taken aback by what he's created, so disgusted by it, he takes off and leaves this newborn to be on its own, not caring what happens to it. Did he not at any point think of this during the long process he went through to achieve such a success?

Maybe the main point of the book is to not let such a deep-seated passion push you forward so far that you don't see what is happening around you, or what might follow. One character from the novel left out of many adaptations is Captain Robert Walton, who is determined to make a name for himself by exploring the North Pole, even at the cost of his crew's lives. Walton is the individual to whom Victor Frankenstein tells his story after he is picked up on the frozen tundra, pursuing his "monstrous" creation. After hearing Victor's story and seeing the creature for himself, Walton realizes that maybe this blind drive isn't worth the cost.

Some speculate that the story voices the desire to replace the need for the female body to reproduce, or maybe showing the consequences of man dabbling in things that they shouldn't (an oldie but a goodie), or even worse, ignoring the results of those actions. Of course, one interpretation often brought up is that it represents the "otherness" of homosexuality, mainly because of director James Whale's own sexuality. I think that is the beauty and the real power of Shelley's tale in that it can be interpreted in so many different ways and still have an impact.

I feel there is a much simpler and broader theory, one that resonated for me in my younger days (and still does today), that encompasses many of these ideas. At its core, the story is about two things. The first is taking responsibility for one's actions. In the novel, Victor creates this new being and then immediately abandons it, leaving it to learn about life on its own. To me, there is no greater tragedy than that. Does that have anything to do with the fact that my parents were divorced when I was very young so that I didn't really have a father figure for the first part of my life? At that point in a young mind, it is very easy to develop that double-sided love/hate relationship with someone that you barely know. You hate them for leaving you like that, but there is still a love for them that you can't explain.

Secondly, I feel that the creature represents someone who is an outsider, one that doesn't fit in with "normal" society. Sure, being gay can fit into this category but so many other differences can as well, such as being of a different race, religion, or something as simple as being a fan of heavy metal music, or even loving horror movies. You don't intend to stand out in a crowd, but you still draw those strange glances from total strangers because of how you look or things you say, with them pre-judging you right there on the spot, without actually knowing anything about you.

The first decade of my life, I grew up in a small town where because I was from a large family, everyone knew who I was. But after moving to a completely new city, I had to start over again, trying to make new friends. This was very difficult. I honestly didn't know where to begin. How could I even relate to these new people? As a result, my own insecurities started to rise. Then, a year later, we moved again to another part of the city and I had to start all over again. Any friends that I had made during that last year were now, for all intents and purposes, gone. That time around, trying to make new friends seemed even harder. Though I did make a few, we were basically a group that didn't fit into the normal groups of a 6th grade class. I liked movies. A lot. But having a strong passion for something like that instead of something more common, like sports, made it so much easier for me to be put on the outside, not fitting in with the rest of the crowd.

I'm sure there are some therapists out there that could read a lot into this, and I'm sure some of it might even be true. At that time in my life, the main thing I knew about Frankenstein's creature was that he was a man-made monster, stomping around villages and wreaking havoc. I did know that he had a bad brain and that's why he did what he did. He just couldn't help it. Deep down, that resonated with me. I felt that he really wasn't the monster that everyone thought he was. There was something hidden deep within that massive frame. Here was this 11-year-old kid that just wanted to be accepted for who he was, and not to be constantly ridiculed and bullied because of his interests. I wasn't like most other kids, and those differences really took their toll on my young mind. Maybe unconsciously I felt a kindred spirit with this other unwanted creature. The more I read and learned about it, the more I picked up on the similarities, which honestly made the bond even stronger.

For years, seeing people at conventions with horror tattoos, I always thought about getting one. I had seen some amazing pieces of work over the years, including a ton of Frankenstein ones. Being that my career as a production scheduler usually required me working in the office, having a horror tattoo that was visible could have potentially caused some issues with my superiors. So it took a very long time. In fact, I was in my early 40s before taking the big step. By this time, tattoos were a lot more common, plus I had stopped caring what people might think anyway. When it came to getting my first one, I went with a very simple and somewhat common design, but something which had a very deep and personal meaning for me. It was just a circle of stitches around my right wrist, a small tribute to the poor creature that I felt such a strong connection with. Finally, I was at peace with who I was and what passions I had incorporated into my life and I was so proud of it! I didn't care if this marking prompted people to stare or think differently of me, or set me apart from society. For once in my life, I was more than okay on the outside. Funny thing was that once I got to this point, it turns out that the outside has gotten pretty crowded these days!

4

Becoming a Cinematic Archeologist

"The process of deviling into the black abyss is to me the keenest form of fascination."

H.P. Lovecraft

Throughout your life, you'll come across many different terms describing a person's fandom. Terms like "movie buff," "sports fanatic," and "foodie" are frequently used these days to describe the extent of a person's passion or their degree of interest in a topic or subject. For movie lovers, these terms can run the gamut, from a casual viewer to the die-hard watcher.

To better understand the different levels or degrees of fandom, let's set up a baseline, a foundation of terms to describe the depths of a person's interest within the genre. These terms could be used for all film genres, but obviously horror is the one I'm focusing on here. Now, don't worry, this isn't about trying to pigeon-hole anybody, saying one level is better than another. This is just a way for us to explore the levels of film fandom from a shared perspective to avoid any confusion or repetition later on. Again, this is just my opinion, so lighten up, Francis.

Your basic "fan" is someone with a casual interest. They might enjoy a horror movie every now and then. Maybe they have even bought a few DVDs or Blu-rays of some of their favorites. They go to a movie theater and enjoy what they watch, but it starts to fade from their memory as they walk back to their car. That's about as far as it goes. It's something they like, but it is not a passion by any means.

A "movie buff" is the type that *really* likes movies. A lot. They know a lot about their favorites, but they tend not to wander too far from camp. The movie buffs that I've run across over the years generally follow newer titles coming from Hollywood, or maybe a mainstream foreign title every now and then. But ask them if they've dug a little deeper into the genre's past... not so much.

Then we have the (dramatic music cue) "fanatic." This type of fan tends to be blindly devoted to a certain subject, such as maybe the *Halloween* films or a certain director, and knows all there is to know about the subject. They also refuse to take any sort of critical look at what they're passionate about, denying any flaws or issues. For example, I enjoy *Van Helsing* (2004) well enough, but I wouldn't try and defend it as high quality entertainment. A reasonable fan, of anything really, is able to take a closer and more critical look at something, even if it something they love. Fans that tend to be fanatical don't always have the ability to do that.

Sounds kind of shallow, I know, but I've run into more than a few fanatics over the years that have that unreasoning passion burning inside of them, burning so hot and fast that they can't stop and really appreciate what they are watching. Luckily, this tends to be a phase and they either move on to something else completely or slow down enough to really start to look a little deeper into the films.

While there is definitely nothing wrong with any of the categories I've mentioned, there is still one left that I use to describe the far end of the fandom spectrum, a "Cinematic Archeologist." Sounds impressive, doesn't it? Let's "dig" into that term a little more, shall we? The dictionary defines archeology as "the scientific study of historic or prehistoric peoples and their cultures by analysis of their artifacts, inscriptions, monuments, and other such remains, especially those that have been excavated." As die-hard movie fans, specifically horror fans, isn't that what we do on a regular basis? We research, explore, and/or seek out titles that we haven't seen before. We are always searching for something new to take us down a darkened path. Even if the film is decades old, if we've never seen it before, then it is as new to us as the latest Michael Bay remake... except probably a lot more entertaining. Even if it is a film we already know, we dig deeper to learn more about it.

Cinematic Archeologists are a special breed. At some point in our lives, cinema really made an impact on us, far more so than your average fan. For some of us, it has literally changed our lives and affected us to our core. A film can sometimes become almost like a religious experience, and probably did at some point early on. Sure, everyone can go see *Raiders of the Lost Ark* and feel the excitement and experience the thrills. To most, it is just a short break from reality that starts to fade away as the credits roll. But for the Cinematic Archeologist, it can actually change who we are. We take away a message, a feeling, inspiration, a connection which could last for days, weeks, or even for the rest of our lives. We want to experience as much about the genre as we can, seeing as many films as we can. We also try to learn as much about the genre as possible. When discussing films, we can give you a good explanation as to why we didn't like a film as much as why we liked another one. Plus, we actually listen to different opinions with an open mind, even if we don't agree with it. (Well, most of the time.)

For me, my path towards being a Cinematic Archeologist started as I was growing up watching TV and movies and really loving the places they took me and the stories they told. In August of 1977, I went to see a new movie in the theater that would have an effect on me like no other had before: *Star Wars*. I know what you're thinking, "This is a horror guy. Why is he talking about *Star Wars*?" Let me explain. While George Lucas showed me a world that I had never seen before and characters that I never could have imagined, he also gave me a story that really hit me at a gut level. That a nobody farm boy could do amazing things and become a true hero. For a 12-year-old kid who felt alone in the world, struggling to find his way, it made me realize even an underdog could still be the hero. But it also showed me how a movie can really make you feel, giving you that sense of incredible wonder, that I think a lot of people lose when they get older.

I went to see *Star Wars* in the theater thirteen times. By today's standards, seeing a movie that many times is nothing, but remember this was in 1977, years before VCRs were around that would allow you to watch your favorites over and over again. There were a couple of times that I paid to go see it and then stayed in the theater for the next screening. So, yeah, you could say this really made an impact with me. I still loved the scary stuff, but this somehow grabbed a hold of something deep inside me and showed me the power of cinema. I can still watch this movie to this day, forty-plus years later, and I still get the same feelings and emotional reaction as I did as that adolescent boy sitting by himself in the movie theater being transported through the stars to a galaxy far, far away.

Star Wars affected a lot of people, so much so that it made them want to be part of the film business. They wanted to learn how to become a director, a screenwriter, or learn how to create the makeup effects for all those different characters like the ones in the Cantina scene. Others wanted to learn how they did all the special effects with the spaceships flying around and blowing up in space. It made people want to get involved, to do something that looked so cool and make a living out of it.

I didn't think about any of those career paths. Instead I decided that I was going to learn as much about this film as possible. And I did just that, buying any books and magazines I could find, absorbing all the information within. My obsession with movies started to flourish: I learned who the actors were underneath the makeup and costumes and inside the droids. I learned not only who the director was, but what they did, as well as other jobs behind the camera. It opened my eyes to not only the film world, but the world of making film.

That fall, I started the seventh grade at Washington Middle School. I only had a couple of friends that I had made the previous year, but my passion for this movie wasn't something that I hid. Honestly, I was amazed nobody else was as impressed as I was about this incredible film. Needless to say, in the late 1970s, being a *Star Wars* fan isn't like what it is today. In fact, being anything different than the pre-selected groups or cliques that had developed, you were pretty much screwed if you were thinking of being accepted. Individuality meant nothing back then, other than getting ridiculed. So getting a reputation for being the "*Star Wars* kid" didn't bode well for a young teenager's self-esteem, which wasn't helping my already lacking social skills. This led this young movie fan further down the path of being anti-social with most people, mainly because they just didn't get it. Or me, for that matter. But I didn't care. The story in *Star Wars* gave me hope. Or should I say... a New Hope?

At this time, I also started collecting anything that I could find on *Star Wars*. Posters, magazines, soundtracks, you name it. If I could afford it, I collected it. My room was entirely covered at one point with posters and pictures from the film. Oh, how I wish I would have kept all of that stuff. I probably could have retired by selling it on eBay!

Even after 40-plus years, I have never lost my love for *Star Wars* or the two sequels that followed. Each one of them made an impact on my life. Watching one of them today can still make me feel like that little kid again, making me tear up each and every time Ben sacrifices his life to help Luke, Leia, and the rest escape from the Death Star, or giving me goose bumps during certain sequences like the final assault at the end of *Return of the Jedi*. That is some serious cinematic power. For a small movie to still have the same impact on a viewer, all these years later. Was it the movie or the person watching it? Or both?

While my love for this trilogy never lessened, in the early '80s I did eventually turn to the dark side, so to speak. That same undying passion for learning as much as I could about the *Star Wars* films continued but with a new path, granted a much more sinister one... the horror genre.

I started learning everything I could about these monster movies that I'd been watching since I was a kid. It started with buying magazines and books, reading through them, learning about movie titles, both old and new that I hoped one day I would be able to see. I wanted to learn about the different actors, the directors, the special effects artists. With each new person I learned about, more titles were added to my "Whoa! I have to see this movie!" list.

That is the real beauty and wonder of being a Cinematic Archeologist, these quests we'd undertake in search of different films. You would be reading a biography about an actor or director where a film is mentioned that sounds really interesting. Then you would set out to find it. These days, it might be as quick as adding it to your Netflix queue or even finding it on YouTube. Back then, it might take several years of searching to finally come across it. The payoff could range from a simple "That's it?" to "Holy Crap... that was Awesome!" No matter the quality of the film itself, the thrill of the hunt could be just as satisfying. At least it was for me. In fact, when I was finally able to see a long-searched-for title, the completion of the "mission" itself usually served as its own reward. If the movie turned out to be enjoyable? Even better! Then you can dig deeper, exploring the making of the film and/or the careers of the actors, writers, director involved, and then seeking out their other projects in turn. See a pattern here?

Here is where this level of film fandom is a little different than the others. Once we've made this discovery, then what? Just like an archeologist that discovers the bones of an unknown creature wants to alert the world of their new find, the same goes for us! While you can be entertained by a film, there is more to be gained if you can pass that joy onto someone else. First, you have to tell them about it. Then, once they watch it, the dialogue begins. What affected you most about it? Did you both like it? If so, you can share your mutual enthusiasm for its merits. If not, why?

While finding another person that was entertained by the same movie could be viewed as a simple act of self-assurance, merely confirming your thoughts about what you liked about it, I've also found that discussing a film with someone who has a different opinion makes me think more about the film, forcing me to articulate exactly what made me enjoy it (or not). Whether it's revealing the personal effect it had on you or just that you liked it when "the guy killed that other guy with a chainsaw," it's the conversation that is the best part. The sharing of different ideas and opinions might make you think about something you may have missed before, and though it still might not change either of your respective opinions, odds are you will both walk away with more ideas in your heads about that particular title. To me, that is always a good thing.

One additional thought: If you are really impressed with a film that you don't see getting the attention you feel it deserves, you need to change that! This could mean writing about it on a blog, posting your thoughts online in a YouTube video, or submitting a review to IMDB or Amazon. This process can also have a snowball effect – if two people hear/read your thoughts and look for this movie, and they both love it and share their thoughts, then the attention for this obscure film grows and grows. Next thing you know, we have a nice fully uncut and re-mastered Blu-ray coming out with interviews with the cast and crew who all talk about how amazed they are that people are still talking about this little film they made decades ago. It can, and does, happen.

I've always felt that learning as much about the genre is a key into discovering and finding these lost gems that are scattered about from the last century of cinema. There are thousands of titles out there that people should be aware of that still haven't gotten a legitimate release. Many of these films are on the verge of being forgotten about forever. No matter how long you've been a fan, those treasures are out there, just waiting to be discovered. Some of them might only have a slight shine to them, while others will blind your senses (and sensibilities) and make you wonder how you could have missed this treasure your whole life.

Same goes with the people involved with these productions, from the actors to the directors to even the guy wearing the rubber monster suit. By doing this research, learning about those involved, we are not only championing the film itself, but also those individuals who put their blood, sweat, and tears into getting it made. I feel it is our job, our duty, to make sure that not only are these films kept alive, but also the memory of the people responsible for their creation. No matter if we're talking about some Hollywood blockbuster or some black-and-white exploitation film made for $10,000, we need to make sure it is there for the next generation of film fans to experience and enjoy.

This is what sets Cinematic Archeologists apart from normal society, or your average movie fans. We recognize the importance of these titles and the need for them to be remembered. Being an avid movie geek is a little more socially acceptable these days, more so than it was forty years ago. Some of these geeks have grown up and become big names in the industry, giving hope to new generations of fans, showing that not only it is okay to be a movie nerd, but someday you might be able to make a living out of it!

Sure, we're still looked at a little strangely by the average sports fan. But then again, most of us don't get drunk at a movie theater and get in a fight with someone because they didn't like the same movie. Yet somehow they say we're the ones not acting like adults. Go figure.

So, as you take on your official title of Cinematic Archeologist, remember to never stop digging and searching for these lost treasures. Then when you do discover one, make sure you do your part to share it with the rest of the world. Or at least your fellow movie buddies.

5

Sharks Come Cruisin'

"Is it true that most people get attacked by sharks in three feet of water about ten feet from the beach?"

Chief Martin Brody (Roy Scheider), *Jaws*

There were only two movies that I remember giving me nightmares. One of them was *The Exorcist* (1973) after seeing it on regular broadcast TV, years before we had HBO or the like. Even edited for television, it still got to me. Every time I closed my eyes, all I could see was Regan's demonic face. But that only lasted one night and I was fine. Watching it now, I still admire how great and effective the movie is, and it can still get under the skin every now and then. As good as that film is, it did not have the same effect as another one.

I mentioned earlier how much *Star Wars* had made an impact on me, but there was a second movie that I saw the same year that also got to me, though in a much different way. That film was *Jaws* (1975). Seeing Steven Spielberg's famous shark movie in the theater changed my life forever. It made an impact on me like no other film I'd ever witnessed before. It terrified me to the core.

I didn't get to see *Jaws* when it first hit theaters in its original release, but I can remember driving by the theater in town and seeing the line of people wrapped around the side of the building. In 1977, when it was re-released, my sister took my neighbor friend and me to the Isle Theater in Aurora to see it. I don't recall knowing what it was about other than a shark attacking people. I must have wanted to see it or I wouldn't have gone – I don't remember being frightened or apprehensive – but I don't think I had a clue what this experience was about to do to me. Once the movie started, however, it didn't take long to realize that I might have just made the biggest mistake in my young life.

As it started, with teenagers partying on the beach, I was doing fine. Even better when the girl took her clothes off and started down towards the water. As she swam farther and farther out, we got the underwater shots.

And then the music started. When she was first jerked underwater, a knot in the pit in my stomach started to form. As goose bumps started to appear on my arms, I started becoming more and more uncomfortable. When she came up to the surface, gasping for air in between the screams, I couldn't move. In the past, if something on TV made me feel uncomfortable, I could just turn it off. But I couldn't do that here; it was as if I was trapped in the water with her. While I made it past that opening sequence, I started to think that seeing this might have been a mistake and I really didn't want to be there, but I knew I couldn't say anything because my next-door neighbor would probably tell everyone that I was too scared. So I had to stay planted in my seat, sinking down more and more, waiting to see what was going to happen next.

Thankfully, there was some humor in the film which helped break the nervousness that I was feeling. Richard Dreyfuss as Matt Hooper was a lot of fun, as well as Quint, played by the incredible Robert Shaw. But anytime the scenes with the shark came up, or even any time in the water when Spielberg wanted you to think the shark might appear, it wasn't funny anymore. A perfect example is the two guys on the dock, using a huge pot roast and a hook to try to catch the shark, using a tire for a bobber. With one of them whining about wanting to go home, it was pretty light hearted... until the tire jerked under the water and the dock they were standing on ripped apart and was pulled out into the ocean. The lump in my throat started to rise as that part of the dock started slowly spinning around, now heading towards the shore... where one of the guys was still swimming back. Of course, the music was pounding again, helping to emphasize the building terror. As the guy on the dock desperately tried to grab his friend's hand, with his legs kicking frantically in the water, I was waiting for the attack. When the guy finally got back on the dock, letting out a huge breath of relief, I was doing the same thing. When his buddy said, "Can we go home now?" I was ready to leave with them!

One of the masterful things that Spielberg did here is create that tension, that suspense. Like Hitchcock's bomb theory, where you let the audience know that something is going to happen, then make them wait while you put the characters onscreen in danger, Spielberg has the beach scenes filled with people having fun and swimming around. The second we see a shot from under the water, we know that bomb has started ticking. I can remember sitting there in the theater so nervous about what was going to happen, what we'd actually see (which is even more terrifying because we don't know at that point), or who was going to be the one. When the Kintner boy gave a quick scream before being dragged down into the depths, blood and bubbles moving towards the surface, hitting the air like a geyser, I was trembling.

The more I look back on that sequence now, I wonder which part was more terrifying: the wait or the actual attack. I'm thinking it was the anticipation, bringing me to the edge of my seat, that delivered the chills.

In the scene where Dreyfuss and Roy Scheider come across the half-sunken boat, Dreyfuss goes underwater to check it out. You know the scene, right? Well, when that head came popping from the hole in the bottom of the boat, all I can remember seeing was the face of my neighbor. The reason his face was all I could remember seeing was because he had done the same thing I had done, turned away from the screen, not wanting to see what had happened or what else might happen! That jump scare did just what it was supposed to do and worked perfectly.

Once Shaw, Dreyfuss, and Scheider are out on the ocean hunting the shark, and you get to see it a lot more, it didn't seem to be as scary, maybe because it wasn't as hidden as it had been before. That didn't mean I wanted to jump in the water, but at least it was visible. But then there was the famous sequence where Quint tells the true-life tale of the *U.S.S. Indianapolis*. Compared to all the attacks in the entire film, nothing scared me more than listening to Quint's story. Even though it was just a story he was recalling, maybe it was the slight emotion in his voice, or the way he told it, but just hearing how the sailors waited for days and days before they were rescued and how the "sharks come cruisin'" dug deep into my psyche. This is a perfect example of how your own mind can come up with something way more terrifying than what you actually could see.

Once the film was over and the shark was dead, I was happy that I survived it. Now I could hold my head up proudly and brag to my fellow school mates in the fall that I had seen *Jaws*. No big deal. But that night, I realized how much this film had terrified me. I had nightmares for two weeks straight, either re-living parts of the movie or reinterpreting the onscreen events into whatever new story my brain could come up with.

I can still remember to this day one nightmare in particular that visited several times in those two weeks:

Remember, this is a dream of a 12-year-old, so logic doesn't play a big part here. I never remember how the dream started other than there was a group of us on a boat in the middle of the ocean. We were stranded and another boat had come up next to us to rescue us. For some strange reason, the other boat couldn't pull up right next to us, but about 10 to 12 feet to the side. Why was it so far away? Because there was a metal grid or type of ladder thing that was going from the top of our boat to the other one. Hanging from this grid was a huge killer shark that had somehow been caught and was hanging there by its tail, flopping back and forth. So... while this giant, ferocious, ravenous child-eating machine was swinging back and forth, we had to jump in the water and swim over to the other boat. For some reason, dreams don't have editors or someone telling them "uh... this doesn't make any sense." I remember being scared as I watched other people jump into the water and swim to the other boat. Then it was my turn. As I stood on the edge of the boat, the very second I started to jump into the water, passing the point of no return, something snapped that was holding the shark and it hit the water the same time I did.

And that is when I would wake up, teeth chattering, shivering so badly that you'd think I was lost somewhere wandering the open tundra of Antarctica. I couldn't go back to sleep because the very second I would close my eyes, I would be right back in that scene and it would again just terrify me to no end. This went on for a couple of weeks before it finally started to lighten up. But the damage was done.

This movie had such an impact on me, that to this day, over forty years later, I have not set foot in any lake, pond, ocean, or anything that wasn't a swimming pool. I've even been to the ocean twice, been right up there to the edge of the water, but would not go any further, not even stepping a toe in there. To this day, *Jaws* is still one of my favorite movies of all time, an incredible piece of cinema that hits all the emotions. I still can't watch it though without getting the same feelings that I did all those years ago. Granted, not to the same degree and no nightmares, but it still has an effect on me. Even to the point that any movie that deals with some sort of fish or underwater creature lurking about and eating people makes me nervous. So films from *Piranha* (1978) to *Open Water* (2003), and the like, all give me a rise in blood pressure.

Even after all these years, recently watching it in the theater on a 4th of July, I found myself hooked once again, being pulled under once again. The sequence leading up to the Kintner boy being attacked gave me that same old knot in the stomach again. Same when right after the two kids with the fake fin get caught and the real shark makes its way towards the pond, it stopped being something as simple as a film production, instead of leaving me wide-eyed, dreading what I already knew was going to happen.

For a film to still have that impact on a viewer, one that has seen it at least a couple dozen times over the last four decades, shows just how effective *Jaws* really is. Even to this day.

6

Working in the Film Business

"To a new world of gods and monsters."

Dr. Pretorious (Ernest Thesiger), *The Bride of Frankenstein*

The summer of 1981. I was going to turn sixteen in August, which meant I could get a job. I'd had paper routes for a few years before then, but this would be a real job. Being that I lived close to West Aurora Plaza, what would now be called a small strip mall, it would be the ideal place to find employment, since it was only a couple of blocks from home and I could just walk to work. There were the usual places, McDonalds, Pizza Hut, a couple of grocery stores, and a few other businesses in the same vein, but working around food really wasn't for me.

At the time, there were five theaters in the Aurora area, as well as two drive-in theaters. In the downtown area of Aurora, there was the Tivoli Theatre, which had opened up in 1928 and could seat over 1,000 patrons! I had seen a few films there in my youth, when I could convince someone to take me there and drop me off. Titles like the 1976 version of *King Kong*, or the great double-feature of a re-released *Jason and the Argonauts* (1963) with *Here Come the Tigers* (1978), a *Bad News Bears* rip-off directed by Sean Cunningham of future *Friday the 13th* fame. When *The Incredible Melting Man* (1977) played there, I desperately wanted to see it, but since it was rated R, my parents would not let me go. A very depressing moment in my life, for sure. (Though, after seeing the movie years later, I wasn't sure if I should still blame them or thank them!) Sadly, the Tivoli closed its doors in 1981, which just happened to be the year I turned sixteen.

Right across the street was the Paramount Theatre, which used to be a movie theater but was converted to a live theater venue at some point. It opened in 1931, and was able to seat 1,885 people! It was restored in 1978 and is considered a historical building in our fine city. Of all of these theaters mentioned in downtown Aurora, the Paramount is the only one still there.

About a block down the street and around the corner from the Tivoli and the Paramount was the Isle Theatre. This was a smaller theater, built in

1938 and seating less than 800 people. I saw a few movies there, including my mind-shattering, life-changing *Jaws* experience. The Isle outlasted the Tivoli, but not by much, closing its doors forever in 1982. (The last few years, it was not a place you wanted to go, for safety's sake.) The entire building was eventually torn down to make way for a Memorial Plaza.

The West Plaza Cinema, located in the West Plaza strip mall that I lived close to, had opened in June of 1970 and was originally just a two-screen theater. I don't recall exactly when, but sometime later in that decade they turned Cinema 1 into two smaller theaters, making Cinema 2 (now Cinema 3) the larger one. This place had already had a huge impact on my life in many ways. I had been a regular attendee for the last six years, seeing a multitude of different movies there, including double-digit viewings of *Star Wars*.

It really was the only place I wanted to work.

About a week after applying, I got the phone call to come in for an interview, where they said I had the job. Being a little excited was an understatement. I was employed as an usher and was informed I needed to wear black dress pants, white dress shirt, and a black tie and they would supply the snappy red jacket that all the ushers wore. My pay for this stellar job was a whopping $2.85 an hour. At that time, minimum wage was $3.35 but for some reason that I never knew, the theater could pay less than that. Maybe it was because of the free movies and popcorn? I know I got my share of both.

My start date was Friday, August 28th, 1981. Opening that weekend was *Body Heat*, starring William Hurt and Kathleen Turner, in the larger Cinema 3, and the two films that had been playing for a while, the Bill Murray comedy *Stripes* and *Eye of the Needle* with Donald Sutherland, were in Cinemas 1 & 2. Yes, I still remember those titles. I guess you can say it was an important day for me. Not only my first day of a real job, but my first real exposure to the movie business, however separated from the actual filmmaking it was.

When I started, there were two managers and one assistant manager. One of the managers, the one that had been with the theater since it opened, only worked a day or two during the week. He seemed like a pretty nice old guy, mainly sitting out in the lobby watching the crowds. Though from what I heard from the girls, he was always keeping an eye on them, especially the front of their shirts. The other manager, the main one, was a crotchety old man who wore suspenders. Rumor has it he started wearing them after his pants fell down one evening as he walked across the lobby. He never seemed to be in a good mood… ever. So making sure you avoided him was one of the keys to the job. We would have bets on how long it would take him to get out of his car and into the theater. Sometimes, this could take up to fifteen to twenty minutes! The assistant manager, the one who hired me, was very laid back and easy to work with. In fact, during the summer months, she spent more time on the roof of the building sunbathing than actually in the theater. Of course, this was only when the other managers weren't there.

Our primary job as ushers was pretty simple, much different than in today's theaters, before anything sophisticated like digital tickets or Fandango. The ushers stood in front of the individual theaters, took the tickets from the patrons as they came in, tore the tickets in half, and gave half the ticket back. The tickets were the ones with a sequential number on them, with each theater having a different color ticket, which told the ushers which theater you should be in, as well as informing management how many tickets were sold. Pretty high-tech stuff, huh?

While the films were playing, we kept ourselves busy by sweeping up the lobby, but another one of our usher duties was changing the five-gallon metal bucket of popcorn oil behind the candy counter which was too heavy for the concession girls to lift. One night during my first few weeks there, I was given this task and when I bent over to grab the bucket, I didn't realize that my tie had flopped down into the oil. In fact, I didn't notice anything until I stood back up and the now-oil-saturated tie slapped back against my stomach with a juicy slurping smack. I looked down and could see the stain slowing spreading out against my white shirt, like I had been shot in the chest, but instead of blood, it was oil. Nice. Thankfully, it was close to the end of the night, so not too many people noticed. One of the hazards of the job and something you learned to never let happen again.

Sometimes, if the theater was busy enough and they were short-handed behind the candy counter, an usher went back there to help out. The last time I was back there ("last time" being the key words here), a very pregnant lady ordered four large drinks. I had all four in my hands, carrying them back to the counter. But I unfortunately misjudged how high the counter was and hit the bottom of the cups on the counter, spilling all four drinks forward, splashing all over the pregnant lady's bulging stomach. No more counter duty for Jon.

Then there was the changing of the marquee sign on Thursday nights for the new movies debuting on Friday. Keep in mind, this was years before any real safety procedures were around – quite frankly, I am still amazed at what was expected of us. The sign for the main theater was not that high, maybe equal to the second story of a building, but it was wide. The ladder we used had two metal hooks on the top to hook over a railing that was at the top of the marquee so the ladder wouldn't fall or move. If you put it directly in the middle of the sign, depending on how long the new movie title was, you wouldn't be able to reach all the letters without climbing down, moving it over, climbing back up, and adding more letters. Unless, of course, you sort of leaned over to the side to reach the end and by leaning I mean basically leaning way off the ladder just barely hanging on. We'd carry the letters for the new title up in a newspaper sack, like the ones carried when you delivered newspapers. If you forgot one or dropped it, your helper would throw them up to you like a Frisbee.

The sign out by the main road, Galena Blvd., was not as wide, but much taller, probably three stories high. Honestly, I'm not sure, but it felt real high. It also had a metal bar across the top where you would catch the ladder's hooks. You could reach the whole sign without having to move which was great. But then you had to move the ladder to the other side of the sign so you could change that. If you only had to change the movie in Cinema 1, which was at the top of the sign, and you had the balls, you could always lean/hang over the top of the sign and change the other side, saving having to walk that heavy ladder to the other side. I always moved it. I wasn't that crazy! In the summer time, it really could be fun. But once it got cold, it became a nightmare and we knew that we were taking chances that we really shouldn't have. It amazes me that no one had ever gotten hurt over the years. Boggles the mind, really, the stuff that I did and witnessed during the years I was there.

But most of my time on duty was spent walking up and down the aisles in the theater or standing in the back, making sure nobody was screwing around, smoking, or carrying on with any other nefarious deeds. It was a sense of pride for an usher to be able to nab a kid trying to sneak into an R-rated movie after buying a ticket for a PG film, or catching people trying to bring in outside food or beverages, especially alcohol. After a while, you got a sense of the ones that were going to cause trouble and kept an eye on them. Today, that would be called profiling. Back then, it was just called doing your job. If you were one of those kids trying to get away with something like that, yeah, we were the assholes that would catch you. Sure, it might have given a slight boost to the ego, but I'm sure that none of us felt that way or abused that power. No sir. No way. Not this guy.

One Saturday afternoon, a group of younger kids walked by the front of the theater, stopped for a bit, then they all walked away except one who came in, bought a ticket, and then quietly went into the theater. The movie didn't start for a little while, so I went into the theater and saw that he had sat down in the very first row. Right. Something was definitely fishy here. So I went into the other theater and went down to the exit by the screen and slowly popped open the door. There were the other kids, standing by the exit door, just waiting to be let in. I went into full "asshole mode" and went back into the other theater and walked down to the front to where he was sitting. I told him that if he tried to let his friends in, he would be kicked out. He said he didn't know what I was talking about. I told him that he needed to sit in the back row, close to the main entrance, where I could keep an eye on him. When he said he could sit anywhere he wanted and I couldn't do that, I told him to read the back of his ticket, because it actually stated that we reserved the right to seat anybody anywhere we wanted. Then this 12-year-old little angel starts cussing at me like he'd been in the Navy for several years, all the while walking out of the theater. Another successful day in the life of an usher.

There were also certain rites of passage that one would go through as a new usher. In the theater lobby were two large chandelier light fixtures, each with what seemed like a thousand light bulbs. One of our jobs was to replace the ones that were burned out. Of course, telling the new usher that he had to get up there and "rotate" the light bulbs, moving each of them to the right until you've switched them all, would have been a cruel joke to play on someone. Good thing we never did that. Or put them on "watering the plastic plants" duty.

As often as possible, however, we'd just stand in the back of the theater and watch the movies. We quickly figured out exactly what time to go in to see certain scenes, usually ones that involved nudity or a nice gore effect. If we knew when a good scare was going to happen, we would go in and watch the audience all jump when it happened. It was amazing to watch the crowds, especially when it was a packed house. If the movie was good enough, they would all react the same way, at the same time, every time. It showed me how effective those filmmakers were in their craft that they could create such an effect. Sure, some of them were just cheap jump scares, but there were other sequences when it drew the audience in so much, that it was deadly quiet in the theater, until the director gave them their release... usually followed by a scream or two and then some muffled laughter.

During my employment at West Plaza Cinema, I was never privy to how things really worked in terms of which movies got booked for our location. The only time we knew something was coming out was when we would be asked to put up a new poster in the "Coming Soon" frames in the lobby. Even then, that didn't mean for sure that it was coming to our theater. However, it was immediately apparent that the management didn't seem to have any issues with playing unrated films. Now, just to give you a little background, movies are rated by the Motion Picture Association of American (MPAA), which is a "voluntary" rating. No film has to have it, but without it certain theaters won't book it because the implications are that any unrated feature is an adult film... meaning porno. There were some horror films that were deemed too gory for an R rating without cutting out the "offensive bits," but the director and/or producer said "fuck it" and decided to release it without submitting it to the MPAA. George Romero's *Dawn of the Dead* (1978) is one that comes to mind. (In fact, *Dawn* actually played at the West Plaza Cinema back when it was released.) Usually this means box office suicide, since some newspapers wouldn't even print ads for them. But that didn't seem to have any effect on what titles we were getting, or management just didn't care.

This worked out great for me because while I worked there, they showed unrated films like *Evil Dead* (completed in 1981 and released wide in 1983), *Re-Animator* (1985), and eventually *Day of the Dead* (1985). These were great times to be a young horror fan and to be working at this theater. We also had the highly edited version of Lucio Fulci's *The Beyond* (1981), then called *Seven Doors of Death*, along with Bruno Mattei's *Night of the Zombies* (1980), *Amityville 3D* (1983), *From Beyond* (1986), and so many more. We even had *Evilspeak* (1981), which was the fully uncut version, with all the bloody pig attacks and head-splitting gore still intact before it was unceremoniously trimmed for its VHS release. Such fond memories. Now if I had only thought about collecting the movie posters back then....

Of course, the other major impact this theater had in my life is that it was where I met my future wife, Dawn. She started there as just another concession/ticket girl and worked her way up to Assistant Manager. We started dating in November of 1983, so there was a point there when she was my boss... and 35+ years later, she still is!

My time in the movie theater business ended sometime around 1985, basically due to the fact that the manager, or the idiot that was holding that position (not my wife, by the way), didn't get along with me too well and decided that we couldn't work together any longer. This guy used to be an usher, a terrible one at that, who I actually tried to train. But when we got new owners and new management, he immediately started kissing their asses and slithered his way up to "student manager" then became a full manager. This showed me at an early age what can happen when you're a kiss-ass. So my illustrious career in the movie business came to an end. Sort of.

West Plaza Cinema went through several changes over the years, with new owners taking over and turning it into a second-run or "dollar theater," showing titles at a discounted price that had already been playing for a while at other theaters. At some point somewhere in the early '90s, they closed down and the building was demolished in 1994. I actually went to the lot during the time they were tearing it down and stole a brick from the rubble. I had it sealed and coated and gave it to my wife for an anniversary present with a little gold plate that had the date we started dating etched on it. People often question why we have a brick on display in our home. I tell them our relationship started with that brick and, one day, when she's finally fed up with me, it will probably end with it as well.

Out of all of the jobs I had in my youth, delivering pizzas, unloading trucks at Sears, or even working security, there was nothing like working at the theater. It was not only a lot of fun, but being around the movies like that was fantastic. Seeing the reactions of the crowds during certain scenes in the movies, whether it was a horror film, action, or comedy, seeing the whole audience erupt with emotions... nothing else like it. I really miss those days.

However, one job that came close was when I got a part-time gig at Y.E.S. Electronics, which was located in the Northgate Shopping mall on Route 31 in the center of Aurora. They were a regular electronics store that was expanding into the ever-growing world of video rentals, which was just starting to explode. I was hired to work in their video rental section. Just like at the theater where I got to see movies for free, now I could take movies home for free. It wasn't long before I was known as the go-to-guy when it came to horror movies. If a customer was looking for one, they would come to me. It was a great way to be able to talk about different movies with other fans of the genre. Granted, none of these people were as fanatical about them as I was, but there was still a common bond. I would often be called upon for recommendations, or help customers remember different actors or directors or movie titles when they couldn't come up with them on their own. Those were good training days for keeping track of all of this trivial information!

Looking back, it seems my years at the theater and video store truly helped cultivate my desire to know more about the horror genre and educate others about it. Watching as many movies as possible, offering suggestions to like-minded fans, making personal connections... these were the early stages of what I would eventually be doing with my website, and all of my writing in general.

Strange how things work out, isn't it?

with Dawn at the Skyline Drive-In 2012

with Dawn, 2011

7

The Bride of Kitley

"Woman... Friend... Wife."

The Creature (Boris Karloff), *The Bride of Frankenstein*

We all hope that we are lucky enough to find someone special with whom to share our life. Just like Dr. Frankenstein's Creature, being different from normal society tends to make that a little more difficult. At least it was for me. During my early years, when I thought about how my life was going to be, I figured my future would be much like that of the Creature: longing for, but never finding that companionship. Oh, how wrong I was.

I was 18 years old and living on my own at the time, working two or three jobs just to make ends meet. Not really sure what my future held, but too young and stupid to even think about it. All I thought about was the right there and now. I had met Dawn while working at the West Plaza Cinema. I don't remember how long it was before we started dating, but I do remember we had our first date on November 22nd, 1983, the date etched on that brick mentioned in the previous chapter. Yes, I remember the date. Sure, it might have been because it was a few days after I saw Black Sabbath in concert, but that is beside the point. We had gotten to know each other from working together at the theater and she was the one that actually asked me out. Five years later, we were married. Little did I know how much she was going to change my life.

Being the wife of a slightly obsessive horror movie fan is not an easy job. Trust me, I know. If you were to ask Dawn that, she would probably laugh and agree, or make some sort of joke about it. But the fact remains that she has been my trusted companion for well over three decades. Over those years she's put up with a lot of my crazy stunts. There was the time I spent the money for our monthly house payment on a shitload of VHS tapes from a video store that was going out of business. She knew these were going to be for resale and that we'd get the money back... eventually. Then there were those strange requests like "Hey, Honey... I need you to make a cake with a large decapitated Turkey head on top." I'm surprised there isn't some sort of a support group for the wives of horror fans, all sitting around in a circle, complaining about the last movie poster their husband just picked up and how much it cost, or what movie they had to sit through the other night.

I have been incredibly lucky to find this person in Dawn. I'll never understand why she has put up with me for so long, and I don't question it. I just wake up each morning thankful that I have someone that loves me enough to let me feed my passion like she does. But it's not like she just puts up with my little hobby. She encourages it! I've known fans that have to either keep their love of the genre hidden or keep it to a minimum. To have a wife that fans the flames of my passion instead of pouring water on it, I consider myself damn lucky.

When we first moved into our house, she told me that I could put whatever posters and memorabilia up in my office, and three posters in our family room, as long as they were in good taste. That was over 20 years now and, like a dark mold, my collection has slowly been creeping out from my office, making its way into the family room, slowly turning it into a horror museum/movie room. Pretty much every spot on the wall has a poster, lobby card, stills, or something from my collection. She even encouraged me to buy a display case for all of my smaller collectibles. Hell, even the bathroom is covered with mini-posters and bloody towels!

At one point, she has commented that this is what defines who we are. Not just me, but us. To me, that is the greatest gift I could ever have in life, a companion that truly understands me, as well as accepts me for who I am. I truly am a lucky man.

When I started having little movie viewing parties, inviting a few friends over, she took it upon herself to feed us. When I decided I wanted to have a birthday party with a drive-in theme, showing a couple of movies outside on our outdoor screen, she made a cake that looked like a drive-in theater! That kind of started a trend for a short time. The following year, the two films I was going to show were *ZAAT* (1971) and *Sting of Death* (1966), both of which feature aquatic monsters from Florida! Dawn decided that she was going to make a cake with these two beasties battling it out, shaping the monsters out of Rice Krispies and fondant, painting them, and posing them on a cake made to look like water. To say it was amazing is the understatement of the century. The fact that this had to be the first time that either of these creatures have been immortalized in cake form was a triumph on its own, but once a photo got online, the responses were even better. Especially when names like Frank Henenlotter, Fred Olen Ray, and even William Grefe, the director of *Sting of Death*, started making comments! Plus, it also proved to Dawn (though she still probably won't admit it) just how talented and artistic she really is. She proved that once again years later when she made the bloody turkey head from *Blood Freak* (1972) sitting on top of a cake for one of our Turkey Day Marathons. (More on those in a bit.) All of this work shows the kind of person Dawn is, willing to go through all this hard work and trouble, just to appease her crazy husband.

When Dawn started joining me at conventions, even though I was thrilled to have her there as my helper, she still felt that she wasn't contributing enough to our little side business. She began exploring ways to showcase her artistic talents, looking into horror or scary-themed material that she could put her spin on for fun and, hopefully, profit. Dawn found her niche making tote bags and pillows and the next thing we know, she had come up with her own business, Horror Slave. Since then, she has gone beyond making just pillows and tote bags, conjuring up baby bibs, neckties, blankets, placemats, and even custom-made bags. I keep telling her how talented she is, even with all the positive comments she gets online from her customers. Maybe one day she'll start to believe it herself!

The reason for this chapter is not to brag or boast that I was lucky enough to find the love of my life. Okay, maybe a little. Had it not been for Dawn, I know I wouldn't be where I am right now, and certainly know that you wouldn't be reading this book. So if you are enjoying this, she should get her own share of praise, for all that she's done and keeps on doing to keep The Krypt carrying on.

with Dario Argento, 1994

with Robert Bloch, 1991

8

You Can't Serve Two Masters

"What's your pleasure, sir?"

Hellraiser

    As it says in the Bible, you cannot serve two masters. Yeah, I know... me quoting the Bible? Never saw that coming, did you? It also doesn't matter if it was referring to God and money as the two masters, the statement does hold some truth behind it. The way I take it is that if you have two passions, and work on both of them, neither will have your full attention. Doesn't mean you can't do both, or more than two, but your time and energy will then be divided amongst them. Pretty profound, huh? Especially when you're reading this book about a guy who loves horror movies? I know there are plenty of people out there that do just that, devoting time to several different interests, and it works for them. I'm just explaining a little further how it relates to me and the path that I took by taking you back to the late '80s.

    Sometime around 1984, being out of high school for a whole year by then, I was working at Sears in the receiving department, where we unloaded all the new merchandise coming into the stores. The trailers coming in looked as if the merchandise was just dumped into it, with stuff all over the place. We'd separate everything onto different skids, one for each of the different departments, and then haul them off to that particular section of the warehouse when a particular skid was full. Not the greatest job in the world, but at least I didn't have to deal with the shoppers out on the floor! In the winter time, it was freezing if you were inside the trailers, but even worse in the summer, where you didn't want to touch the walls of the trailer in fear of getting burned. All this for a whopping $3.25 an hour. Yes, those were the days. But a friend of mine told me about a job working security, where you could basically sit on your butt all day and get paid almost $4 an hour! Plus, it would be a full-time job! I immediately jumped at that chance.

    The job wasn't anything special, and definitely not exciting, since I was assigned to work at a warehouse that housed tractor parts. Of course, as a new hire, I started on the 3rd shift, working 11pm to 7am. My "week" would start on Friday night and go through the weekend to Wednesday. On the Friday and Saturday shifts, the hours were 11pm to 11am. There was only one guard on duty at a time, so other than making your rounds through the plant every two hours, the main goal there was to stay awake. You might think that working by yourself in a huge warehouse, at night, with most of the lights turned off, that your mind could play tricks on you. There were only a couple of times when I scared myself, but not because I thought a zombie or other monster was going to jump out at me. Just not seeing something until the last minute and thinking it was something it wasn't. A slight jump, but no heart attack. The bosses weren't too particular with what you were doing to pass the time, as long as you were awake. So since I was already going overboard on horror movies, I figured why not try reading some horror fiction?

Now let's back up a few years to fill in a little history. All through high school, I probably read a total of two or three books. It was not my favorite pastime. In fact, having to read something for school was always a chore, since if it wasn't something that interested me, it was like pulling teeth. Of course, now I look back on those times and deeply regret all the time I could have spent during those early years diving into some amazing stories. Did all you youngsters out there still in school catch that??? Well... you're reading *this* book, so I guess that's something, right? Sure, we can't change the past, but I think if my teachers would have encouraged me to read something other than what they were demanding, my distaste for it might not have been so strong. Not saying you can't follow their curriculum, especially for certain assignments, but there were plenty of times where they could have been more open, say, for a book report or something. I had plenty of titles that I thought were interesting but were turned down, usually with a stern frown. Reading is reading... if it helps spark that interest or desire, don't pour water on that spark. Hell, pour gasoline on it!

But back to the exciting world of 3rd shift security work. The first book I purchased for this new job was a used paperback copy of Stephen King's *Pet Sematary*, since he was still one of the top horror authors. It had recently come out in the paperback edition, I believe, and figured that would be a good one to start with. I think it took me three days to read it and it scared the crap out of me. I can still remember getting to the chapter when we learn the fate of little Gage, having to quickly back up a few pages because the chapter started so suddenly with the event already taken place, that I thought I maybe had missed something. Because of that novel, I learned right away, especially with King's work, that if a three-year-old boy wasn't safe, then nobody was. What shocked me even more was that just by reading the story could have that much of an effect on me. The part where Louis wakes up in a bed full of mud and leaves after a nightmare gave me chills. This was completely new to me and I loved it. So I started to pick up more of King's work, devouring each new story that unfolded before me.

As I was making my way through King's bibliography, one of the titles I picked up was his 1981 non-fiction title *Danse Macabre*, where he writes about the horror genre, both in film and fiction. For a newer fan such as myself, this was a huge gateway opening up, like a new drug addict given free rein at a pharmacy. King discussed different authors, novels, and short stories that made an impression on him. This prompted me to start a list of authors and books to look for. With names like Shirley Jackson, Richard Matheson, and H.P. Lovecraft among so many others, I started to fill out my newly formed Need-to-Find list of titles and kept it handy every time I went into one of those used paperback stores.

Quick side note... I can't express enough just how envious I am of younger and "newer" fans to the genre, getting to experience H.P. Lovecraft's tales of the Old Ones or reading King's short story "Survivor Type," or reading the opening lines of Shirley Jackson's *The Haunting of Hill House* for the first time. Same goes for the movies too. So never be ashamed of not being as "experienced" as other fans. Just make sure you enjoy the path you're on as you make your way.

Okay... where I was I?

The more I found, the more I read, averaging about two to three books a week, knocking them out as quickly as I bought them. Once I read a book by an author and liked it, I would then look for other titles by them, both old and new. As you can imagine, the number of books in my collection was starting to grow and soon I was forced to buy a second bookcase. Then a third. And so on. As I started this collecting thing, I discovered I was no longer happy with a paperback version, even though they were considerably cheaper. There was just something special about a solid hardcover copy sitting on the bookshelf. This is an early warning sign, my friends, of the dreaded disease *Collector-itis*. It is not fatal, but if left unchecked, it can get very costly. I started buying the hardcover copies of not only the newer books coming out but trying to find the older titles that I liked in that format as well, upgrading from the paperback version. Now, even back in the '80s, this could not only get expensive, but very time-consuming. Remember, this was years before the Internet and places like Half Price Books, so there was a lot of work in seeking out different book dealers, trying to get an idea what a good price would be for something like a hardcover edition of King's *'Salem's Lot*. Lot of living and learning going on then. Some of the editions I see now at places like Half Price Books, selling for pennies compared to what I had paid for them, makes me cringe. But it also makes me jealous of newer fans and how accessible these titles are, just waiting to be added to somebody's library.

During this time, I was discovering so many wonderful and creative authors that were taking me on some dark and twisted journeys, meeting unique and deadly characters in all different forms, from cannibals, vampires, zombies, or some sort of monsters that slid out from the muck and dark crevasses of the authors' minds. Authors like Dean Koontz, Clive Barker, F. Paul Wilson, Skipp & Spector, Robert McCammon, Joe Lansdale, and so many more. It was like a never-ending sea that kept flooding my mind with story after story.

All the time this was going on, I was doing the same thing with horror movies. I was making a list of titles that I wanted to see, once again, getting quite a few of them from King's *Danse Macabre*. I was also picking up any reference books on horror movies that I could find, which made my list of titles that I needed to see grow faster and larger than the Amazing Colossal Man! It was a never-ending treasure hunt that took a lot of time and effort, but was a lot of fun. And in the end, when you finally had a copy of a title that you never thought you'd ever get to see, it was simply glorious, even if the movie didn't live up to the hype that built up in your mind. There was some elusive kind of satisfaction of checking another title off your Need-to-See list, as well as putting another notch in your belt of movie knowledge, waiting to be able to casually tell another monster fan, "Yeah, I've seen that one before."

My collection of movies and books, both non-fiction and fiction, continued to grow, until the fall of 1992, when something happened that changed the path I was on: the birth of my son, Nick. By this time, I had moved on from the security job and was working in a corrugated box plant, so the time spent reading had been cut down drastically, but I still read when I could. It was also around this time that costs of hardcover editions were starting to creep up to the $25 and $30 price range, which was making it harder and harder to keep up with all the different authors that I was following. In other words, it was starting to get expensive. Really expensive. Then along comes Nick. Not only was money in short supply, so was my free time. Instead of sitting on the couch reading, now I was on the floor playing with him, or trying to keep him from getting into trouble. Probably more of the latter.

It was at this point that I had arrived at the crossroads. No, not the kind where legendary bluesman Robert Johnson reportedly sold his soul, but one where I felt I needed to make a decision. As I mentioned in the beginning, the quote says you can't serve two masters. As much as I was passionate about the fiction side of the genre, I was even more passionate about the film side, and I knew that path would be a lot cheaper and would take less time to partake in a 90-minute feature than a 400-or-so page novel. This wasn't an easy choice and wasn't made overnight, but a lot of thought was put into it. Once it was made, there was no looking back. I have to say it was tough to finally let go of that part of my collection, especially when it came to selling 500+ books, some of which were signed editions, most of which I had gotten personally signed. Sure, there are times when I miss those old fiction days. There were so many great literary journeys I'd taken over the years, filling my head with visions that I know I'd never see in any movie, or at least not to the same degree as the written words coming from the twisted mind of the author. But I do know now that it gave me much more time to focus my attention on movies. Not to mention saving me a ton of money.

But I did get rid of them and started down the other path I had chosen. I would now be able to devote all of my attention to the horror film genre. I was on a quest to not only watch as many of these horror films that I could find, but also learn as much about them and the people that made them as possible. Now, almost 30 years later, I'm still on that path.

I am not saying that exploring multiple passions isn't possible. It just wasn't something that I felt I could do, not when the task of learning as much as I could about this huge and never-ending genre was something that I knew I would never finish in my lifetime. But I am bound and determined to do as much as I can in the short time I have on this planet. I will say, since turning down this road, I've never gotten bored with the horror movie genre, or even felt that I needed some time off from it. My passion for it is stronger now than ever before. Because with each step I take down that journey, the more doors open, more excitement awaits, and, of course, more horror!

9

Fango, Weaver, and a Man Called Stone

"Friendship is like peeing on yourself: everyone can see it, but only you get the warm feeling that it brings."

Robert Bloch

While *Famous Monsters of Filmland* was the magazine for monster kids in the '60s and '70s, by the time the 1980s rolled around, fans were reading *Fangoria*. *Fango* was *the* horror movie magazine at the time and remained one of the top mags for decades to come. To celebrate their 100th issue, which came out in March of 1991, they explored the history of horror, having several authors take on a decade or two, reviewing the horror elements from each particular era. Tom Weaver, renowned writer, scholar, and Lord of the Interview, wrote about the '30s and '40s. Now I have a lot of respect for Weaver for what he's done for the genre, interviewing people that most have forgotten about, helping to keep their memories and stories alive and documented. Though, back in the early 1990s, when I was a little bit more arrogant and outspoken (if you can believe that), it was easy to set me off on some tirade if you criticized something or someone that I really admired. Glad things have changed since then.

Anyway, in his article, he made a few unkind comments about Lon Chaney Sr.'s films, ones that felt like sucker punches to me. You see, I was (and still am) a huge fan of Chaney. What this man went through for his craft showed incredible dedication, not to mention the many faces and characters that he created himself doing his own makeup. As a performer, he communicated more about the human condition simply by using his face and body than pages of dialogue could ever do. Yes, he really was that good.

So I responded.

Dear Fangoria -

I have finished reading your 100th issue and enjoyed it quite a bit. However, there were a couple of things I didn't care for. In the article by Tom Weaver, History of Horror: The 1930s & 1940s, he mentioned that "Most of [Lon] Chaney's films were borderline horror (not to mention borderline entertainment) at best." Lon Chaney Sr. was a great actor, dedicated to his trade. The things he put himself through, just for the show, far surpass any of today's actors. I'm not trying to cut down any actors, because there are some great ones out there, but none like Chaney, who took more pride in the film than anything else. Whether or not his films were "boring" or not, Mr. Weaver, just watching the Master at work is entertainment enough!

But wait, there's more. Weaver then refers to Bram Stoker's Dracula as a "crashing bore of a gothic novel." What are you, goofy? Why is it still being printed and adapted into God only knows how many films? Because it's boring? I think not! I wonder if anybody will be reading your writings, Mr. Weaver, after almost 100 years, let alone remembering any of them.

Yeah... full of piss and vinegar, wasn't I? And lo and behold, my letter was actually printed three issues later, in *Fangoria* #103. I always requested that they printed my address with my letters, in hopes of attracting fellow film fans – that maybe thought the same as I did – who would want to correspond back and forth. Once again, you have to remember this was years before the Internet, so communicating with other film fans meant actually corresponding... writing LETTERS. This was how you could connect with other die-hard film fans that, like myself, didn't have too many local friends who were into these movies like I was. Having a passionate conversation about a drill going through someone's head in a Lucio Fulci film with a person I worked with just wasn't going to happen. At that time, I was already corresponding with several people, so adding some more meant all the merrier.

Later that year in November, I received a letter in response to mine. The guy's name was Jon Stone and he lived in Ohio. One of the reasons that he wrote was because we both spelled our first name the same way, but he also understood my frustration and why I was complaining. He had done the same thing before in response to an article in *Gorezone*, one of the spinoff magazines of *Fangoria*. He also seemed to be a big film nut. We seemed to hit it off pretty well and continued to write back and forth.

Around this time, I was also into tape-trading. If you wanted to find a movie that wasn't at your local video store, you had to find someone that either had copies from a TV broadcast, or maybe even a VHS tape that was out of print or just damn hard to find. So you would have a list of your movies that you would send out to other collectors and would trade back and forth. Sure, sometimes the quality wasn't that great, the print might have commercials in there, or weren't the uncut versions, but at this time, that was the only way we *could* get to see them, so we'd take them. Stone and I started to do this, trading two or three movies with each letter. He loved the cult and crazy stuff, especially when it had some outlandish title.

Stone introduced me to so many movies that I hadn't even heard of, but he was *very* familiar with and just loved them. He also loved sharing this love and passion with another film fan. This included the works of a Spanish actor named Paul Naschy. I had heard of the guy before but wasn't familiar with his work. But Stone was. In fact, he was a huge fan. So I asked him to send me one of Naschy's flicks, one that he thought was his best movie. Like any serious (aka obsessive) film fan, he couldn't decide on just one, so he sent me two: *Horror Rises from the Tomb* (1973) and *Night of the Howling Beast* (1975). I popped in *Horror* that night and was just blown away. It featured zombies, a decapitated villain, blood and gore, and a pretty damn original story! I was hooked right away. I was equally amazed by the second feature, which introduced me to Naschy's famous werewolf character, Waldemar Daninsky. Naschy's werewolf was like no other than I had seen, imbuing the character with a physical viciousness that actually made this man-wolf scary as hell. Throw in cannibalistic women in a cave, a sadistic overlord, and skins ripped off the backs of captive females, it made for another highly memorable film. Stone had infected me, just like Daninsky and his lycanthropic curse, with his passion for this Spanish actor's films! And it kept growing from there. The thing about being a passionate film fan is it's not something that you want to keep to yourself. When you find another person that has the same response to these movies as you do, you want to help them discover more and more of them, almost like it is justifying what you are doing. It sounds crazy, but it's true.

After a few years of corresponding and occasionally talking on the phone, I convinced him to come out to a convention that I was attending. Because we had been corresponding for so long, meeting in person was like seeing an old friend. We had such a good time at that show, spending most of the time talking about the movies we loved. Soon, he would not only join me at many other shows, but when I became a dealer myself, he was my helper. He did this for a few years, before getting his *own* table at the shows. Even if the shows weren't that great, we always had a fun time just hanging out and talking about movies. We did shows together for several years, resulting in so many incredible memories and stories, some that put a smile on my face when I think about them still to this day. Sadly though, he stopped setting up at cons and eventually even attending them. We're still in contact with each other, but he is still deeply missed at these get-togethers, not just by me, but several other friends.

Mr. Stone opened my eyes and mind to so many movies over the years that we were trading and corresponding about, becoming great friends along the way. I owe a lot of gratitude to him for helping make me the film lover that I am today. Now, some 25+ years later, even though we don't talk as much or see each other that often, I still consider him to be one of my best and closest friends. All thanks to a few lines in a magazine article that pissed me off.

At a Monster Bash Conference in 2016, I met up with Mr. Weaver, who was gracious enough to sign quite a few of his books that I brought from my library. As he was signing, I related the *Fango* #100 story to him, explaining how – because of something he wrote and my younger, more confrontational attitude – I met someone who ended up becoming a close and personal friend for nearly three decades. He laughed out loud and said that was one of the best stories he's heard and thanked me for sharing it with him. That just made the experience even better.

with Jon Stone, 2016

10

The Birth of the Krypt

"Some men, it seems to me, lose happiness as they grow up. Their entire absorption in their careers and adult responsibilities bring up lines of worry and premature old age. It is not silly or childish to have an interest in hobbies."

Peter Cushing

Kitley's Krypt, my website, blog, or whatever they call it these days, has been running since October of 1998, which means it is probably one of the oldest running horror sites going, possibly *the* oldest in the States. This isn't meant to be a boast or brag; it just means I've been holding the same fort longer than anybody else!

With my love and passion for *Star Wars*, my obsessive compulsiveness really began to show its true colors. Whenever I got into something, I tended to go a wee bit overboard. After the whole *Star Wars* thing, I sold my soul to rock and roll, as the saying goes. In the early '80s, I started listening to heavy metal music, with bands like Iron Maiden, Black Sabbath, Scorpions, and many, many more, which became my next obsession, one that was moving faster than an early Metallica riff (crap... hope I don't get sued for mentioning them) as I tried to find out more and more about the different bands I was getting into. I used the "family tree" method of discovering more bands: I would start with a band I liked, seek out their older albums, learn if a member was in a previous band, and explore those as well. The more I looked, the more I'd find. If I discovered a new band that my friends hadn't heard of, I felt it was my job, my duty, to introduce them to it, hoping that they enjoyed it as much as I did. I think that sharing a strong passion for something with another person, and seeing them enjoy it, is a great feeling, a form of paying it forward. As well as being a confirmation that what you liked really is worthwhile, it is also a way for you to experience that joy of hearing/seeing something again for the first time, watching or hearing another person's expressions and reactions.

When my love of the horror genre finally went into overdrive in the mid '80s, I was desperate to find others that shared my strong convictions.

Of course, this was not as easy as it is today. There was no Internet, and "social media" meant having pen pals! At first, there were not many movie conventions or memorabilia shows around, certainly not in my area, but as the years progressed, I started to attend these gatherings, connecting and corresponding with other like-minded fans from all over the country and the world, loving the fact that I was able to talk fervently about these movies that I loved so much, and have that passion returned, sometimes for days on end. But as cool as this was, I always felt there was something else I could do.

Back in my school days, writing was not a particularly favorite subject of mine. In fact, I hated it. Any written assignment had to be about a subject that the teachers approved, something topical or in the news, which made the whole thing a dreaded chore, reinforcing my hatred. I often wonder what might have happened if the teachers had let me choose a subject that I was interested in, like a band or a movie. Might that have sparked a bit more personal investment in what I was doing? What if the whole point of the assignments had been to get the creative fires started, allowing the students to express themselves on topics they actually cared about, or at least liked? Alas, it never happened with the teachers I had.

As such, I had never considered becoming a writer, not even as a remote possibility. Or should I say, I never thought I was qualified to do it in a public forum. I mean, I had scraped by through school (mainly because I just didn't care to apply myself) and never had any professional training. But... along with all these glossy magazines like *Fangoria* and *Famous Monsters* on newsstands, a bunch of fanzines started popping up, independently created, self-published magazines that people with similar passions were cranking out, spreading their own little soapbox sermons, writing movie reviews, exploring topics within the horror genre. The possibilities of writing as a way of sharing my passions began to fester in my little brain.

I never set out with the goal of becoming a professional writer. I just wanted to write about the movies I loved and the people behind them, passing what I had learned onto others, hoping to infuse this mad passion so that they would join me on the journey. Sure, I might have entertained fantasies of making a living out of writing, having a huge audience. But it really was more about just getting my thoughts and ideas out there for other people to hopefully stumble upon.

Sometime in the early to mid-'90s, I was participating in a sort of communal fanzine/newsletter thing. I honestly don't remember how I got involved exactly, but it was called *Death at Work*. The concept was simple: A group of people would send their "contributions" to one main person, who would then combine them all together and then send them out to everyone. So you would get this stapled-together pile of pages, filled with separate chapters from different members of the group. There was no real unifying concept, so people wrote about whatever they wanted. There were movie reviews, poems, stories, illustrations, and anything else these creative people wanted to share. Even though my involvement didn't last that long (about a year or so), I knew right away that I wanted to start my own version of it.

Since I had several good friends that I'd met over the last few years, from either trading movies or seeing at local memorabilia shows, I had a good pool to draw from. I reached out to a few of them to see if they would be interested in putting together our own little communal newsletter. While I always had illusions of it becoming an actual fanzine, one that we could sell, I figured we'd start out slow.

Visions of Darkness made its debut in the summer of 1995, with contributions from Jon Stone, Eric Ott, Max Meehan, and Mark McConnaughey. It was filled with a wide range of art, reviews, rantings, clip art, ad mats, homemade cartoons, and whatever else these nuts wanted to put in there. (I reviewed *Dark Waters* [1993] and *Accion Mutante* [1993], among others. Years later, I would meet the directors of both films, even interviewing one of them.) The cover was just a bunch of images that I had Xerox-copied from other magazines and puzzled together, and the opening paragraph below explained our reasons behind the project:

"Welcome to our first issue. As most of you probably know, when you're into the horror genre, unless you are lucky enough to have some friends to discuss or talk about different films, it's kind of hard to try and explain your joy and excitement when you saw someone get their head crushed by an elevator in The Fly II *to a person who is looking at you while wondering if you've had your medication today. That is one of the main reasons for starting this. To give us deviants some place to be able to discuss such things, while not being banished to the psych ward. So let your opinions fly!"*

Some things just don't change.

During its three-year run, we had members leave, new ones join, while some just disappeared. In that time we created thirteen different issues, which was something I really enjoyed doing. Putting each issue together, deciding what to put on the cover, and making the intro page with the index highlighting everyone's submissions, I really felt like I was creating our own little magazine, even though there were only a select number of us actually receiving copies. (We never sold or distributed them publicly.)

But near the end, things were changing. It was becoming harder and harder to get people to send in their contributions in a timely manner, and honestly, I was getting tired of it. Some of the members were saying it had lost the personal touch that it originally had. The last thing I wanted was for it to become a chore, you know, WORK. So, after thirteen issues, *Visions of Darkness* slipped away into the shadows forever.

This left a void that I knew I needed to fill. Not just the creative aspect of what we were doing, but the need to communicate my thoughts, opinions, and ramblings on the horror genre out there in the world. I didn't even care if anybody would listen or not, I just needed an outlet, one that I had more control over, where I didn't have to wait on anyone else. This feeling goes back to the different aspects of fandom. I wasn't content with just sitting back and watching the movies. I wanted... no, *needed* to be able to talk about these films.

The year was now 1998 and this "Internet" thing had been slowly taking off, with different websites popping up all over the place. Any average Joe could actually create their own website, giving them their own little soapbox to preach whatever they wanted for the whole world to see. Hmmmm. Granted, I didn't really have a format figured out, didn't know what the content was going to be, and knew nothing about how to even start. But that didn't stop me from jumping in head first.

Around this time, a good friend of mine, Tom Sueyres (aka Tom Simmons), a dealer in rare and obscure video titles, was running his own website and magazine titled *Video Junkie*. (With fellow cinephile William Wilson eventually joining the ranks after a brief hiatus, *Video Junkie* is alive and well, delivering incredible knowledge and insight as well as some damn funny ramblings.) Tom was essential in helping me bring the Krypt into the online world. Over the first few weeks, there was many a phone call that started with, "Hey Tom... uh... how do I do this?" which was then followed a short time later with "Hey, Tom... uh... how do I do that again?" Tom was always there to help, as well as point out little mistakes I had made. That would usually mean a phone call in the morning (okay, more like early afternoon, since mornings and Tom went together like Kane Hodder and a *Freddy vs. Jason* reunion) with the time-honored statement, "You worked on this update late last night, didn't you?" This meant that I hadn't been proof-reading what I was writing before posting – there would be sentences that would just stop in the middle and others that made no sense whatsoever. This is what happens when you try and be "creative" without a lot of sleep; a habit that has taken me about 15 years to break (though I still bend it from time to time).

Tom was also there to give me guidance as to the content I was creating and posting, holding me to a higher standard. One of the best pieces of advice that he gave me dealt with doing "what was right instead what would be popular." When I would run a thought or an idea by him, his response would be "Would you want to read about that? Would it get your attention to stop and read it?" He really showed me that by following your own heart and passion, you can be much truer to yourself and know that you won't be in fear of copying anybody because it comes right from you. If it wasn't for Tom, I'm not sure if the door to the Krypt ever would have been opened.

In October of 1998, to the sounds of the concrete slab grinding open, Kitley's Krypt came to life.

I used Microsoft Front Page 1998 to build the site, made things simple; nothing too fancy. I always felt that the content should be the real draw, not the bells and whistles. So while it wasn't anything special in format or design, it was my soapbox and I stood proudly on it. In February of 2015, I moved it over to a WordPress format, mainly because Front Page was no longer compatible with the newer versions of Windows.

Over the years, I have been asked a few times on why I put my name in the site's title. Being a little egotistical, maybe? Sure. Why not. In reality, the reason for that is plain and simple. Everything I was putting on this site was coming from me. Not from some silly fake name or persona that I was going to hide behind or to try and be hip and cool. It came from me, Jon Kitley. I would stand behind whatever I posted on the Krypt. I wasn't going to worry that I might piss off some studio and lose any special privileges, movie set visits, free screenings, or anything else that would sway my decision to post my true feelings on any subject matter. In other words, my integrity wasn't for sale. It's a shame more sites even today don't follow this motto. If my opinion didn't match someone else's, so be it. It doesn't mean I am going to change it, but I am always willing to discuss it further, always willing to hear another side. As the saying goes, being fans of horror movies doesn't mean we have to agree on every single movie.... we just need to agree on the genre.

Another point that I made clear right from the beginning was that there would never be any advertising on the Krypt. I know most sites out there have about as many ads and banners as they do content. Just like I wanted visitors to know that I wasn't personally trying to sell them something, I also wanted them to know that by coming to the Krypt, they weren't going to be bombarded by annoying ads, banners, and all sorts of other nonsense to keep them from the reason they came there in the first place. Besides, I always considered it was bad enough that most of these sites not only had the same content, but that they all looked the same because they all were running the same ad banners! Maybe it's just me, but I've always felt that a little journalistic integrity was more important than a few $$ that could be made from selling ad space. Nothing against those that choose to do it, but it wasn't for me or the Krypt.

In the early years, I had listed merchandise that I sold at conventions, but eventually closed down that part of the site. Even to this day, I still have people ask why the stuff I sell at shows isn't listed on the site. The first reason was because I seemed to be spending more time updating inventories than actually working on the other parts of the site, such as reviews and news updates. But mostly, I wanted everyone coming to the Krypt to know that the only thing I was trying to give them was education (and maybe my opinions every now and then) and that was free. I didn't want anyone thinking that deep down, I was really trying to sell them something. If I was singing the praises of a movie or a book, it was because I really liked it, not because I had copies of it that I was trying to sell. In all of my years of being a dealer at these conventions, I've come across more than a few dealers that were there simply to make money and couldn't care much about what they were selling, as long as they could convince you that you needed to buy it. I wanted to make sure that the Krypt was not like that.

In the beginning stages, most of my updates consisted of DVD release announcements. This was a big part of my content because at the time, there were still plenty of titles that had never come to that format yet, so that was pretty big news for us collectors and fans. Bit by bit, news of those releases were being spaced out by other little tidbits of news happenings, death notices, convention reports, movie marathons and other screenings, as well as my little rants and ramblings. The more time that passed, the more of myself poured into the site, and it slowly started to change.

When the site first started, I had used different tag lines like "Where Horror Dwells," trying to be all professional sounding and shit! But the site's focus and intent started to evolve. It started to be less and less about news and reviews and more about education. There were a lot of sites out there that were posting the latest announcement, plus review after review, which is great, but I still wanted to be something different. I would still post little news stories but it was going to be on items that I thought needed to be talked about and not the same old story that would be on every other one of the bigger sites. Or if it was something everyone was mentioning, I would make it a point to put my own personal take or opinion on it.

Because of my love for the genre, with the history so vast, I always considered myself a student. Still do. With most of the other sites out there, especially the top ones, there was always more of a focus on what was new and what was coming out next, that fans either tend to forget about the past, or never even know about it. Sure, there would be attention to an older movie, but that was usually because it was getting a new special edition DVD or Blu-ray release and not just because the movie is awesome and needs some attention. Because there were just so many titles getting released in whatever format, the market was becoming so flooded, that it was easy for things to be forgotten, even in a matter of weeks. So I wanted to make the site a place where a fan could come and hopefully either learn something about the genre, or maybe just get that itch to dig a little deeper into the bowels of the history. To help push that theory, I came up with "Discover the Horror" and immediately knew I had a winner.

What I really liked about the "Discover" tag line was that it had a double meaning. Sure, at first glance it meant to discover the website, but it really meant to discover the genre itself. With it being one of the oldest film genres around, not to mention one of the most profitable, there are countless titles out there, both old and new, just waiting to be discovered by both younger fans, as well as maybe even some of the older ones. Even being a student of the genre as long as I have been, I still come across older movies that I have never heard about before. So no matter what is coming out that is new, there are always a ton of older titles just waiting for you. All you need to do is just look a little.

Plus, it wasn't just discovering the movies, but also the people behind it. Sure, everyone knows Boris Karloff, Bela Lugosi, Robert Englund, and Kane Hodder. But what about the hundreds and hundreds of other actors, directors, makeup and special effects artists, and cinematographers that all worked in the genre, giving us such entertainment that they need to be remembered as well? Names like George Zucco, Lionel Atwill, Ted V. Mikels, Ray Dennis Steckler, H.G. Lewis, Doug Hobart... the list goes on and on. These are the people that worked their collective asses off, just as hard as big-budgeted filmmakers (sometimes much more), to produce something entertaining for a variety of different reasons. Because of that, we need to keep their memories alive and well so their movies can be passed down to the next generation of horror fans. So starting in July of 2008, I started have a semi-regular posting called "Horror History" to help get their names out to newer fans who might not have heard of them. All the time, hoping that some reader might decide to follow that post one step further and check out one of the films these people had worked on. All you need is for someone to take that first step.

The thing about feeding this beast inside you, whatever your passion might be, whether it is writing, painting, or whatever creative output you have, is to please yourself first rather than others. Yes, there are certain constraints and guidelines one must follow, especially when talking about writing, and especially if you are doing professionally. I mean, it's important to have a point and to be understood. But if it comes from your heart, the rest will follow. As corny as it sounds, be true to your own voice. It is the one thing that is different than the thousands of other writers or artists out there. Everyone can state fact after fact, but it will be your own feelings, your own thoughts, your own life experiences, and observations that will make it different, and uniquely you.

In April of 2006, the Krypt finally got an official logo. I had been trying to come up with one that would really capture the spirit of the site. Enter Joseph Vargo. I had met Joe through a mutual friend at one of the Cinema Wasteland shows, when he was putting out a musical CD from a band called Nox Arcana. It was a collection of gothic and creepy soundscapes, like a soundtrack for a movie... just no movie. Since I've always been a sucker for soundtracks, I was immediately interested and ended up loving it, as well as the multitude of other releases Nox Arcana put out over the years. I got to know Joe quite well from these, and getting to chat with him at the cons, about movies, music, and all things that go bump in the night! Joe was also highly talented artist, creating some amazing gothic imagery. When he learned that I was looking for a logo design, he offered up his services. I gave him an idea of what I was thinking, something that would visually present the whole "discover" part and he said he'd be happy to see what he could come up with. A short time later, he sent me the design and it just blew me away. Sure, while some people tend to think it is an image of Lovecraft's Cthulhu, I still think it is a perfect representation of what the Krypt is about. People recognize the logo now and I am constantly getting comments about it, as well as being recognized because of it from the site and my column in *HorrorHound* magazine. (I'll get to that a little later.) I will be eternally grateful to Mr. Vargo for this, as well as his friendship. People like him are a rare breed.

Looking back on the site now, hitting its 20-year anniversary in 2018, I've often pondered how much time I've spent working on the Krypt, time that I could have used watching more movies or reading more of my ever-growing library of reference books. There were times (many of them really) where I thought about throwing in the towel and going back to just being a fan. This would usually happen anytime my computer crashed, which has happened several times over the last two decades... more times than I even care to remember, in fact. But then I would get an email from someone that had just read something on my site, maybe a review, news of a book coming out, or one of my many rants or ramblings, and it really made a connection with them. Sometimes it was just a quick note to say that they really liked the site and to keep up the good work. As short as those emails or comments might be, it was fuel to the fire to keep the doors of the Krypt open a little longer. Maybe there's a little lesson there, folks. When you see someone putting their soul into some kind of outlet, whether it is writing or some type of artwork, if you like what you see, just take a moment and let them know. Who knows... maybe that person is on the verge of giving up on their path because of being discouraged or even worse, thinking what they are doing isn't "good enough." So a quick "Hey... nice job on that," or "I really like your work," could really do wonders for them.

Case in point: Stephen Thrower is a writer and scholar about the genre, who had previously penned a great book called *Beyond Terror: The Films of Lucio Fulci*. In 2007, Thrower wrote an even bigger volume on the wonderful world of cult cinema, *Nightmare USA*. This massive tome (500+ pages) covered so many cult and obscure titles that your average horror fan had never heard of, let alone seen. I ordered this as soon as I heard about it and had slowly been making my way through this enormous volume. Now here's the funny thing: one night, I was talking to a buddy about it and he casually says how cool it was that I was mentioned in the book. "Uh... what did you say?" was my bewildered reply. It seems that near the back of the book, on the section on *Simon, King of the Witches* (1971), Thrower had used a quote from an interview I did with actor Andrew Prine... and credited Kitley's Krypt! I can't tell you how that made me feel, except that I wasn't just some idiot with a website, but an actual journalist.

It was moments like this that really showed me a couple of things. First of all, that someone without any official schooling, but with practice, trial and error, and fueled with enough passion can become something that he once thought impossible. It also proved to me that this isn't just a hobby, but a way of life, a path that I have chosen and continue to follow. A path where I found purpose helping pass on my obsession and love for horror movies with other like-minded fans. Yeah, sounds a bit silly, I know. But silly or not, I do believe it to be true. And it is a path that I'm still following to this day, twenty years and counting.

with Aaron Christensen, 2015

11

They Came from the Krypt!

"Writing is not a serious business. It's a joy and a celebration. You should be having fun with it."

Ray Bradbury

I have known Aaron Crowell and Nathan Hanneman, the creators of *HorrorHound* magazine, since sometime around the early 2000s. I believe it was at one of the Cinema Wasteland shows where they were set up selling different toys and horror collectibles, as well as their book, *Tomart's Price Guide to Horror Movie Collectibles*, which was an evil little thing. It showed a ton of different horror collectibles, ranging from classic Universal monster stuff to more modern-day items. It would make any collector drool at some of the items in there, wondering if you'd ever be able to add some of them to your collection, or beam with pride if you already had it in your collection. Even if you weren't a collector, it was still a fun book to page through, just seeing all the different items out there. Of course, if you were one to partake in the buying of such merchandise, this was a huge checklist! Lucky for me, I have only dabbled in such things on rare occasions. True story. Well...

Anyway, our friendship grew from then and they became part of my convention family that we'd get to see once or twice a year. But in April of 2006, something changed. Aaron comes walking up to the table and hands me the premiere issue of *HorrorHound*, their new project they are doing. Paging through it, I immediately loved it because it wasn't like other magazines out there. It not only dealt with movies, but also with toys, collectibles, as well as interesting articles like "10 Reasons to Own an Import DVD Player." He asked me if I'd be interested in writing something for them. I replied that while I appreciated the offer, my website kept me pretty busy.

Over the next year or so, however, I found myself helping them out here and there with different pieces for the magazine, supplying some poster art or other such memorabilia. With each issue, the audience grew and grew. I would look forward to each new issue because I just really loved what they were doing and how they were doing it. They offered interesting article topics, such as ones on the VHS explosion of the '80s, as well as some kick-ass retrospectives that not only covered the particular movie(s), but also included amazing photo layouts of the different collectibles tied to that film(s). One of the things they didn't do was review movies because they felt that it was done by other mags as well as so many places online, that they wanted to be a little different. And they were.

I believe it was in early 2009 when I got a phone call from Aaron. He said he and Nathan had been talking and were looking to have a regular column in the magazine that would cover a couple of different films each issue. They would be sort of like reviews, or just about the films themselves. The titles didn't have to be new or old, but any two random choices. Would I be interested in doing it?

As I had said before, for some stupid reason, I felt that if I was going to write something, I would want it on my own website. Honestly, I think that was me convincing myself that I wasn't a real writer. I mean, I just ran a website that had a little bit of traffic, but it wasn't like it was drawing huge hits. Writing for a real magazine, where a lot more people would actually be reading what I was saying... well, that was a pretty big step. As much as I tried to convince myself that I wouldn't have time for another outlet besides the Krypt, I finally decided that it was time to put myself out there for the world to see... or read, technically. It would not only bring more attention to the Krypt itself, but it would also give me a chance to do what I've been doing on the site already, only to a much wider market: introducing movies to an audience that might not be familiar with them! When Aaron said that I could pick whatever two movies I wanted with each issue, it was really hard to pass up. So I accepted.

"They Came from the Krypt" made its debut in *HorrorHound* #16 (March/April 2009). My first column was about two of my favorite films featuring Nazi Zombies, *The Frozen Dead* (1966) and *Shock Waves* (1977). This was well over fifty issues ago now and my only regret is not starting sooner. In that time, I've covered made-for-TV movies, Mexican horrors, Italian zombies, shark movies, '50s giant monster flicks, obscure grindhouse features, and so much more. Any doubts that I may have had about taking this plunge were washed away the first time someone came up to me at a convention and thanked me for my column because they had checked out one of the movies I wrote about and really enjoyed it. There's that term "runner's high" when they get that burst of adrenaline. Well, hearing a comment about your work like that is definitely a "writer's high." It also showed that maybe, just maybe, I did have something to say. Since that column, I have also written other articles for them, including a couple of interviews, several retrospectives, including two about a couple of my favorite films, *Frankenstein* and *The Thing*, as well as some other bits here and there.

Then something even more amazing happened.

In 2013, the long-running Rondo Awards added a new category, "Best Column." For those not familiar with the Rondos, it's a fan-based "People's Choice" award program that has been celebrating different contributions in the genre, as well as those who are doing that work, since 2002. There are categories like Best Film, Best Writer, Best Artist, Best DVD Extra, Best Interview, Best Magazine, Best Magazine Cover, and so on. When they started this new category, much to my amazement, "They Came from the Krypt" was one of the nominees. When the final votes were tallied, John Bowen from *Rue Morgue* was honored with the top prize… with the Krypt as the Runner-up! I have to say, if there was anybody I was okay "losing" to, it would be Mr. Bowen, who is a class act and a damn funny writer.

My column was nominated again the following year. Even more shocking: I actually won.

Had my father or step-mother been alive to hear this news, they surely would have been more shocked than I was. Throughout my early school years, there were countless hours of working on different essays, with my step-mother (who not only was an ex-teacher, but also an ex-nun!!!) standing over my shoulder watching and reading the scrambled thoughts I was trying to put to paper. The fact of the matter is that I was just a terrible writer. Trying to get my thoughts down, in a manner where someone could gather some sort of clue as to what my point actually was, was like trying to shave your face with a cheese grater. Sure, it gets the job done, but it's also just a bloody mess.

This is a great lesson for you younger fans out there with thoughts, hopes, and dreams of becoming an official writer. Just practice. Over and over. Once you're finished writing something, come back the next day and read it again and see if it still sounds okay. And then read it again. Also, not trying to sound like a jerk, but make sure what you're writing about is accurate. Do your research and double check and triple check. Opinions can be as varied as much as fans of the *Friday the 13th* sequels. But facts… well, they don't change. So, make sure you have them right. It also helps if you are writing about something you enjoy. (Try writing a retrospective on mummy movies… ugh.)

The most important part is simply to just start writing. Write a little review of a movie you watched. Write why you liked it, or didn't like it. Get your thoughts down on paper (or on a computer screen, as the case may be). But keep writing. Keep re-reading and refining as you do it. Passion doesn't always equal talent, and practice may not make you perfect, but both are invaluable as you travel down the path.

12

New Eyes

"The great horror movies are like Frankenstein's Monster, considerably more than just the sum of their tacked together body parts."

Anne Bilson, *BFI Modern Classics: The Thing*

"You can never see the same film twice with the same eyes."

I believe I first heard this saying from my friend Aaron Christensen. (I'm not positive it was from him, but I'm going to give him the credit anyway.) It's a twist on the old "You can never step in the same river twice," and simply means that no matter what, once you have watched a movie for the first time, there is no way you are going to have that same experience again. I agree with that statement 100% of the time... well, almost.

Before we get into more depth about this, let me get on my soapbox real quick and make sure we're all on the same page when I talk about "watching" a film. When you are seeing a film for the first time, it is imperative that you are actually WATCHING it. One thing that would drive me crazy when my son would sit down with me for a flick was that he'd be on his phone, or his laptop, or a handheld game of some sort, or sometimes more than one of those. He always claimed that he could multi-task, which I'm sure he can, but if you're not looking at the screen, you are not seeing what is happening, plain and simple. That would be equivalent to reading a book, but only reading every other paragraph. Sure, you might get the gist of what is going on, but you're missing a lot too. Just think about a sequence that maybe the cinematographer, director, and lighting guy worked hours to get one particular shot set-up to look fucking amazing, or a makeup effect that took weeks to create to make it perform correctly on camera... but did you see it? No... you're staring down at a cat video. Not only is it just wasting your time if you're not going to watch it, but it is also pretty disrespectful to the filmmakers. So put down the damn phone, turn off your computer, and watch the movie!

Okay. Off the soapbox.

With the first viewing of a horror film, you really don't know what is going to happen. Yes, this could be for any kind of genre, but the name of this book isn't *Discover the Romantic Comedies*, is it? So upon that first time, if there's a mystery or killer on the loose, until the plot reveals it to us, we're as much in the dark as the characters on the screen. We could also be surprised by a particular scene, or maybe a character getting killed off we didn't expect. Or maybe just how the story might take a left turn out of nowhere. Of course, we also have the jump scares too.

During those subsequent viewings, the game has now changed. You already know who the killer is, so the big reveal isn't going to have the same impact. You're not as surprised at the twists and turns of the story because you've already been down this road. Jump scares? You know where they are so you see them coming a mile away and they have lost their impact. Yes, you can still be entertained by the movie, but you're not looking at it the same way as you did the first time.

Don't get me wrong. I'm not trying to say it is useless to watch a film you've already seen before. On the contrary, it's just now you're seeing it through a different set of eyes than before, possibly more "educated" eyes. Meaning, just possibly, you can start to see it a little differently, looking further into it than you did the first time, maybe seeing things you missed, or even picking up little nuances that you didn't catch the first time around. Upon multiple viewings, you start to notice the atmosphere a little more, or how the camera is either positioned or how it is moving. Maybe there are lines of dialogue that you didn't catch the first time around that really was giving you some clues to what was going on. Maybe since that first viewing, you have read some behind-the-scenes account about how the monster was designed and created and now find it a lot more fascinating how it all came together. That's the amazing thing about being a cinephile. The older you get and the more movies you watch and absorb, the more your cinematic palate expands and becomes more refined. The more you learn about these movies and the people behind them, the more you'll start to notice things.

Upon a second or third viewing or more of, say, a giallo film, you know right away who the killer is, so that surprise is already gone. You might even remember who is going to be the next victim, so a lot of the suspense and surprise might be gone. But, hang on, it's not as bad as all it sounds. My point is that this is when those "new eyes" take over. While watching this giallo, since you already know who the killer is and that he's waiting behind the bathroom door, maybe now you're paying a little more attention to how the camera is slowly moving through the apartment. Or how the lighting is used to cast shadows a certain way. Or even how the music is helping to build the suspense. All of this you may have caught upon that first viewing, but maybe not as much during repeated viewings. Maybe you were so entranced by the story and when the killer was going to jump out, it didn't sink in as much as the second time.

Let me give you a couple more examples.

In Alfred Hitchcock's classic *Psycho*, unless you were seeing it when it first hit theaters back in 1960, everyone pretty much knows that Norman Bates is the disturbed killer. If you didn't... oops! Sorry. My point can be used for any film on a repeat viewing, but I'll stick with *Psycho* since everyone has pretty much seen it. So after the first time, and you know the big reveal, you could focus your attention more on different things, picking up little nuances, such as Perkins' performance, the dialogue, or just little cinematic shots that maybe, just maybe, Hitchcock put in there on purpose.

For example, let's take the part where Bates makes the comment about his mother, "It's not like my mother is a maniac or a raving thing. She just goes a little mad sometimes. We all go a little mad sometimes. Haven't you?" Without knowing who the killer is here, we might miss that remark of who really is the "mad" one he's talking about. Or better yet, when he is referring to his mother and says, "Oh, but she's harmless. She's as harmless as one of those stuffed birds." Since we now know that Mrs. Bates really isn't a maniac and is as harmless and more akin to one of those birds than not, it means a lot more knowing that fact then when we first heard those comments, not knowing the real state of Mrs. Bates. That's a nice little nod to the audience, giving them little hints about what is really going on, knowing full well they won't pick up on it.

In the visual aspect of this, during the scene when Norman and Marian are talking outside the motel, there is shot of them standing there, and you can see a reflection of only Norman in the window, possibly showing his split personality??? On a repeat viewing, it might just bring a little smile to your face, knowing that Hitchcock (and screenwriter Joseph Stefano) might just be winking at you.

Now I'm not suggesting that if you go back and look at the likes of *Sleepaway Camp 3* or *Friday the 13th: Part 7*, you'll see these same sort of cinematic "winks," but then again... you just never know, do you? Don't automatically discredit a filmmaker just because of the title they might be working on. Just saying.

In the 1963 film *The Haunting*, directed by master craftsman Robert Wise and based on the novel *The Haunting of Hill House* by Shirley Jackson, we get one of the best haunted house movies ever committed to celluloid. Now for those of you who haven't seen this movie, put this book down, go find a copy of this movie and watch it. Then come back. I'll wait. Not because there might be spoilers ahead, but just because the movie is sheer genius and belongs on any Must Watch list of horror films.

Back? Good. Let's continue then.

In this story, we don't get the traditional floating ghosts with chains wandering the hallways in search of a warm body to scare. In fact, we don't see any kind of ghosts throughout the running time. So as a youngster, you might find *The Haunting* a bit slow, tedious, or even, dare I say... boring? I know such a statement is blasphemy for most die-hard horror fans, but in this day and age of the video game generation, where instant, constant, and continuous gratification is expected, or even demanded, viewers might get bored with the lack of non-stop action. Going back to it with expectations managed (i.e. you are expecting a slower-paced story this time), you might find you don't need that mile-a-minute stimulation, and that you have the patience to be absorbed into the characters onscreen and let this incredible story unfold before you. You start to experience the frightening panic right along with Eleanor as she hears the muffled whisperings outside her bedroom door, or as the door starts to bend and bulge inwards. It is a terror that you actually feel as she does.

In other words, you are watching it through a different, or at least a more experienced, set of eyes. Eyes that have become more mature. Eyes that have learned to look for different things, such as atmosphere, subtext that might be in the dialogue, or things in the background scenes that you might have missed the first time around. Little tidbits like this can and will help you appreciate the film and the filmmakers a lot more.

Here is another example, kind of on the other end of the spectrum. Larry Buchanan was a Texas-based filmmaker whose budgets made Roger Corman's look like Michael Bay's. He produced a plethora of low-budget films from the 1960s through the 1980s, in many different genres, both for TV and for the drive-in market. His films are not generally known for being well-made. In fact, some of them even hard to get through the full running time without hitting the fast forward button. So your first experience with a Buchanan feature might leave you a little less-than-amused. In fact, some might be angry that you'll never get those 90 minutes back.

Now, I'm not trying to be a Buchanan defender... okay, actually I am. I've loved his work, even though I know how inept they might seem and it's mind-blowing that they ever got released. While I am in 100% agreement that his films are not well made, usually pretty cheesy, and poorly written, I still find them entertaining. Why? Maybe it has something to do with me reading his autobiography, *It Came from Hunger: Tales of a Schlockmeister*, where he talks of his struggles with having very little time and money to produce the films that he was hired to make, but yet he always seemed to get them finished. Most of which, by the way, turned a decent profit. Having read these astonishing tales, it makes me view his final products with a little more respect and appreciation than I had before. The monster in his 1969 made-for-TV movie *"It's Alive!"* looks very similar to the one used in his 1967 film *Creature of Destruction*, and it sure wasn't because it was such an amazing monster suit. But I give him credit for being frugal and using whatever means he had as his disposal. Does it make them better films? Not even close. But knowing a little about what went into making these low-budget features, you tend to overlook things that I would normally shake my head in bewilderment and wonder why I'm wasting my time. Well... sometimes I still think that, but his films still put a smile on my face, even if it's because I can't believe what I'm watching.

Paying attention to how the camera is moving is also an important part of the movie-watching experience because it shows you exactly what the director and cinematographer *want* to show you, as well as *how* they have chosen to show it to you. While the screenwriter and the editor are worried about the storyline, the pacing, and making sure it flows, what the audience sees, especially in the horror genre, can be just as important. Why? Maybe because it is how and where the camera moves that can create atmosphere and mood. It could be the angle of the shot can make the viewer feel disjointed or off-balance from the angle or direction. Atmosphere and mood are often used when describing a ghost story or haunted house movie, but they can also be created just by how either the camera is moving or where it is located.

Two examples, both from the same movie:

In Tobe Hooper's 1974 film *The Texas Chain Saw Massacre*, there are a couple of shots where cinematographer Daniel Pearl elevates this little low-budget exploitation film to a level of high art, for which most critics will never give it credit. The first shot is right after the character Kirk has wandered into the house where our friendly cannibalistic family lives, and gets a mallet to the side of the head for his troubles. Right after Leatherface slams the giant metal door, the shot transfers back to Pam sitting on the little wooden swing, with the camera behind her. As she gets up and moves towards the house, the camera follows right behind her in one continuous shot, even moving underneath the swing, all the time keeping a low angle behind Pam with the ominous house in the background as we move closer, stopping short, as if to say, "Fuck that... I know what just happened and I'm not going in there." It is something simple but highly effective in building that tension as we follow her up to the house of death, and stop before getting too close.

The other shot, a much simpler one, is when the Cook is bringing Sally back to their home, where she is tied up on the floor of his truck. One of the camera angles is on the floor looking up at the cook as he drives, as if you, the viewer, are poor Sally being driven off to your probable doom. Again, a simple shot, but it creates a scary bit of mood for viewers, that we are trapped with her as well. Some of these things you might not have picked up the first time you watched it. But on repeat viewings, your "older eyes" just might start to.

Earlier I mentioned that I *almost* believed that statement about never being able to watch movies with the same eyes. But I recently discovered something that made me re-think the whole theory. There could be a particular film that could be a favorite of your childhood that you know is kind of cheesy or just not geared for an adult viewer. As you push "play" and the movie starts, there is a small part of your brain already declaring that you must have been jacked up on a bunch of sugar-laced cereal and junk food, since it's the only way to possibly explain how you found this movie "amazing."

Then, something happens that you didn't expect. Those older and more educated eyes, the ones that you've been training over the last few decades on the finer points of cinema and filmmaking techniques and theories, suddenly take a backseat to a pair of ten-year old eyes. They seem to have taken control, somehow filtering what you're watching, altering your cranium, jettisoning your brain back in time, creating those same feelings and emotions that you had when you first watched it, all those years ago.

It's almost like your adult brain has been hijacked. It's still there, completely aware of this inferior product passing through its orbital sensors. But somehow that rational part of your brain is tied up and gagged in the corner, unable to shout out, "Hey, this film is silly, stupid, terrible, all of the above!" Instead, those same thrilling feelings of excitement wash over you just as they did all those years ago. You can't explain it or defend it, but for some reason, it is really like watching it through the eyes of that little kid parked in front the TV for the very first time.

For example, every time I watch *Jaws*, even having seen it countless times before, I still get a little choked up hearing Quint's speech about the *U.S.S Indianapolis*. When the Kintner boy gets attacked, the hair stands up on my arms and that cold feeling starts rising in the pit of my stomach. Even though my adult mind appreciates all the technical skill and camera tricks, remembers all the behind-the scenes mishaps with the giant mechanical Bruce shark, and knows exactly what's going to happen and when, I'm still watching it through my child eyes every time, having that same emotional response I did the first time.

Why do some films have that ability to take us back in time, whether it is a masterpiece or a schlocky made-for-TV movie? How do they still have the power to grab hold of us and our emotions? This effect is more powerful for some, and others are never really affected by it. Even those that are can have a different or deeper impact than the next guy. It all comes down to a personal level. That, my dear friends, is the real beauty of cinema.

So what have we learned? That the more movies you watch, the more you can see? Maybe. Or how about that the movies we loved as a child may seem silly today? Possibly. Or even if they seem juvenile today, they can still teleport us back and remind us why they entertained us in the first place. The bottom line is that the more you watch and learn about them, the more you can not only see, but also understand, especially when we view them with an open and interested set of eyes. Just make sure you keep them on the screen!

13

You Can Never Have Too Many Reference Books

*"I can hardly describe to you the effect of these books.
They produced in me an infinity of new images
and feelings that sometimes raised me to ecstasy..."*

The Creature, *Frankenstein; or The Modern Prometheus* by Mary Shelley

The above quote was taken from a novel written over 200 hundred years ago, yet those words describe my feelings perfectly when it comes to horror reference books. In my younger days as a fan, before the Internet, these books were a treasure trove of trivia and tidbits about films that I had never heard of, let alone seen. Reading through the different synopsis, some with outlandish plots which made them sound even more amazing, I always hoped that one day I would get to actually see them. There were the photos that littered the pages like splatters of blood in a giallo flick, showing screen monsters from over the previous decades, some hideous and terrifying, which burned into my psyche. Images such as Leo G. Carroll's seemingly melting face from *Tarantula* (1955), Mr. Hyde's beastly facade from the 1931 version of *Dr. Jekyll and Mr. Hyde*, or Boris Karloff as the menacing-looking butler with a busted nose in *The Old Dark House* (1932) were faces that I would look at over and over again. From a variety of vampires, werewolves, and other creatures of the night, even without knowing the movie plots, my brain was coming up with my own wild stories just from the images alone.

The very first horror reference book I can remember being enamored with was *The Films of Boris Karloff* by Richard Bojarski, originally published in 1974. I would check it out from the Washington Middle School library, paging through the volume, mesmerized by the different images and the many faces of this amazing actor. I knew Karloff had played Frankenstein's creation, but had no idea just how many movies he appeared in. Here I discovered he had been in quite a few silent titles before breaking into the "talkies," even making several of those before his big break. I also learned that he played in countless other genres besides what made him famous, even playing a Chinese detective in the *Mr. Wong* series of films. This book was a gateway, and I spent many hours thumbing through its pages. In fact, I checked it out so often that I was told by the librarian that I could no longer take the book, to give others a chance at it. Every time I was in the library, I found myself drawn back to it though, partially to see if anybody else had checked it out (which it seemed no one ever did because it was always there) as well as refreshing my memory of the images within its pages.

When I made the decision to become a Cinematic Archeologist, I would go to these reference books. I learned about the actors, the directors, the makeup artists and set decorators, all the people that worked on making what we see on screen come to life. The more I learned about those people, the more I found myself being interested in more than just the story on the screen, almost seeing past it, or deeper into it. When you realize that there are scenes in a film where the background is actually a matte painting and not a real landscape, it fires your imagination and appreciation. Little things like that make you start to see these films a little differently.

Two of the earliest titles that I remember adding to my small library were Denis Gifford's *A Pictorial History of Horror Movies*, first published in 1973, and William K. Everson's *Classics of the Horror Film*, published the following year. Gifford's book had a gloriously green montage of a cover, with images of different screen monsters on the jacket: Frankenstein's Creature, Dracula, Chaney's Phantom, and even Hammer stars Peter Cushing and Christopher Lee. I would later find out this image was created by famous poster artist Tom Chantrell, who had done a lot of work for Hammer Films. It really was a history lesson through pictures, schooling my young brain about so many movies.

Everson's book followed suit with another plethora of photos from the classic movies. Not only were the Universal monsters covered, but plenty of creatures from other studios. While I was always fascinated and intrigued by most of the images, there were a few here and there that I would try to avoid, such as on one page in the chapter on *King Kong* that featured a poor guy hanging on a tree right before getting eaten by a huge dinosaur. Not sure why, but that one always gave me the chills. As cheesy as it looks, it still packs a punch even to this day. These titles were just two staples of my beginning library, but ones that I would go back to time and time again. They were, and still remain, an important part of my early horror education.

If you were a fan of the classic Universal films, such as *Dracula*, *Frankenstein*, *The Wolf Man*, and all their descendents, a series of books started to appear in 1989 that were simply a must for your library. They were called *Universal Filmscripts Series* and were edited by Philip J. Riley. Each volume focused on one title in the series and gave you everything a fan could want. You'd have background information about the film itself, the production, the actors, and the locations. They had behind-the-scenes shots, production illustrations, publicity stills, and then, of course, the actual script. One part of these series of books that I always enjoyed was the press material. Not only would we get to see the original advertising, but also newspaper articles about the pictures. Riley would continue to put new volumes out, covering all of the classics. Every time I'm doing any writing on one of these titles, I am always going back to these for information.

In the mid 1980s, when VHS was a booming business, there were video stores with a huge selection of horror titles to choose from. With such a wide variety of lurid titles, how could one know what to choose other than going by the box art? That's where the reference books came in. There were volumes like John Stanley's *Creature Features Movie Guide*, where he covered a lot of titles, though some of his synopses got the plots wrong. My two go-to books when I needed to look up a movie were Michael Weldon's *Psychotronic Encyclopedia of Film* and Phil Hardy's *Encyclopedia of Horror*.

Weldon's book, a thick oversized paperback that came out in 1983, covered not just horror, but sci-fi, fantasy, camp, beach party movies, and just about every other type of strange movie that wouldn't even begin to get past the velvet ropes at the Oscars! The reviews were short, but it gave you an idea of what you might be in for. Plus, while many video guides went a little deeper in their reviews or discussion of the films, they also missed a lot of obscure titles. But, more often than not, Weldon mentioned them. I still have my original edition, which is now more a collection of pages than an actual book, since the binding has long since fallen apart after being opened and closed thousands of time over the last 35 years.

Phil Hardy was the editor for the massive tome *Encyclopedia of Horror*, first released in the UK in 1986, and then in the U.S. in 1987. It was later reissued in 1993 as *The Overlook Film Encyclopedia: Horror*, expanding on the original content to the current year. This book was not only vital to my early days but helped open so many new doors. Not only did this book go through each decade, starting with the early days of silent cinema, but Hardy also covered films from all over the world. You could find the works of Paul Naschy, Coffin Joe, Hammer, Mario Bava, and so many more within its pages. Each selection gave us a synopsis (most of the time), the cast and crew, and also all of its alternate titles, from its original moniker in its home country to all of the variations for foreign markets. This was very important to fans that were taking those first steps into sub-genres outside the norm. Most video guides only mentioned the bigger names, but Hardy's book went deeper.

One unfortunate drawback of Hardy's book was that it caused confusion amongst film collectors since he also listed the running times of each of the titles. The problem was that some of these running times were taken from PAL import tapes where the run speed was a bit different than over here. Also, some films were released in different versions, some edited, and some edited more than others. So trying to find a version that was "uncut" didn't mean it was necessarily going to fit the running time listed in this book. It had to come down to knowing the film and its history well enough to know which particular scenes were cut or missing from the version you had. Trust me, it wasn't easy.

I learned about so many new movies because of these two volumes. But it didn't stop there. I would pick up other video guides to see what films they mentioned, as well as what they said about them. These days, you can find themed guides covering just about every sub-genre out there: mummy movies, ghost stories, TV horrors, zombie films, or the Italian giallo, the list keeps growing and growing. Trust me, I know, because these titles keep getting added to my library each year.

A bit of warning though, when it comes to reading reviews in these books. There are going to be some reviewers that simply don't like a particular movie. I wouldn't take this to heart, but maybe compare it to a few other books and see what they say. I've read more than a few "bad" reviews on a title that I avoided seeing for years because of what an author has written about it, only to find out that when I actually did watch it, I really enjoyed it. Make sure you take someone's OPINIONS as just that. It really comes down to what YOU think about a particular film that is most important.

There are also many wonderful biographies that shed light on industry veterans that aren't necessarily considered legends (though I think they should be). In 1997, author Randy Palmer wrote *Paul Blaisdell: Monster Maker*. Does that name ring a bell? Hopefully it does, because Blaisdell was the guy who created the monsters, aliens, and creatures for AIP's sci-fi / horror films, such as *The Day the World Ended* (1955), *It Conquered the World* (1956), and *Invasion of the Saucer Men* (1957). Some of the creatures he conjured may seem a little silly these days, especially when the likes of *MST3K* make fun of them. But when you read about what actually went into the making of these films, and how little money and time Blaisdell had to create such things, it gives you a little more appreciation for his accomplishments. Just hearing what Blaisdell went through designing the alien invaders from *Saucer Men*, being given a different direction for the project each time he talked to the producers, it would be enough to make you go nuts! But no matter the money or the stress, he was still able to create some highly memorable movie monsters. Reading Palmer's biography on Blaisdell fills in the history surrounding a highly talented, unsung hero of that era.

It Came from Hunger: Tales of a Cinema Schlockmeister is not just a biography about a filmmaker, but an *autobiography* from the man himself,

Larry Buchanan. I know I've mentioned him before in this book, but Buchanan's autobiography is a great example of how you can see a film so differently once you know more about it and the people behind it. Buchanan's films redefine the term "low-budget," but they almost always all turned a profit at the drive-ins. When you have a distributor call you up and say, "I want to make a drive-in picture with lots of nudity and very little dialogue and all I can spend is $8000!" what is a starving independent filmmaker going to do other than take that challenge? The end result? *The Naked Witch* (1961). The details of what Buchanan went through to make it happen is something that all up-and-coming filmmakers should hear. Then you read about the struggles he would go through to try and get his films made under incredibly short schedules, you start to understand even more. His story of making his first real exploitation film, *Venus in Furs*, only to have it dropped to the bottom of Lake Dallas after it was completed and never seen or released by anybody other than the director and the man who paid for it, is one of the best stories *not* to come out of Hollywood. I don't see how anyone could read these tales and not look at Buchanan and his films a little differently. All because of a book.

There are those subjects that you think you know a lot about, whether it be an actor or a film. Then along comes along a book that shows you that there is always more to learn. Since Boris Karloff is one of my favorite actors, I was always reading a lot about him and his films. Then in 2011, *Boris Karloff: More Than a Monster* by Stephen Jacobs comes out. This massive volume shed more light on Karloff, his work, and personal life than I had ever read before. From stories of different movies and early years when he was a stage actor to so many great personal tales, it made me appreciate him even more.

Gunnar Hansen, as most fans know, played Leatherface in Tobe Hooper's infamous *The Texas Chain Saw Massacre* (1974). Now there have been more than a few documentaries made on this notorious film, with countless interviews from the cast and crew about the ordeal they went through to make this picture. So did we really need yet *another* retelling of the production? I sure didn't think so. Then I started reading Hansen's book, *Chain Saw Confidential* (2013). Even though I knew the stories, Hansen gave us even more insight and behind-the-scenes tales that would make the hairs on your neck stand up. The fact that this project even got finished, let alone released, is beyond me. Not to mention that it's a miracle nobody died in the process! Afterwards, while I still held this film in high regards, I saw it a little differently. It made me appreciate what the cast and crew went through to bring us all of this onscreen insanity. Again, because of a book.

Passion is the driving force behind many of these books. That all-consuming need an author feels to educate others about a particular actor, director, special effects artist or film... even if that film is considered to be one of the worst ever made. When I discovered that someone had written a book called *I Cannot, Yet I Must: The True Story of the Best Bad Monster Movie of All Time – Robot Monster*, I knew I had to add it to my library. Then when I discovered this title was close to 700 pages long, I knew the author had to be just plain crazy! Why would anybody invest that much time and effort to write about a movie that is essentially laughed at all over the world? Author Anders Runestad felt the need to bring light to this 1953 film and its creator, Phil Tucker. I reached out to Runestad, mostly to ask what would possess him to put in this much time and effort. He told me, "There are other bad monster movies, but nothing quite matches a gorilla wearing a diving helmet (that is not really a diving helmet) while talking to himself about his feelings between bursts of making ineffectual threats to the last people on Earth." So instead of waiting for someone else to write the book, Runestad decided he would be the guy. There is so much information within these pages, about the film itself, those involved both in front of and behind the camera, as well as what else they worked on before and after this picture. It really is a great historical lesson on a movie that most people wouldn't give five minutes of their time for. And for that, I will forever give authors like Runestad praise and gratitude.

There are some authors that I follow, usually purchasing whatever their new book is, because I've enjoyed their previous work immensely and I trust that each new volume will open up even more doorways. Tom Weaver is one of them. He has released over a dozen books collecting interviews that he's done over the years with countless directors, actors, and others that have worked in the horror and sci-fi genre. Not just the big names either, but even the lesser-known stars. He always gives the reader a chance to hear from someone that was there working on these sometimes obscure pictures. With titles like *I was a Monster Movie Maker* (2001), *Earth vs. Sci-Fi Filmmakers* (2005) and *A Sci-Fi Swarm and Horror Horde* (2010), Weaver continues to help educate us movie fans about the genre and those involved.

Gregory William Mank is another author that has dedicated his life interviewing different cast and crews of these films, pouring hours and hours of research into volumes of books for us eager fans to eat up. Whether it is *Bela Lugosi and Boris Karloff: The Expanded Story of a Haunting Collaboration* (2017) or his incredible moving biography, *Laird Cregar: A Hollywood Tragedy* (2018), I always tear through Mank's books simply because they are so fascinating, well written, and full of great stories.

Of course, when you're dealing with subjects outside of the classics, one of the top authors would be Stephen Thrower. I first became aware of his work with his book *Beyond Terror: The Films of Lucio Fulci*, originally released in 1999, but has since gone through a few updated and expanded editions. I mean, when a huge hardcover book comes out on one of your favorite directors, giving him and his films a serious look, you just can't pass that up! It gives fans of Fulci a little more credibility that a scholar like Thrower is taking the time and effort to research and discuss the filmography that most critics would dismiss as exploitative garbage. Speaking of which, American exploitation films were the subject of his 2007 book *Nightmare USA*, which is a large 500+ page tome of American independent films that, again, most critics would never even take time to watch, let alone research and appreciate like Thrower did. Titles like *The Deadly Spawn* (1983), *Screams of a Winter Night* (1979), *The Strangeness* (1985) and so many more, all laid out with plenty of poster art and images from the films discussed. If you ever needed to add films to your Need-To-See list, then you'll find plenty in here. You might be familiar with some of the titles mentioned within these pages. You might have even seen some of these films. But guaranteed you'll want to see them all over again once you've read Thrower's book. And if you're looking for more Thrower books, you can always check out his two-volume set exploring the cinema of Jess Franco!

One last author I'd like to mention, one that I'm lucky enough to consider a friend, is Troy Howarth. I had become online friends with Troy around the time he was working on his book *Splintered Visions: Lucio Fulci and His Films* (2015). I already had a few of his previous books, such as *The Haunted World of Mario Bava* (2002) and the first volume of *So Deadly, So Perverse* (2015), so I was already impressed with his work. We chatted online about the Fulci book, where I mentioned that I had some photos of Fulci from his one and only American convention appearance back in 1996, and that he was more than welcome to use them if he wanted. That following spring at the Monster Bash convention, Troy was set up as a vendor, as was I, so I got the chance to meet him in person, as well as pick up a copy of the Fulci book. He was just as friendly in person and we had a great time chatting about Fulci. We quickly discovered we shared a passion for the work of Paul Naschy as well, and he mentioned he was thinking of tackling a book project about him. I told Troy not only was that a great idea, but if I could be of any help, such as offering up some rare Naschy titles or more convention photos, I was more than willing. As the project came to be, Troy was gracious enough to ask me to write a little piece for the book, which I was not only honored by the offer, but eternally grateful for the opportunity. *Human Beasts: The Films of Paul Naschy* was released in 2018, and I was so thrilled to see a book about Naschy come out, since the only other book about him was Naschy's own autobiography. Troy's books are always filled with so much information about the subject, as well with things connected to it. His *So Deadly, So Perverse* series, which covers the giallo film sub-genre, is simply a must for fans of Italian cinema. The first volume goes into the history of the giallo, where and when it started, as well as defining what in fact giallo truly is, and then goes through each of the films from 1962 to 1973. (Vol. 2, in case you were wondering, picks up at 1974 and does the same thing through 2013.) If you ever wanted to learn about Italian giallo and know which films to look for, then this is your first stop! Troy has also done several audio commentaries for Blu-ray releases of different Euro-Horror film titles as well and, just like his books, fills them with so much information and trivia that they are always worth your time.

Truth be told, I could go on for days about these books. It really is my passion. There is just something special about holding a physical copy in your hand, knowing that there is a world of information lying in those pages. It doesn't stop there. Even though there's always the lament that printed media is dying or dead, I'm here to tell you that is a bold-faced lie. My Amazon "Want List" is proof of that! Some people seem to think you can find anything on the Internet, so there's no need to buy a book. I hate to break it to you, but not everything on the Internet is completely true. Yeah, yeah, I know. Hard to believe. I'm not saying every book is 100% factual either, since I've found more than a few titles that were definitely in need of fact-checking. That said, there tends to be more research and fact-checking for a book that is going to be published than there is by a guy uploading the latest review to his movie blog.

As I mentioned earlier, my school days were sadly wasted without having developed a passion for the written word. It depresses me when I think about all of that time I could have been filling my head with information about these movies that I love. Maybe I'm just trying to make up for all that lost time. But when you find a subject matter that you are very passionate about, there is nothing more driving than the desire to learn as much as you can about that particular subject. That is how I am about horror movies. I want to learn as much as I can about them, as well as the people that made them. And really, there is no better place than these reference books. There are thousands out there. Trust me... I'm still adding them to my library.

14

The Curse of the Critics

"I don't worry about what critics say. I make pictures people want to see."

B-Movie Producer Robert Lippert Sr.

Even though horror is one of the oldest film genres around, it never has and probably never will be taken seriously. No matter how much money it pulls in every year, no matter how popular it is, it will always be the red-headed step-child of cinema. It is just something that we fans have learned to deal with, even though it can still drive us crazy.

There are some "normal" film critics out there that are horror fans, but for the most part, mainstream critics tend not to be able to see past the gore, the thrills, or the darker places that these movies take us. These critics are unable or unwilling to look beyond the stigma of horror to see anything that could be considered artistic, well-crafted, or even inspiring therein. For that, I really feel sorry for them, because they are missing out on so much beauty in that darkness.

As followers of this devious genre, we proudly carry and wave the flag for the films within it, championing titles that came out decades before we were even born or the next anxiously awaited production. Whether it is the actors, the director, or other craftsmen behind the scenes, we sing their praises and make sure that others know about them as well. We see and appreciate the talented actors that put themselves through hell to make this picture, either from wearing an ungodly amount of prosthetic makeup or by exploring the darker recesses of their own mind to create a character. We are enthralled by the way the cinematographer has shot the film, choosing strange angles or using special lighting techniques to present the director's unique vision. We value the composers who create an audio soundscape to add a unique dimension to accompany the images that we're seeing. We celebrate the unusual stories, characters, and creatures the writers have created that come to life on the screen before us. We don't have to wait decades to realize how great a movie might be. We tend to know right away.

Back in 1982, the only theater in my hometown where I could go see John Carpenter's *The Thing* was at the Skylark Drive-in, where it played on a double bill with *Enter the Ninja* (1981)! Like most horror fans, I immediately fell in love with this movie. The over-the-top gore was jaw-droppingly unbelievable, appeasing the gorehounds with effects we'd never witnessed before, but aside from all of that, it was a really good movie. The characters and the story were woven together perfectly, creating a pulse-pounding sense of paranoia, tension, and suspense. Even if you were to take out the gore and effects, the story would still work. But that is not what most critics thought when this was first released upon the world. In fact, they trashed it. They trashed it so much that it crippled Carpenter's career for a period of time.

"There's a big difference between shock effects and suspense, and in sacrificing everything at the altar of gore, Carpenter sabotages the drama. *The Thing* is so single-mindedly determined to keep you awake that it almost puts you to sleep." David Ansen, *Newsweek*.

No drama? No suspense? Really? Did he see the same movie?

"What the old picture delivered – and what [director John] Carpenter has missed – was a sense of intense dread." *Variety*

Howard Hawks' 1951 version generates more dread than Carpenter's...? Seriously?

In his review for *The New York Times*, Vincent Canby wrote, "[the film] is a foolish, depressing, overproduced movie that mixes horror with science fiction to make something that is fun as neither one thing nor the other. Sometimes it looks as if it aspired to be the quintessential moron movie of the '80s." He also goes on to write that "...it should be immediately pointed out that this new film bears only a superficial resemblance to Howard Hawks's 1951 classic *The Thing*, though both were inspired by the same source material, John W. Campbell Jr.'s story *Who Goes There?*"

I might be being a little picky here, but maybe it should also be pointed out that, first of all, the actual title of Hawks' film is *The Thing from Another World*. And if Canby had actually read Campbell's story, he would have known that Carpenter's version is much, much closer to the story than the Hawks version. But I digress.

Even in the science fiction magazine *Starlog*, Carpenter couldn't get a break. Writer Alan Spencer wrote that the film "...has no pace, sloppy continuity, zero humor, bland characters on top of being totally devoid of either warmth or humanity." He goes on to say that Carpenter would be better at directing "traffic accidents, train wrecks, and public floggings." I know plenty of fans, myself included, that think there is a LOT of humor within this film. Spencer's comments about the characters not having any warmth or humanity are just ridiculous. Plus, characters like this, choosing to live in the middle of nowhere, surrounded by thousands of miles of snow and ice, don't tend to be people that are super-friendly. They are loners. So maybe these actors were trying to, I don't know, *portray that in their characters.* Maybe I'm wrong, just throwing that theory out there.

Over 35 years after its release, *The Thing* is no longer looked upon as "a virtually storyless feature composed of lots of laboratory-concocted special effects," as Canby called it, but a piece of cinematic gold. Director Guillermo del Toro referred to it as a "game-changer and one of the finest horror films ever made. It cannot be matched." *Empire Online* dubbed it a "peerless masterpiece of relentless suspense, retina-wrecking visual excess and outright, nihilistic terror."

But this wasn't the only film in our horror history where critics just didn't get it at first. Far from it. In 1957, when Hammer Films released *The Curse of Frankenstein*, their color version of Mary Shelley's famous tale, *The Observer* stated they "could not discern one moment of art or poetry," while the *Daily Telegraph* just said "For sadists only." *The Tribune* flatly said that it was "depressing and degrading for anyone who loves the cinema."

These classic Hammer films are now regarded as important pictures in film history. In a 2013 retrospective for *The Guardian*, Michael Newton wrote that the early Hammer color films "are among the loveliest-looking British films of the decade," and that they offer fans a "last gasp of British romanticism, the solid sets drenched in a soft brilliance of shadows of grays, reds and blue."

A little over a decade after Hammer started their color remakes, a film made by "some people in Pittsburgh" using "non-professional actors" not only changed horror cinema, but created its own subgenre: George Romero's *Night of the Living Dead* (1968). Now some major critics did pick up on the talent within this little black-and-white film. Roger Ebert is always getting slammed for his negative review, when his criticism was really that kids were allowed into the theater, not against the film itself. On the other hand, Vincent Canby, once again writing for *The New York Times*, found little merit, saying it is a "grainy little movie acted by what appear to be nonprofessional actors, who are besieged in a farm house by some other nonprofessional actors who stagger around, stiff-legged, pretending to be flesh-eating ghouls." *Variety* stated that Romero "appears incapable of contriving a single graceful set-up, and his cast is uniformly poor."

Strange, really, that this little amateur effort seems to have inspired so many other films, filmmakers, makeup artists, and actors, not to mention going on to have this "incapable" director make five features continuing the series, as well as all the remakes and many other *Night*-inspired titles. Even more confusing, why would The Library of Congress Film Registry induct it into their archives in 1999? Wait... could it be that maybe those critics couldn't see past the Bosco syrup to see the real merit that lies within?

Michael Powell's 1960 film *Peeping Tom* got such a bad rap when it came out that it ruined the director's career. Len Mosley, writing for *The Daily Express*, claimed the film "is more nauseating and depressing than the leper colonies of East Pakistan, the back streets of Bombay, and the gutters of Calcutta." I wonder how much time Mosley spent in those leper colonies. And why? Of course, in 2004, *Total Film* magazine named *Peeping Tom* the 24th greatest British movie of all time.

They don't stop there. Bosley Crowther, writing for *The New York Times*, calls Hitchcock's *Psycho* (1960), a "blot on an honorable career." *Time Magazine* said it was "stomach-churning," while Caroline Lejeune from *The Observer* said "I couldn't give away the ending if I wanted to, for the simple reason that I grew so sick and tired of the whole beastly business that I didn't stop to see it." Wait... so you didn't even watch the whole picture and you're giving it a negative review? Right... seems fair.

Of course, *Psycho* was also inducted in The Library of Congress Film Registry in 1992.

But it isn't just the classic films we're talking about either, where critics just don't seem to get it. Roger Catlin, writing for *The Omaha World-Herald*, didn't care for *The Shining* (1980), writing that "Jack Nicholson is simply too lovable to be a murderer." Uh... has he seen any of Nicholson's other movies?

Jim Delmont, a staff writer for *The World-Herald*, said that the 1991 film *Silence of the Lambs* has "almost no entertainment value and is not even a true crime story." You remember *Silence*, right? The one that was nominated for seven Academy Awards and won five of them, including Best Picture, Best Actor, Best Actress, Best Director, and Best Screenplay. Granted, this is when Hollywood started calling these types of films "thrillers" to try and keep away from the negative connotations it gets, such as the year before with *Misery*.

So what happened? Why are these movies trashed when they are first released, but then years or decades later, are now considered classics and getting inducted into The National Film Registry? How come the critics didn't see what the fans did, or that the critics see now?

Maybe the answer lies within that last comment. Maybe the critics of today that are singing the praises of these films are the kids that saw these either at the theater or late night on TV or cable, and witnessed the beauty within through their younger and more impressionable eyes and minds. They were being entertained, amazed, terrified, and even inspired by what they were seeing. Now, those fans are adults and are making sure that the records are set straight on these films and how they should be remembered. These days, in the era of the Internet, any aspiring writer can have a website or blog and be a film critic. Sometimes these sites can become really popular where a critic's opinions are followed and trusted. Take *Rotten Tomatoes*, for example. More and more people are turning to this type of outlet run by people who like these kinds of films, more so than some guy at a newspaper who probably isn't a horror fan, uninterested in giving a film a proper chance to begin with.

At the end of all of it, fans know not to listen to what the mainstream might say about the genre they love. We will continue to follow these films and keep their memories alive and well, even without the support of the "normal" critics.

Maybe it's better that this genre is never taken seriously. It's worked for us so far for the last hundred years.

15

What Is Your Favorite?

"A man who limits his interests limits his life."

Vincent Price

When you are a fan of horror films, or any kind of film for that matter, one question that comes up in conversation at some point is the famous "What's your favorite movie?" I actually dread hearing that question, even to this day. It's not that I'm trying to sound elitist or anything, because in case you hadn't noticed, I LOVE talking about horror movies. But trying to choose one single title as my favorite from the hundreds and hundreds of films that I love? There is no way I could narrow it down to a Top 10, let alone to a single title. Even if I tried to come up with ten, they would constantly be changing back and forth, adding new ones in, and it would just end up in frustration (and probably a headache) because I would always remember another title to throw into the mix.

I do think there are some films I would say are "perfect," meaning that they really would be a 5-star rating. Films that you couldn't find flaws in, such as Carpenter's *The Thing* (1982), Romero's *Creepshow* (1982), Cronenberg's *The Fly* (1986), or Wise's *The Haunting* (1963), just to name a few. Granted, this is all personal opinion, but I could watch those films over and over again. And just as I'm writing down those titles, about four or five more pop into my head. So yeah, coming up with ten would be an insane quest for me.

That said, I love looking at other people's lists, or in books like *Top 100 Horror Movies* by Gary Gerani, because I find it interesting to hear/see/read other people's thoughts and opinions. Whether or not you agree with them, it will make you think, like why would they chose that particular title, or give you some suggestions that you either have never heard of or maybe had forgotten about. It brings about a discussion, even if it is just inside your own brain. And really, isn't that one of the points about being a fan of this genre? Getting together with other like-minded film nuts to discuss movies, bouncing our thoughts off of each other, getting to know someone else's opinions and theories, and maybe learning about some titles that you hadn't heard of or knew little about. That's the best part, when you come away from a conversation with a bunch of new titles that you need to seek out. They don't need to be new films either, because in reality, any title you haven't seen is a new movie... no matter what year it came out, right?

That is what this chapter is about. Instead of coming up with a list of my all-time favorites, or some sort of Best Of list, I figured I would go through some of my favorite subgenres. Some of these might pertain to a certain studio, or maybe a specific country or two, or maybe a certain point in time. But they are ones that I find myself drawn to, time and time again, for a variety of different reasons, which I'll explain as we go along. If there is one subgenre that you are not familiar with, then maybe when I'm done you'll decide you will want to wander down that path and discover what I'm talking about. At least, I can only hope. Got your notepad? Let's get started.

Silent Films

For any person that calls themselves a horror cinephile, they better have watched more than a few silent films. Because if you've never seen Robert Wiene's 1920 classic *The Cabinet of Dr. Caligari*, starring Werner Krauss and Conrad Veidt, or F.W. Murnau's *Noseratu* (1922), starring Max Schreck as one of the most iconic cinematic vampires ever, then you have not done your homework. But on a good note, if you haven't, boy are you in for a treat with those two! And the best part... that is only the beginning!

There's a theory going around that cinema narrative was destroyed with the advent of sound. Now that actors could talk, it meant there would be long stretches of dialogue to help explain the story to the audience. No longer would filmmakers have to tell their stories through images and facial expressions from the actors. Nothing would be left up to the audience to figure out or interpret on their own. Sounds a little silly at first, but think about it and it does make sense. That really comes into play these days, especially in Hollywood, where everything has to be explained to death.

Watching these older films now is a real treat because you can just sit and gaze at the incredible imagery they are showing you, using techniques that were probably just invented on the spot. There were no rules to follow, no guidelines, other than whatever the filmmaker wanted to do and as long as he could figure it out. But the imagery... wow. Just look at the two films I mentioned, *Caligari* and *Nosferatu*. In *Caligari*, the sets are designed at weird angles and corners, giving the viewer a skewed sense of reality, and the shadows are used in *Nosferatu* to create a sense of dread. But it wasn't just the look of a film. It was also the acting. Performances were much different in the silent era because the actors had to be so over-the-top when they emitted their emotions making sure audiences understood without them saying a word.

Of course, one of the all-time best actors in that era, in my opinion, was Lon Chaney Sr. I quickly learned who he was because of his horror roles, like *Phantom of the Opera* (1925) or his tragic performance as Quasimodo in *The Hunchback of Notre Dame* (1923). The more I read and learned about this fascinating man, the more of his non-horror films I sought out. Trust me, that was not an easy thing to do before DVDs and Blu-rays. But I would find a title here and there, or from trading with other collectors. Watching Chaney on screen always put me in awe. He could emit so much feeling and emotion just with a snarling glance or a tragic smile that is hiding a broken heart. Sure, the silent film actors had to overact to make sure they got their point across, but Chaney was a master of making his characters come alive. There are certain scenes in *Phantom*, like right after his deformed face has been revealed to Mary Philbin's Christine, where we get to see this terrible visage riddled with anger and hate. Chaney was a master of turning himself into so many different characters with his trusty makeup kit. He would transform his looks and his body into completely different and sometimes unrecognizable characters, even putting himself through some excruciating pain for his art. The stories of how Chaney would put his body in forms of discomfort, or even severe pain, just to develop a character are legendary. Some have been slightly over exaggerated over the years, but some were not. Just watch his performance in *The Penalty* (1920).

Thankfully, a lot of his films have been found and archived in digital formats and are now easier to find. While I would pretty much recommend any Chaney film, one that I would consider a must-see, besides the three mentioned above, is *The Unknown* (1927), where Chaney plays an armless circus performer. While not technically in the horror genre, there are enough dark elements to it that I think you'll enjoy it. Plus, anytime you can watch the master on screen is well worth your time.

Black-and-White Films

Over the years, during discussions with other fans (though mainly younger ones), I occasionally would come across someone that remarks that they are not a big fan of watching "one of those old black-and-white movies." Every time I hear that, a little piece of me dies inside and I want to knock some sense into this supposed cinema lover. I have learned over the years that this method, yelling and ridicule, is not the best way to help expand a fellow film lover's palate. If you really want to help them to think outside of their initial preconceptions, sometimes you just have to politely question them. Ask them which films have they seen that they didn't care for? They might name a few that they did like, usually classics like *Night of the Living Dead*, but maybe they've just missed out on the real attraction of black-and-white films. By being non-confrontational, you might be able to persuade them to put aside their harsh feelings and maybe give a few titles another chance. Like with all movies, excluding yourself from a particular subgenre just keeps you from some amazing cinema. In reality, a black-and-white movie is the same as a color one since it really comes down to the story, the acting, mood, and atmosphere, and all the other elements that made good movie. The color, or lack thereof, should have no bearing on it. It just becomes part of the style.

What exactly is it about a black-and-white film that still attracts my attention? Maybe it's because I grew up watching these old flicks on television, so they possibly bring back a little sense of nostalgia of my childhood. Hundreds upon hundreds of innocent hours spent sitting in front of the television, eyes glued to the dark and strange tales unfolding before me. It's like a small part of my psyche stepping back in time.

Even today, there are plenty of times when I want to travel back to those innocent days and have those feelings again when I pop in an old movie. Whether it's one of the Universal classic monsters, or one of their many cousins from another studio, there is just something about them that makes me feel comfortable, almost like slipping into a nice worn-out pair of shoes. It just fits. In these films, monsters were still being invented (and quite a few used and reused) and crazed mad scientists were always coming up with new ways to rule the world. The actors played their roles completely straight, giving a performance like it was for the Oscars. In the case of Fredric March with his role in the 1931 film *Dr. Jekyll and Mr. Hyde* (where he actually did win an Oscar), for a film that is coming up on being a century old, March still breathes life into both of these characters on screen in a manner that packs a one-two punch, even today.

Charles Laughton was an actor that played in all sorts of genres, but made a few in the horror field, such as James Whale's *The Old Dark House* (1932) or Erle C. Kenton's *Island of Lost Souls* from the same year, where he played the maniacal Dr. Moreau. One film he did that seems to be forgotten, or at least passed over, is his role as the deformed Quasimodo in the 1939 remake of *The Hunchback of Notre Dame*. Now it was years after becoming a Cinematic Archeologist that I finally sat down and watched this version. I had seen it before but had dismissed it because I was such a huge fan of the Lon Chaney Sr. version. I felt there was no way that anyone could surpass his performance in the original film. Then one day I came upon the realization that it was my duty to watch this other version with more of an open mind. What I didn't expect was the stunningly tragic performance that Laughton gave as the simple-minded hunchback. As the film progressed, I had tears welling up while watching this poor creature come to life. Whether you want to consider *Hunchback* as a horror film or not, Laughton should have not only been nominated for an Oscar, he should have won. Thankfully the film still exists and we can still enjoy it and be drawn in to this sad tale and be in awe of this amazingly talented actor.

Okay, okay... maybe not all of these performances were worthy of Academy Awards. While most gave it their all, others just seemed to be having fun with it. From watching the tortured performance of Colin Clive's Henry Frankenstein to Ernest Thesiger chewing the scenery (and spitting it out) or the underrated George Zucco underplaying his characters to the point of sheer creepiness, they all held my attention as a kid, and still do today. And it wasn't all fun and silly cheap thrills. Some titles could and were actually downright scary, even terrifying. Yes, even a black-and-white film could be scary. Hard to believe? Read on.

In the 1940s, producer Val Lewton was in charge of making low-budget B-movies for RKO Radio Pictures. The studio wanted quick and easy cheap thrillers, giving Lewton some silly exploitation titles to work with. He hated those titles and refused to do what the studios wanted. Instead, he put a lot of style and talent in front of and behind the camera, producing some highly original and innovative pictures, such as *The Cat People* (1942), *I Walked with a Zombie* (1943), *The Body Snatcher* (1945), and several others. With talented directors like Jacques Tourneur, Robert Wise, and Mark Robson, what they lacked in budget, they excelled in talent, style, and atmosphere. Instead of coming up with cheap and tawdry programmers, these are prime examples of how black-and-white films can be as powerful and gripping as any color film. In the film *The Leopard Man* (1943), there is a sequence where a young girl is coming home and is being chased by something. Terror builds the closer she gets home, coming to a terrifying ending right outside her front door, with her mother on the other side, listening in horror. Tourneur created a powerful piece of cinema that proves to us that you don't need to show much to keep the audience on the edge of their seats.

Another great example of Lewton's work happens to be one of my favorite Boris Karloff movies, where I feel he plays one of the scariest characters in his career. *The Body Snatcher*, directed by a young Robert Wise, takes place in 1831 in Edinburgh, at a medical school run by Dr. MacFarlane, who is sort of following the path of his former instructor Dr. Knox. (In real life and in the film, Dr. Knox had employed the infamous grave robbers/murderers Burke and Hare to acquire bodies for his medical classes to study anatomy and the basics of surgery.) A cabman named Gray knows Dr. McFarland's little secret and constantly uses it to torment the doctor. Gray seems such a friendly man on the outside, but behind the wide and happy grin, is a very dark soul. The only real monsters in this film reside inside this character, and

Karloff gives one of his finest performances. The dialogue sequences between Karloff's Gray and MacFarlane (played wonderfully by Henry Daniell) are one of the many highlights of the film. The juxtaposition of the characters, the way they seem on the outside and what they are on the inside, is a perfect display of some top-notch acting and characterization.

That same year, another film came from the shadows to encircle and enthrall audiences in its sublimely dark atmosphere. Based on the Oscar Wilde novel, *The Picture of Dorian Gray* (1945) was directed by Albert Lewin and starred George Sanders with Hurd Hatfield in the title role as the young man that sells his soul to stay young and beautiful, while a portrait he had commissioned would grow old. Dorian soon finds out though that his portrait is not just aging, but it is also showing the effects of his cruelty towards others. This one definitely is a slow burn but it is an excellent example of black-and-white film, with amazing performances by Hatfield and Sanders.

By the time the '50s hit, the traditional horror pictures were starting to dwindle and lose their popularity. Then, things got bigger. And by bigger, I mean HUGE! In 1954, a movie about giant ants was released with the simple title of *Them!* This started a whole chain reaction of giant monsters running amuck all over the theater screens for the next few years. After the success of *Them!*, all the other studios quickly jumped on board the big-bug-bandwagon. Scorpions, grasshoppers, mollusks, octopi, spiders, praying mantises, no creature was free from exploitation, growing to gigantic proportions (and hopefully gigantic box office profits) as fast as writers, directors, and special effects teams could unleash them. As a child, it was so much fun seeing these gigantic creatures wreak havoc and how the protagonists would figure out a way to destroy them before the world was completely demolished.

Granted, if you grew up during this time, when atomic power and radiation was still such a mystery to most people, the writers had free rein to come up with some of the most ludicrous and fantastic theories on how these behemoths could grow to such an enormous sizes, as well as how to defeat them. I mean, when you hear that putting something that is radioactive in water in order to dissipate its dangerous effects, well... it is more than laughable today. But back then who was going to argue, let alone know any different? It was a time when there really weren't any rules when it came to writing these stories, and that is exactly what they did. While much of the "science" in these films would make a real scientist's head spin, we youngsters figured it had to be true.

As I got older, I wanted to know more about not only these movies, but the people responsible for creating these wonderful childhood memories for me. It wasn't just the directors like Gordon Douglas, Jack Arnold, Nathan Juran, and Bert I. Gordon, to name a few, that I wanted to know more about but also the talented and unsung creators of the actual creatures. These are the guys that had to create these giant beasties, decades before CGI, when special effects technology was still being invented. People like Ray Harryhausen, Augie Lohman, Larry Meggs, Cleo E. Baker, and Fred Knoth worked hard at creating the look of these creatures, and more importantly, figuring out how to try and make them come alive on screen. Sure, some of these creatures may look a little cheesy these days, especially when compared to what they did in Spielberg's *Jurassic Park*, but for that time and the tools they had to work with, using a lot of ingenuity, I think they knocked it out of the park on many occasions.

Titles that you should seek out include *Them!*, *Tarantula* (1955), *Black Scorpion*, *The Deadly Mantis*, and *The Monster that Challenged the World* (all 1957). There are more, but those are a good place to start. I can guarantee that after you get through these films, you'll be hooked and will start making your own path in search of next big-bug B-movie!

But it wasn't all towering terrors coming from that decade. I can still remember sitting in my room and watching Don Siegel's *Invasion of the Body Snatchers* (1956) for the first time, on my little 13" black-and-white TV, terrified when it was revealed that the invading alien wasn't a weird-looking green creature, but could look just like someone I knew! This idea that people we knew, our friends and neighbors, were being replaced by some sort of duplicates that grew from a large seedpod, looking exactly the same, but somehow different, less emotional, less human, and they wanted everyone else to become just like them? It was terrifying, even for a little 12-year-old kid. And that ending? Wow! What a kick in the nuts! I think that might have been the first time I can remember a movie that didn't really end, instead playing almost like a beginning. The fact that there wasn't a happy ending here, but that this invasion had only just really started slowly creeping across the world was pretty damn scary for this kid. Sure, there were all these hidden meanings and messages in there, depending on how you wanted to read it, but that didn't mean squat to me at the time. All I knew was that the terrifying look in Kevin McCarthy's eyes at the end as he screamed *"YOU'RE NEXT!"* just scared the crap out of me.

1957's *Night of the Demon* (released as *Curse of the Demon* here in the U.S.) starred Dana Andrews as a professor doing battle with Karswell, brilliantly played by Niall MacGinnis, a man who knows a thing or two about the occult. This is a film centered on the question, "Is the supernatural real?" Granted, the producers changed the ending proving it (in the film at least) really did exist. But then again, did it? A subtle, eerie film, well-crafted with strong performances, it really is one of the best supernatural horror films of that decade.

To prove the point even further that an older film could still be scary, even if there is no monster, or at least one that we never see on screen, let us take a look at one that came less than a decade later, 1963's *The Haunting*, also directed by Robert Wise. I can remember seeing this for the first time, which must have been around my late teens, at my girlfriend (and future wife) Dawn's house. She had already seen this one and knew that I'd love it since it was pretty creepy, so we sat down to watch it.

The story is a simple one, with a group of people going to a haunted house to investigate if evil really does live there. There are no ghosts with rattling chains wandering the halls of Hill House, where our story takes place, but there is something definitely there. What Wise does, as did author Shirley Jackson in her book, *The Haunting of Hill House*, is build characters that we follow along with as strange things start to happen, never tipping a hand on what is really going on. While we might not know what is causing all of these strange noises and actions, we do know that it will send chills up your back and make the hair stand up. There are several sequences that even today can get under my skin. The camerawork here is stunning, with close-ups, spinning shots that will make you dizzy, and quick edits with some incredible jump scares that will have you doing the same. There is even a shot where we are simply looking at a wall, but as it slowly starts to zoom in, at what seems like a snail's pace, we hear muffled voices coming from outside. Is that a face we see in the pattern on the wall? What are those voices saying? All the while, the hair rises on the back of your neck and goose bumps are forming on your arms.

One of the beauties of *The Haunting* is the ambiguity of the story. Even when all is said and done, it is up to the audience to decide what they thought really happened and what they want to take away from it. It is really a masterpiece, epic in its subtlety, and remains one of my favorites to this day. If you haven't experienced this movie yet, you need to. You owe it to yourself as a horror fan.

Another ghost story that has that same uncertainty is *The Innocents* (1961), Jack Clayton's version of Henry James' 1898 novella *Turn of the Screw*, starring Deborah Kerr as a governess hired to take care of a couple of youngsters. Seems like a simple enough story, right? But something darker is going on under the surface here and we're unsure what exactly it is, or where it is coming from. The stunning cinematography by Academy Award-winning DP Freddie Francis is just amazing. This is a prime example of how beautiful and effective a black-and-white movie can be. With its the powerful performances, especially by child actors Martin Stephens and Pamela Franklin, it is a film that will leave you on the edge your seat, particularly during the final minutes.

Mexican Horrors

While we're still on the subject of black-and-white films, there is one subgenre that generated quite a number of titles in the 1950s and 1960s that doesn't seem to get a lot of attention.

Actually... before we get to these films, let us remember that there was a Spanish-language version of *Dracula* shot on the same sets as the Lugosi version back in 1931, filmed at night with a different cast and crew. Some (including me!) say that it is even superior to the American version, with a much more erotic undertone in its take on Bram Stoker's story. Well worth your time, and the first of many highlights on your path south of the border into the Mexican horror genre.

After the success of *Dracula*, other Mexican fright films appeared, such as the *La Llorona* (*The Crying Woman*, 1933), based on a famous folklore tale, and *El Superloco* (*The Super Madmen*, 1936), the first Mexican mad scientist flick, as well as a few more horror-related titles appearing in the 1940s. Once we got into the 1950s, the masked wrestling films of El Santo started, which became its own subgenre known as Lucha Libre! El Santo, as well as the Blue Demon and a variety of other wrestling heroes (and villains), crossed over into the horror genre, fighting vampires, mummies, Martians, Frankenstein's monster, all familiar to U.S. audiences, but with some surprising differences, in the years to come.

But in the late 1950s, producer Abel Salazar wanted to do his own version of Dracula. Hiring Fernando Mendez to direct, they came up with a completely new vampire tale, one set in modern-day Mexico. A somewhat well-known named actor had already been cast for the title role in *El Vampiro*, but at the last minute, Salazar felt he needed to make a change. He figured that, in 1931, Universal used unknown actors for both their monsters in *Dracula* and *Frankenstein*, so he wanted to do the same. Going to a local theater, he came across Germán Robles in a play and decided on the spot that he would be their vampire! *El Vampiro* was released in 1957 and is filled with so much atmosphere and style that it just oozes from your TV. Robles even beat out Christopher Lee as the first screen vampire to wear fangs, though that is a point of contention still up for debate amongst worldwide vampire cinema buffs. Salazar and company followed it up with a sequel the next year, *El ataúd del Vampiro* (*The Vampire's Coffin*), not only producing these pictures but starring in them as well, in titles like *El barón del terror* (*The Brainiac*, 1962), *La cabeza viviente* (*The Living Head*, 1963), and my personal favorite, *La maldición de la llorona* (*The Curse of the Crying Woman*, 1963). While still black-and-white movies, similar in many ways to the Universal efforts from the 1930s, Mexican horror films of this era were inspired, never derivative of the U.S. horror films that came out before. Their unique vision is something well worth exploring.

Hammer Studios

Ah yes... The Studio That Dripped Blood, as they were known. Where to start....

While, since we were talking about black-and-white films, let's start there, shall we? We all know that Hammer was known for their glorious color remakes, but in the years before those, they were making the usual mono-chromatic pictures, as everyone else. In fact, they continued to do so even into the 1960s. But let's back up a bit.

There have been several books written on the history of Hammer Films that I would highly recommend to help you better understand the importance of this studio to horror history and why fans love them so. Denis Meikle's *History of Horrors: The Rise and Fall of the House of Hammer* is required reading, as well as any book by Wayne Kinsey on the subject. Of course, there is also the magazine *Little Shoppe of Horrors*, which is an incredible source of information about the studio, the films, and the people involved with them. All of them I would consider necessary reading for newer Hammer fans.

While some fans might think that Hammer started with *The Curse of Frankenstein* (1957), or potentially stretching back to the Quatermass entries of the mid-'50s, they were producing films as early as the 1930s. In fact, the second picture they ever made, *The Mystery of the Mary Celeste* (1936), starred Bela Lugosi. As I said, there are several sources to go to for a more detailed account of the birth of the studio, but they had started originally as a distribution company before figuring out it would be more lucrative to produce and release their own films. They made dozens of pictures between the 1930s and 1950s, mainly crime dramas, action films, and science fiction tales. They often created film versions of radio programs that were popular at the time, like *Dick Barton, Special Agent* (1948). Since the name itself was already in the public's mind, promotion was already started. It was using this plan that started them down the path of success, when in 1953, there was a six-part serial broadcast on the BBC, titled *The Quatermass Experiment*, about a lone survivor of a rocket-into-space journey who comes back to Earth... a little different.

Since this series was extremely popular, with each new installment clearing the local pubs, Hammer knew it would be perfect to adapt into a feature film. Granted, taking a six-part series and condensing it into a much shorter running time for a theatrical release would be quite a feat. But director and co-writer Val Guest took on the task and created the picture that really started the ball rolling for Hammer. Released in 1955, *The Quatermass Xperiment* starred American actor Brian Donlevy in the role of Professor Quatermass. This was also Hammer's usual game plan, having an American star in their picture (even if they were past their prime) to help bring a little more publicity to the title. This film was a huge hit, really putting them on the map. When the BBC started to broadcast *Quatermass 2* in October of 1955, Hammer jumped on buying the film rights for that as well and had a script started by the next month.

They had some other well-made black-and-white features during the beginning stages of their rise to power, such as *X-The Unknown* (1956), *The Abominable Snowman* and *The Snorkel* (both in 1957), but later that year, things blew up when *Curse of Frankenstein* hit the screens. From there, they tended to stay with that type of programming: full-color gothic thrillers.

After the success of Alfred Hitchcock's *Psycho* in 1960, Hammer began tinkering with their formula, trying their hand at black-and-white thrillers, usually with some sort of twist. The first of these was a top-notch thriller starring Susan Strasberg and Christopher Lee called *Taste of Fear* (1960), released here in the States as *Scream of Fear*. Other titles soon followed, such as *Paranoiac*, *Maniac*, and *Nightmare*, all in 1962. While they more often stayed with their more successful color format, Hammer occasionally returned to this style with projects like *The Nanny* in 1965, starring Bette Davis. These lesser-known black-and-white thrillers, filled with great characters, moody atmosphere, and twisting plots, still can hold the attention of today's audiences, given half a chance.

But it was Hammer's color remakes that truly got horror fans to stand up and take notice. Never before had we witnessed the exploits of Dracula and Dr. Frankenstein in bright and bloody color and fans couldn't get enough of it. Hammer continued their reign of cinematic terror well into the late 1970s though production did begin to slow down considerably by the middle of that decade. Modern-day horrors like *The Exorcist* and *Jaws* were becoming more and more popular and fans were growing tired of the Count and the Baron. But for three decades, Hammer sailed a bloody sea of success with wave upon wave of amazing films, many of which are still considered classics today. Why is that? What makes a Hammer Films so special?

Right off the bat, there was the color. Not just color, but eye-popping bursts of bright red splashes of blood and flesh-toned body parts, it filled in all the objects on the screen that we were used to seeing in black-and-white in the old Universal classics. We could now see how the victims of Dracula actually looked pale and bloodless, a subtle effect that made an impact on the screen.

Another indispensable element was the amazing work of production designer Bernard Robinson and the locations where these pictures were shot. Once again, growing up on the Universal flicks, you knew the backgrounds were just huge backdrops and any village was just one from the Universal lot. But the pictures coming from Hammer seemed more realistic for some reason. Sure, they did use matte paintings now and then, usually to show the castle looming in the background, but the surroundings always looked like they were real places. The work that Robinson did turning Bray Studios (where a lot of the early color films were made) into so many different locations, from Dracula's Castle to the town square of a Cornish village or the home of the infamous Rasputin, is not only amazing, but when you realize how short on time and funds these productions usually were, it is even more impressive. Robinson is one of the true unsung heroes of Hammer.

Helping these monsters look as good as they did, as well as some of their victims, was due to the hard work of makeup maestros Phil Leakey and Roy Ashton. Now there were others that helped out on the makeup side, but it was Leakey and Ashton that created most of the memorable monsters, such as Christopher Lee's distinctive visage for the Creature in *Curse of Frankenstein*, or Ashton's work on Oliver Reed in *Curse of the Werewolf* (1961). Just stunning. These guys worked with very little money, even less time, but still managed to create some amazing effects time after time. Even something as simple as the voodoo mask that John Carson wears in *The Plague of the Zombies* (1966) could be striking and menacing. It is one that I never forgot, and never will, since I now have it tattooed on my arm!

But I think the main reason that these British terrors are so memorable to most fans comes down to one simple thing... the actors. Two of the most famous names helping the studio make their name were of course, Peter Cushing and Christopher Lee. Cushing was somewhat familiar with British audiences because of his appearance in the BBC's adaptation of Orwell's *1984* (1954), but his portrayal of Baron Frankenstein was like nothing we'd ever seen before. This guy was a real bastard! In adapting Shelley's novel, making sure he stayed away from anything from Universal's original in fear of copyright infringement, screenwriter Jimmy Sangster decided to make the Baron the real monster, not the creature. And with Cushing in the role, it worked. For Lee, this was his big break. He'd been working as an actor for over a decade but after *Curse*, he was an overnight star. When these two teamed up once again for their next feature, *Horror of Dracula* (1958), Lee's place in the horror genre was now set in stone, as much as he tried to undo it in later years.

If a film had either of these names in the credits, fans would come out to see them. Whether they were fighting the beasties or playing them, Cushing and Lee always put their heart and soul into their roles, never giving anything less than their all to make their characters believable. Lee took on the role of the most famous vampire, made it his own, and made him terrifying. Same goes with his performance as Kharis the mummy in Hammer's 1959 production of *The Mummy*. No longer was this thousand-year-old creature just shuffling around looking for someone to strangle who was dumb enough to stand there long enough to come within his grasp. Lee's portrayal of him made the famous monster scary again, breaking down doors and busting through windows, showing the victims that they were utterly helpless against him. Cushing also showed audiences the darker side of the human soul, whether outwardly exposing corruption and rescuing the world from the plague of vampiric horror as Dr. Van Helsing or by revealing an inner, personal corruption of the soul as Dr. Frankenstein, challenging the world with his scientific drive and reckless ambition, pushing the limits of science and knowledge, no matter the cost.

There were plenty of other actors and actresses that helped make these films what they were. Andre Morrell, Frances Matthews, Barbara Shelley, Andrew Keir, Veronica Carlson, and Ingrid Pitt, to name just a few, gave wonderful performances in whatever roles they were taking, making the story we were watching believable. Even in the smallest of bit parts, innkeepers, barmaids, or whatever, Hammer had the benefit of talented character actors in supporting roles. George Woodbridge, Richard Wordsworth, and, of course, Michael Ripper were important pieces to the puzzle, a strong foundation that made the picture whole.

Of course, there were just as many important names behind-the-scenes just as noteworthy, including directors like Terence Fisher, John Gilling, and Seth Holt, composer James Bernard, music supervisor John Hollingsworth, and producers like Anthony Hinds and Anthony Nelson-Keys. (The multi-faceted Jimmy Sangster ultimately made his way from the bottom of the industry to the top, moving from assistant director to production manager to screenwriter to director and producer.) Everyone at Hammer, from the wardrobe people to the guys in charge of the props, consistently to turn out high quality entertainment.

If you're not familiar with The Studio That Dripped Blood, then I suggest you start down that path. There are a ton of great movies under Hammer's banner just waiting to be discovered.

Spanish Horror

With all the different regional horror subgenres out there, such as Italian, Japanese, British, etc., one country that doesn't seem to get as much attention is Spain, though that does seem to be slowly changing. Let's take a look into this country's wonderful output of horror cinema over the last five decades and maybe convert a few new fans along the way

I can't mention the Spanish horror genre and not start with writer/director/actor Paul Naschy. The man made quite a few titles in his career and I've enjoyed many of them. He made all sorts of horror films, usually filled with plenty of monsters, both human and of the supernatural kind, especially the wolf man. He was waving the genre flag at a time when most were not, and did so in a country that really didn't like or want those kinds of films being produced there. But he made them anyway. Naschy's output is just staggering, making over a dozen films featuring his lycanthropy-cursed Waldemar Daninsky character alone. Naschy was a huge fan of the genre, playing just about every one of the classic monsters over his career as well as many new ones of his own creation. Here's a little taste of Naschy's filmography: *Frankenstein's Bloody Terror* (1968), *Hunchback of the Morgue* (1973), *Horror Rises from the Tomb* (1973), *Blue Eyes of the Broken Doll* (1974), *Night of the Howling Beast* (1975), *The Mummy's Revenge* (1975), and *Night of the Werewolf* (1981).

But Naschy wasn't the only guy. There was Jesus "Jess" Franco who was making films all over the world, not just Spain. While today, his films might be known for being cheesy schlock, or just plain bad, there was a time when this highly crafted filmmaker could turn out some well-made pictures. Films like *The Awful Dr. Orlof* (1962) and *The Diabolical Dr. Z* (1966) are artistic achievements and standouts in Franco's filmography, while on the other end of the spectrum, titles like *Dracula, Prisoner of Frankenstein* (1972), *Female Vampire* (1973), and *Bloody Moon* (1981) might not be as skillfully directed, but I find them highly entertaining. And at the end of it all, isn't that what it is all about?

Spanish horror has their own brand of famous monsters as well, such as the infamous Blind Dead from the mind of Amando de Ossorio. Taking the myth/legends of the Knights Templar, he re-wrote their history to create the spectral monsters that would first appear in 1972's *Tombs of the Blind Dead* (*La noche del terror ciego*). With the slow-motion sequences of them galloping across the countryside on horseback, Ossorio came up with an unique and disturbing icon of Spanish horror, whose popularity expanded to three films debuting over the next three years: *The Return of the Evil Dead* (*El ataque de los muertos sin ojos*, 1973), *Horror of the Zombies* (*El buque maldito*, 1974), *Night of the Seagulls* (*La noche de las gaviotas*, 1975), cementing the director's place in horror cinema. But Ossorio wasn't finished there. He also gave us entertaining titles like *The Lorelei's Grasp* (*Las garras de Lorelei*, 1973), *The Night of the Sorcerers* (*La noche de los brujos*, 1974), and his last film, *The Sea Serpent* (1985), which is not an Oscar contender for sure, but is still a damn fun movie and perfect for any Turkey Day screening!

There are also many notable figures like León Klimovsky, Eugenio Martin, Juan López Moctezuma, and a few others continuing to work in the genre. Some of the more gothic titles, from directors like Naschy, Klimovsky, and Ossorio, were perfect for fans that were following those same kinds of pictures coming from Hammer in England. Like those, the ones made in Spain also had the benefit of using real landscapes that were readily available, giving an added sense of realism to these films, especially to a younger audience. Spanish productions were also pushing the limits of sex and gore, going even farther than what Hammer was doing, usually having plenty of flesh and blood on display. Still others, like Naschy, fueled by a passion for Universal's classic monsters at an early age, incorporated these U.S. productions into their own work, but putting their own spin on things, making these films much different than what had come before.

Over the last couple of decades, there has been a huge resurgence of horror films coming out of Spain that are continuing the tradition of creepy cinema. Director Álex de la Iglesia isn't one to really fit into one single genre, usually hitting several in one picture but they are always over-the-top and make for a very entertaining trip. His first feature, *Acción mutante* (1993), about a group of handicapped terrorists that are out to get the rich and famous, is about as crazy as you can get. He's built his career with great titles like *The Day of the Beast* (*El dia de la bestia*, 1995) or the more recent *Witching and Bitching* (*Las brujas de Zugarramurdi*, 2013) and shows no signs of caving into mainstream movie pressures, relishing instead his outsider status making the kind of films that he wants. Something that is dearly missed in Hollywood.

In 2007, J.A. Bayona directed one of my favorite films, *The Orphanage*, a touchingly atmospheric tale full of secrets and dread. I only hope, since he's been making bigger Hollywood films lately, that he doesn't lose that sense of creativity and originality. Judging from his last couple of features though, I think he's on the right path.

Also in 2007, Paco Plaza and Jaume Balagueró gave us one of the few POV/found-footage movies that not only worked for me, but also gave a great boost to the dying zombie subgenre, *[Rec]*. Making the inspired choice of confining most of the film to a single location, Plaza and Balagueró's story of a television reporter trapped with the tenants of an apartment building suddenly quarantined by the police is an exercise in suspense as events spiral into chaos. There's a lot at work here beyond the basic narrative – it took three sequels (of varying degrees of quality, depending on who you ask) to figure all of this out – but the film leaves its mark.

Balagueró's first feature, *The Nameless* (*Los sin nombres*, 1999), showed us he was serious about his work. His 2002 follow-up, *Darkness*, starring a young Anna Paquin, despite its flaws, still showed a great sense of not following the traditional rules. My favorite film he has made so far has been 2005's *Fragile*, set in a children's hospital on the verge of shutting down, starring Calista Flockhart and Richard Roxburgh. If you're a fan of classic ghost stories, then you will love this one. His segment in the *6 Films to Keep You Awake* series, *To Let* (2008), is my favorite of them and a non-stop terror ride, starring the amazing Macarena Gómez. If you want to really get creeped out, check out *Sleep Tight* (*Mientras duermes*, 2011).

What this current wave of directors has shown is that Spain has come a long way when it comes to the horror genre, compared to where they were back in the early Naschy days. And that is always a good thing.

Italian Films

When I really started to take my horror education seriously, there were some films that were considered Must-See and Must-Have titles for one's collection. At that time, in the early '80s, for most young horror fans (meaning in experience, not age), it was all about the gore. And nobody did gore like the Italians. Spanish director Jorge Grau really started the color flesh-eating zombies phase with *Let Sleeping Corpses Lie* (1974); four years later, George Romero and Tom Savini upped the ante with *Dawn of the Dead* (1978), not to mention all the slasher films that Savini was providing ground-breaking effects for, like *Friday the 13th* (1980), *Maniac* (1980), or *The Burning* (1981). But it was the Italians that took gore to a gourmet level. Okay... maybe more like a buffet.

One of the directors leading that charge was Lucio Fulci. A highly talented craftsman, Fulci's career encompassed many genres, including comedies and action films, but he found his greatest success in horror with legendary films like *Zombie* (1979), *City of the Living Dead* (1980), and *The Beyond* (1981). Thanks to Fulci, we got to see wood splinters slowly penetrating an eyeball, a drill bit cutting its way through someone's skull, acid pouring over a woman's face, and so many other dementedly delightful sequences.

Let me give you an example of his genius when it came to gore. In *The Beyond*, there is a scene where one of the undead attacks a woman in one of the rooms of a cursed hotel. The creature grabs her by the face and slowly pushes her back towards the wall. Now the camera shows us a shot of a huge nail sticking out of the wall directly behind her, so we know that he is going to push her head right on it, hitting the head on the nail, so to speak. With quick shots edited between the nail on the wall and the woman's head being pushed back closer and closer, back and forth, closer and closer, we're nervously anticipating this character's demise, until BAM! It is slammed up against the nail, just like we knew it was going to. But where Fulci shines, where the real payoff is, is not the head hitting the nail, which the audience was expecting, instead it is the shot of the nail going through the head and pushing the eyeball right out of its socket, giving the viewers a little extra stab of shock and adrenaline! It may seem like a cheap gag, but it is effective and took the audience farther than was expected.

The Beyond is a perfect example of a film that threw logic right out the window. Some of us seeing it in American theaters under the title *Seven Doors of Death* might have thought it didn't make sense because it was cut. (Granted, at the time, we probably had no clue that there was actually an uncut version out there.) But even so, there are still plenty of things that just don't add up or make sense. And that was the whole idea. Fulci wasn't interested in making a linear plot line. He wanted atmosphere. He wanted gory effects. As he put it himself, "My idea was to make an absolute film, with all the horrors of our world. It's a plotless film: a house, people, and dead men coming from the beyond. There's no logic to it, just a succession of images."

Of course, Fulci wasn't the only one to be assaulting our young minds. Aristide Massacessi, better known as Joe D'Amato, gave us plenty to shudder about with the very dark and disturbing *Buio Omega* (1979), the sex-crazed *Erotic Nights of the Living Dead* (1980), and the ultimate (and literal) gut-muncher *Antropophagus* (1981), where George Eastman's character chomps on his own intestines, not to mention the famous fetus-eating scene. (Yep. You read that right.) Of course, there were plenty of other directors doling out the gooey red stuff, like Michele Soavi with *Stagefright* (1987) and *The Church* (1989), Lamberto Bava with *Demons* (1985), and even Bruno Mattei with *Hell of the Living Dead* (1980), just to name a few. These were the kinds of titles that we young gorehounds were ravenous for. We didn't care if the movies were well-made or didn't make any sense. We just wanted to see the juicy bits, the over-the-top blood 'n' guts, and they always delivered. As it turned out, some of these were actually highly crafted features!

Now, anyone who was thinking that stories should start at the beginning, have a middle, and then be tied up nicely at the end, might have had difficulties with the European sense of filmmaking. As Fulci stated, sometimes the stories didn't make sense, or they didn't have an ending that really explained what we just watched, or the narrative was completely disjointed. This can be known as "style over substance," where there was more importance placed on the look and feel of the picture than the story. Italian directors didn't care if there was an explanation as to why the black-gloved killer was stalking and slashing his victims, as long as he looked cool doing it! Not all European films followed this process, but it definitely wasn't an unusual path to follow.

What they may have lacked in story or plotlines, they made up for with style. Big time. Of course, one of the directors leading that parade in the 1970s was Dario Argento. He was one of the bigger names that younger fans sought out, finding plenty of red stuff, like the brutal murder of the doomed psychic Helga in *Deep Red* (1975), the over-the-top double murder at the beginning of *Suspiria* (1977), or the arm-severing conclusion of *Tenebre* (1982). The "style" that I mentioned was always evident within the frames of Argento's work. He gave us some incredible visuals, using intricate camera shots, incredibly long dolly shots, almost microscopic close-ups, showing our eyes cinema like we'd never seen before. Surrounding all of these amazing visuals was incredible scores from the likes of Ennio Morricone and the band Goblin, taking us on a unique cinematic ride.

Take his 1987 picture *Opera*, for example, which happens to be one of my favorites. There are quite a few different sequences here that put the spotlight on this particular director's camerawork. Some shots are minor and quick, while others are longer and more elaborate. One of my favorites is a simple one. During a sequence where the camera is acting as the killer's POV, when we hear his heart beat, the camera actually trembles or flutters with the sound of the beating. Nothing mind-blowing, and yet something so simple that it adds so much to the look of the film.

There is also the amazing sequence with the peephole. (Before I go further, have you seen this movie? If not, then you're going to want to skip to the next paragraph. In the meantime, go find yourself a copy of this movie. You need to see it. Okay... back to the scene.) The way Argento sets up this shot is just brilliant. As someone (who we think is a cop) is knocking on the door, Mira (Daria Nicolodi) shouts at him while looking through the apartment door's peephole. Camera shots cut back and forth from Mira's view, to a profile shot with her head pressed up against the door, to a shot we see the gun pointed right at the camera. Then we see a bullet coming down the chamber of the barrel, then cut to seeing the hair on the back of Mira's head blow out with the bullet going right into her eye and out the back of her head, to the bullet hitting the phone on the floor down the hall at the back of the apartment. Pure genius with such a great payoff. Dark and twisted, yes, but beautifully shot. (No pun intended.) Just think of the work involved in pulling off that one little sequence.

Here is another great sequence: Near the end of the film, close to the climax at the opera house, there are crows that are flying around loose. Argento had a huge apparatus built that would swing the camera around in circles while moving up and down from the ceiling to the floor, giving the audience a bird's point of view as it flew around the auditorium. Again, another shot where a lot of time and money went into just for one little sequence, but it shows the visual talent that Argento had and wanted to put in his film.

Another example of Argento's visual talent is the glorious use of colors in *Suspiria*, where it becomes almost surreal with its kaleidoscopic use of colors, bright and vibrant blues, reds, and greens to add a fairy tale quality to the story. Hard to forget.

Of course, Argento wasn't the first Italian to paint his horror film with that kind of palette. A decade before Argento made his directorial debut with *The Bird with the Crystal Plumage* (1970), another Italian director made his official debut with a black-and-white film called *Black Sunday* (1960). And while it wasn't in color, the way he painted the screen with style and atmosphere, you'd think it was. That director was Mario Bava and once he moved to color films, it was if the visible spectrum was made just for him. Just watch some of the films he made in the '60s and witness the incredible use of colors, such as in *Black Sabbath* (1963), *Blood and Black Lace* (1964), or even the campy *Planet of the Vampires* (1965). It will hopefully open your eyes to the power and beauty of cinema.

These are only a few of the many talented filmmakers Italian horror has produced. The first steps on a long and winding path. If you're a beginner to the genre, then these guys are a great place to start. If you've dabbled with a few of them, seek more out. Or if you're already familiar with their work, then I encourage you to search on, discover new directors and find their work. You will be amazed at how much wonderful cinema is out there. Once you can let the need for a structured, linear plot go out the window and embrace what these directors are doing with the camera and graphic visuals, you will start to enjoy these films for what they are: incredible pieces of cinema made by stellar craftsmen.

Hong Kong

Back in the '80s, there was a short-lived British TV series called *The Incredibly Strange Film Show*, hosted by Jonathon Ross. Encompassing about a dozen episodes spread over two seasons, Ross interviewed cult filmmakers like John Waters, H.G. Lewis, Doris Wishman, Sam Raimi, George Romero, Jackie Chan, and others, discussing their work, their lives, and the impact they've had on the world of cinema. Ross was a fun host, with his over-pronounced lisp calling them "how-wor movies." But seeing his reaction to some of his guests, their strange films and sometimes even stranger life choices, such as Ted V. Mikels and his tales of living in a castle, was the best part of the show. Even if you didn't care for Ross as host, the show was still a great place to learn about some of the fringes of crazy cinema. Case in point: one of the episodes was on Hong Kong producer/director Tsui Hark. He had worked with John Woo on the features that really put their names on the map, such as the *A Better Tomorrow* films and *The Killer* (1989). But he also produced a wide range of films, with a few scenes from some of them shown on this TV series.

One of the films he produced that they showed clips from was simply called *A Chinese Ghost Story* (*Sien nui yau wan*, 1987). What I saw just blew me away. For someone who was used to the same old stereotypical monsters coming from Hollywood, this film was bat-shit crazy, with stop-animated zombies, giant tongues, flying heads, demons with huge mouths like giant alligators, and some of the most beautiful ghosts I've ever seen! I immediately set out to find a copy. Since Chicago had a very large Asian population, I figured I'd try to find some video stores in those areas that might carry some of these films. Most of these stores were little hole-in-the-wall places that were basically renting bootleg VHS copies, usually with a hand-written label scrawled across it, usually not in English as well, or with markings at all. All of the boxes would be on the shelves, somewhat like a video store and you'd pick up the empty box and show it to the person behind the counter, putting that quizzical look on your face as to say, "Do you have this one in stock?"

Some of the places seemed a little put off by some crazy white guy coming in asking for movies that weren't even in English. One store in particular, which had a younger guy working there, told me that every single movie I was asking for wasn't available each and every time I asked. Needless to say, I never went back to that one. But for the most part, I never had any issues at the different places I found, and when I learned more and more about the movies and the people in them, would often surprised the workers there when I would ask for a movie with Chingmy Yau or Wang Tsu Hsien, or one of the many other actors or actresses I had soon begun to admire.

It was a crap-shoot if the tape you were renting was going to have subtitles or not. But I soon discovered that a lot of these Hong Kong films had storylines that were pretty easy to follow though you may not get every last detail of the story. No matter what, visually it was amazing. And at that point, I was going to be happy with any version of these films that I could get my hands on.

When I finally was able to track down a copy of *A Chinese Ghost Story*, which ended up not having subtitles, I still watched it awe. The cinematography was unbelievable, as well as the outrageous special effects and creatures. A thousand-year-old tree demon with a huge tongue that would go right down your throat and drain the life out of you in seconds. Didn't matter if I couldn't understand what was being said. Once I upgraded to a copy that actually did have subtitles, it was nearly the same story I originally deciphered on that first viewing. Leslie Cheung stars as our hapless hero who happens to fall in love with the stunningly beautiful Joey Wang. Unfortunately for him, she is a ghost that is being used by a demon to draw in victims to feed it. So basically this is a love story, but one done with so much style and atmosphere and beauty, that you can't help but fall in love with this movie. Sure, it might have something to do with the charming

Ms. Wang that attracted me to the movie, but I'd like to think it was much more than that.

I soon learned that there was actually a trilogy of these films, all directed by Siu-Tung Ching. *A Chinese Ghost Story II* (*Sien nui yau wan II yan gaan do*, 1990) continued the story of Cheung's character, with Joey Wang playing another person that just happens to look like his lost ghostly love from the first film. The final part of the trilogy, *A Chinese Ghost Story III* (*Sien lui yau wan III: Do do do*, 1991), takes place 100 years after the first film with a new hero, a fumbling apprentice monk played by Tony Leung who, along with his old master, battles the tree demon from the first film. Joey Wang is back once again as another ghost luring the attention of the young monk. Both of these sequels are filled with the same kind of crazy action/horror as the first one. The first film was so successful that it basically started a whole subgenre of films in Hong Kong with a ton of similarly-themed films following suit with some even going the sexy route like *Erotic Ghost Story* (*Liu jai yim taam*, 1990), which also had a few sequels.

The deeper down the hole I went, I found more and more outrageous horror films coming from that small part of the world. Titles like *Centipede Horror* (*Wu gong zhou*, 1982), *Dr. Lamb* (*Gou yeung yi sang*, 1992), or three of the best of the lot, *Seeding of a Ghost* (*Zhong gui*, 1983), *The Seventh Curse* (*Yuan Zhen-Xia yu Wei Si-Li*, 1986), and *The Untold Story* (*Bat sin fan dim: Yan yuk cha siu bau*, 1993), which I would consider well worth seeking out. I will warn you that these last three titles are very dark and grim in some cases, especially *The Untold Story*, but they are worth it. Even the action/comedy/horror vampire film series, which started in 1985 with *Mr. Vampire* (*Geung si sin sang*), are a lot of fun. This was another film that gave birth to a whole subgenre after its huge success.

These Hong Kong films revealed a world that I might not have ever experienced, both on screen, watching the films, and in the real world with my many quests taking me to Chinese video stores in search for the next film. All because of *The Incredibly Strange Films Show* inspiring me to step onto that path.

Presumably by now, you've found a few new titles to seek out and maybe start digging a little deeper into one of these subgenres. If you have, then I have done my job. Hopefully you enjoy them as much as I do. As a true student of the genre, you should never be afraid to try something different. Seeking out new films and subgenres is just as important as re-watching your old favorites. Without that new blood, your viewing can grow stale, even downright boring. So take it from me, explore, take a chance on something different, or out of the ordinary. Sure, it may kill a few hours of your future, but the adventure will be worth it.

with Barbara Steele, HorrorHound 2015

with Dawn and William Grefe, Cinema Wasteland 2016

with Bryan Martinez, Dawn, and Alan Tromp, Monster Bash 2016

Pieces cake by Dawn

Mariano Baino, Bryan Martinez, Coralina Cataldi-Tassoni, Music Box of Horrors 2017

Blood Freak *cake by Dawn*

Drive-In cake by Dawn

Z.A.A.T. vs Sting of Death cake by Dawn

with Richard Johnson

with Jon Stone and Mark McConnaughey, Horrorfind Weekend 2004

Turkey Day in May 2017

with Bryan Martinez and Scott Bradley, Cinema Wasteland 2016

Evilspeak *crew*

with Ken Johnson

with Alex de la Iglesia and Phil Meenan

Hidden Horror book launch

Corndog + Drive-in = Heaven

16

The Drive-in Experience

"The drive-in people love this stuff. They'll sit and watch this for 10 minutes. And then go get their hot dog."

Larry Buchanan, on his film *The Naked Witch* (1961)

The drive-in theaters are definitely a thing of a different era. For those us who grew up in the 1950s through the '70s and maybe even into the '80s, going to the drive-in wasn't the same as going to the movies. Sure the picture and sound quality might not be as good as the local hardtop, but it was so much more than that. It was the experience that made it so special, at least for me.

Richard M. Hollingshead, Jr. was the man responsible for creating the very first drive-in theater, The Automobile Movie Theater, which opened in Camden, New Jersey, on June 6th, 1933. That's right, kiddies, the drive-in has been around for over 85 years. It was a place where the whole family could go and, even better, for a cheap price. The parents didn't have to get a babysitter, or worry about the kids being too noisy or rambunctious, since they were in the privacy of their own car and wouldn't bother their neighbors. By the 1950s, drive-ins were all over the place. No longer a place just for families, it was now the perfect place for teenagers to take their dates, giving them the privacy that they wanted. Sometimes, they'd even watch the movies! Some things have never changed over the years either.

Unfortunately, this mobile movie experience is something that is almost lost on most people these days. While some of these theaters are still around, their numbers have dropped considerably. There used to be thousands of drive-in theaters across the U.S. Now, there are only a little more than 300. This is such a sad thing to think there is a generation that might not learn and experience the joy and excitement of going to one of these classic outdoor theaters. It isn't just going to a movie, but truly a whole entertainment experience that can't be replicated anywhere else.

Thankfully, there are a few of these places still around, usually struggling to keep afloat, where we can still go, taking a trip back in time to enjoy a double feature under the stars. For me, there is just something special about a drive-in that I love. From seeing the movies through the front seat of your car, or out in a lawn chair in front of your vehicle, taking a trip to the concession stand for a corn dog and a root beer... it's like you stepped into a different world, a world filled with a warm and nostalgic feel that I always enjoy. There really is nothing quite like it. I'm so thrilled that I've been able to share this experience with my son quite a few times over the years, but we'll get into that a little later.

The very first time I got to go to a drive-in as a kid was when my brother-in-law took me to see *Infra-Man*. This had to be around 1975, making me close to ten years old. I can remember being in the backseat of the car, waiting for this film to start. It was a Japanese movie about a robotic superhero going around battling all sorts of monsters, with tons of karate action and lots of jumping and flipping around; something any ten-year-old boy would love. But before it started, there were some trailers for the coming attractions and for some strange reason, I can vividly remember the two that were screened. The first one was for *Gumball Rally* (1976), sort of a precursor to *Cannonball Run* (1981). The second was for René Cardona's *Survive!* (1976), the real-life story about the 1971 plane crash in the Andes mountains with a Uruguayan rugby team. This version of the film really hyped up the cannibalism aspect of the story in true exploitation manner. Not sure why, but these two trailers stuck in my head.

Once *Infra-Man* started, it was just awesome. There was a lot of kung-fu fighting, all sorts of Saturday morning cartoon action that I grew up with, but this wasn't a cartoon, it was real live action! Then when the monsters started to appear, I have to admit, some of them scared the crap out of me. These are the same type of creatures that one might see in the *Power Rangers* TV show, and yeah, it scared me enough to duck down behind the seat so I couldn't see the monsters. Boy, how things have changed! But it still remains one of my favorite childhood memories, sitting in the backseat at a drive-in, eating up the action (and popcorn) that played before me.

It was around that time when I moved to Aurora, IL. Since I was only 10 years old at the time, even if I had realized there was a drive-in theater near me, there was no way I would be able to convince either of my parents to take me to one. So I would have to wait until I was not only old enough, but had my own car.

Aurora had two drive-in theaters, the Skylark Drive-In and the Hi-Lite 30. The Skylark was open from 1962 until it finally closed down in 1985. Not sure why but I didn't get out to this one that often. The one time I do remember going to this particular theater was in 1982 to see John Carpenter's *The Thing*, inexplicably paired with *Enter the Ninja*, starring Franco Nero. But then again, I enjoyed the hell out of both of them!

The other drive-in was the Hi-Lite 30, or as it was known in town as "the Dirty 30." The reason for that was because not only was there an outdoor screen, but also an indoor theater on the premises that was built sometime later, that, at some point, started playing adults-only features. Apparently the outdoor theater used to have its own concessions area or building, but that was before my time. When I started going to the drive-in, the concessions building was already part of the indoor theater. The actual outdoor part had opened in 1947 and was the oldest drive-in in Illinois before it closed in 2006. In fact, I was there the very last time this theater was open. But before we get to that, let's back up a bit.

Before I ever had my own car, my buddy and I would convince his mom to take us to the Hi-Lite 30 on the nights when they would show kung-fu triple-features, screening titles like *Fist of Fury* (1971), *The Chinese Connection* (1972), and *Enter the Dragon* (1973). We would pitch in some money for her to buy herself some beer and she would sit in the back of the car and drink while we sat in the front and watched Bruce Lee kick some major ass. Great times.

I still visited this place after I had my own car, seeing more martial arts flicks like Joe Lewis' *Force Five* (1981), as well as a few horror titles. One evening in particular, I was there to see *Evil Dead 2* (1987) on its initial release. Once again, here's another title that wasn't playing at any of the indoor theaters in my area, so this was my only opportunity to get to see it on the big screen. Much to my dismay, my first screening of this wasn't as enjoyable as I'd hoped. Since I was a huge fan of the first film, especially because of all the gore, and because of all the gruesome photos from this new sequel that I'd been eating up in the pages of *Fangoria*, I was expecting another onslaught of blood and guts. What I wasn't expecting was it to be more of a comedy. (Obviously, once I changed my expectations, I learned to enjoy the film for what it is.)

At some point, the indoor theater closed down for a while, opening up sometime later as a second run theater. This is where they would screen one or two films that had already made the circuit a few weeks earlier, but for a much discounted price, like $1 per title. The only time I went there was for a double feature of *Child's Play* and *Hellbound: Hellraiser 2* (both 1988). By then, the "screen" looked more like a quilt than an actual screen, with many large patches over different parts of the screen. When my buddy and I got there, as we were looking for our seats, we noticed one aisle was covered with a thick layer of that kitty litter stuff that is used to put over an area where someone had vomited. And from the amount they had on the floor, this person must have emptied his entire stomach... twice. So we moved a few rows back and sat down. A few minutes later, these two kids are running up and down the aisles, being noisy and obnoxious as hell. Then we see them start down "puke alley" and we both watched with bated breath as this little kid was flying down the aisle, only to have both of his legs slide out in front him going right though the onslaught of upchuck! He got up completely covered with a sickening combination of vomit and kitty litter, even mashed up in his hair. I have to say, I can't remember a time when feelings of disgust and laughter came together with such force.

Not sure what the official date was, but by 2005, the entire Hi-Lite Theater was closed. I know the outside theater ran for a little while after they re-closed the indoor screen, but it didn't last too long. In September of 2005, an event was held there that would be a very memorable night, one filled with joy and happiness, as well as sadness, even though we didn't realize it at the time. Mike and Mia Kerz, who run the *Flashback Weekend* conventions in Rosemont, IL, had decided to put on a one-night event at the Hi-Lite 30, throwing a dusk-til-dawn marathon, just like the old days. My family and I had known Mike and Mia since we'd been dealers at the *Flashback* shows since they started. We were very excited about this drive-in event because we had never had the chance to experience one of those epic evenings filled with popcorn and horror; even better it was only about fifteen minutes from our house. The lineup for this event was going to be five different movies: *Last House on the Left* (1972), *Evil Dead 2* (1987), *The Beyond* (1981), *Dead and Breakfast* (2004), and *Pieces* (1982). They were also going to have some special guests there as well, such as the star of *Last House*, David Hess, and Tom Sullivan, the man responsible for creating all the effects on the first *Evil Dead* film. I knew I was going to be at this event no matter what, but quickly contacted Mike to see if he was going to have any vendors there, because I'd love to be one of them! The answer was "yes" and we were in! This was going to be my first time (of many) that I was going to be setting up at an event like this. The chance, not to only see some incredible films on the big screen, but also to get to hang out with other like-minded film fans; how could it be anything but a glorious night.

Now there are a few moments in the life of a parent that are forever etched in your brain. For some, it might be when their kid hits the winning run in a little league game, or maybe them coming home from school with a report card full of As. Of course, for me, it wasn't going to be as traditional as that, because it happened that night at the drive-in.

This all-night horrorthon was taking place on Sept. 24th, just two days after my son Nick's 13th birthday. I brought him along to be my helper this time out because I knew he was a huge fan of *Evil Dead 2* and *Army of Darkness* (1992), though he had never gotten around to seeing the first one in the series... yet. We tried once, but it was still a little too intense for him at that time. So this night would be special for the fact that he would be getting to see *Evil Dead 2* on the very same screen that I had, some 20 years earlier. Talk about some father-son bonding! Since Nick was a huge fan of these movies, I knew that he would get a kick out of meeting Tom Sullivan. I had met Tom a few years earlier at the first Cinema Wasteland show (where he has become a regular staple) and we had become good friends over the years. Plus, he usually would bring props and memorabilia from the original film for fans to check out, so I knew Nick would just eat that stuff up.

Shortly after we get to the drive-in, unload our stuff at the concession area and set up our vendor table, the skies open up and it starts to pour. And I mean POUR! Just like the amount of multi-colored blood gushing down on Bruce Campbell in the *Evil Dead* films. But just as I started to think that this perfect evening was going to literally go down the drain, as quickly as the rain started, it stopped. After that, it didn't take long for people to start arriving either. Before the movies were going to start, there was going to be some sort of magic show and maybe even a band playing as well, which was cool because it made this more than just about watching movies, it made it an actual event.

The first movie in the lineup was going to be *Last House*. I knew this was not a film Nick needed to see at his current age so it worked out perfectly. My plan was to keep our table open until about halfway through *Last House*, then breakdown and get things loaded back into the van, so we'd be ready to watch the rest of the movies. Once it had started to get dark, someone had set up a projector and was screening *Evil Dead* against one of the walls inside the concession area. So Nick stood over there and was able to get through the entire movie this time. Maybe the environment made it a little less scary? Who knows? I just know that he was pretty proud of himself to finally check it off his list.

After the movie had ended, I figured Nick would be back at the table with me. But then I noticed that he was over at Tom Sullivan's table. I could hear him grilling Tom on how they did some of the different effects and Tom was gracious enough to fill his head with all those great stories of low-budget filmmaking. After a while, I went over there to tell him to stop bothering Tom, but as I walked over there, this is when my Hallmark Parent Moment happened. As I got closer, I noticed that Nick was standing between two older adults and he was going on and on about different horror movies, telling them different things about them. One of them asked him, "How do you know so much about these films?" Nick replied, in a very proud voice, "Because my dad knows everything about horror movies." I had to stop a moment to wipe away the small tear forming in my eye, which I'm sure was from some salt floating around from the popcorn. It was a damn proud moment for me, but it didn't stop there.

When I finally went up there, I told Nick to stop bothering Tom and to let other people have a chance at him. Tom graciously said it was no problem and asked Nick if he wanted to get a photo together, which he quickly replied with a big "YES!" Tom then told Nick to come behind the table, turn and face me. Tom had turned to the side and then turns back around with the original severed head from the original *Evil Dead* in his hands, and quickly holds it out to Nick like it was nothing special, which he takes, then quickly realizes what he is holding in his hands. A piece of movie history that most people have never even seen up close in real life, and yet, here he is standing there, a 13-year-old kid, holding the actual prop from this famous movie. The look on his face was like he was holding the Holy Grail. His face lit up, eyes bulging wide, with a smile on his face big enough to make Mr. Sardonicus jealous. Out of all the conventions that I've attended with Nick, seeing various guests and celebrities, that moment in time, with the glowing look on his young face, still brings a smile to my face.

And, following in his old man's footsteps, Nick told me days later that he tried to describe to his friends at school what had happened at the drive-in that night and what he got to hold… only to be met with the usual reaction of someone that had no clue of that historical moment and what it meant. He learned that lesson early.

Once *Last House* was coming to a close, we had our stuff packed up in the van, turned facing backwards with the hatch up, and sat in the back with blankets and snacks waiting for *Evil Dead 2* to start. I think Nick crashed sometime after that one and slept through most of the other ones. I tried to nap during *Dead and Breakfast* mainly because I wanted to stay awake for the last film, *Pieces*. I have to say, if there was ever a movie made for the grindhouse or drive-in market, *Pieces* is it. And I guess it is only fitting that it would turn out to be the very last film ever to be screened at the Hi-Lite 30.

Mike and Mia Kerz were planning to purchase the drive-in, put some work into it and bring it back to life, in order to make a great family-orientated place for people to enjoy the drive-in experience. But due to some political bullshit, they were denied the chance to do that, since the property was going to be turned into housing, parking spaces, or apartments, according to conflicting reports. On the morning of Friday, July 21st, 2006, this historical attraction came crashing down as demolition crews started their work, officially ending the life of this 58-year-old landmark. Most people from this area probably never even thought twice about it, which really is a shame. Just imagine the thousands and thousands of eager film fans sitting in their cars over the last five decades, eating popcorn, being entranced by what was being projected on the giant movie screen (or maybe more entranced by what they were doing in the backseat). For a lot of us, the Hi-Lite 30 had a special meaning and was a special place. Thankfully, while that would be the last time I was to enjoy the exploits of the Hi-Lite Drive, it would not be the last time I'd have the opportunity to delve back into the past to enjoy many other all-night, from dusk-til-dawn movie marathons at a drive-in.

In 2007, Mike and Mia purchased the Midway Drive-In located in Sterling, IL, spending quite some time renovating it, breathing life back into, what is now the oldest running drive-in in the state of Illinois. And it wasn't long after the Midway was up and running before they held the first (of many) "from dusk-til-dawn" horror movie marathons. I think we've been to just about every single one of them and have always had a great time. These events are usually packed with avid horror fans excited for the chance to see some of these classic films on the big screen. Thanks to the Kerz family and the Midway, we've gotten to see films like *Phantasm* (1979), *Dawn of the Dead* (1978), *A Nightmare on Elm Street* (1984), *The Texas Chain Saw Massacre* (1974), *I Drink Your Blood* (1970), *The Town that Dreaded Sundown* (1976), *Psycho* (1960), and more, on the big screen, surrounded by fellow drive-in and horror fans. I know there are many more events like this coming, and I plan on being there.

It wasn't long before I started looking for other drive-in theaters that were still up and running that also hosted all-night marathons. The Riverside Drive-In in Vandergrift, PA, has been hosting Monster-Rama marathons since around 2007, with two nights of classic horrors, all from 35mm prints. I would see these advertised every year and stated each and every time, "I'm going to this one!" but never made it. It would always come down to the fact that I'd be driving over 1000 miles there and back, just to watch some movies that I already owned on DVD. The cost of that trip would always override the desire. Until 2011, when we made a little family vacation out of it and made the trip, which was well worth it.

As I began my search for other drive-in theaters, I came across one that was much closer that was also doing these two nights of classic horror films. Enter the Skyline Drive-in in Shelbyville, Indiana. This place is located right off I-74, about 30 minutes south of Indianapolis. I believe it was in 2011 when they began holding their Super Monster Movie Fest in August, screening an assortment of classic titles both Friday and Saturday, then replaying some of them on Sunday. Since this was so much closer than Pennsylvania, it would make for a much easier trip, and in 2012, we did just that.

The first year we went, on Friday they screened *Chamber of Horrors* (1966), Amicus' *Vault of Horror* (1973), Antonio Margheriti's *Castle of Blood* (1964), and *Scream Bloody Murder* (1973), which featured a young Angus Scrimm. Then on Saturday, they featured *Tell Tale Heart* (1960), *The Ghost* (1963) starring Barbara Steele, *Face of the Screaming Werewolf* (1964) featuring Lon Chaney Jr., and *Kiss of the Tarantula* (1976). As expected, it was a lot of fun. We got a hotel room close by, so after the last movie ended we'd head back to catch a few hours of sleep, then head back into Indianapolis to hit the different bookstores, as well as a few of the amazing restaurants in the area, meeting up with good friends and having a great time.

In 2016, Dawn couldn't make it, so it was just my son Nick and me making the trip. Always trying to save a buck, I figured we could just sleep in the van there at the drive-in and save a couple hundred bucks on a hotel. The Skyline allows people to camp overnight so I thought it would be perfect. Well... almost perfect. During the day, the temperature was in the upper 80s, so by the time the sun went down, it was still hovering above 70 degrees. This meant that our hopes that the van would be rather cool at night just weren't going to happen. Instead, it felt like an oven. There were times we had to turn on the A/C just to break some of the heat, but the minute you turned off the engine, the heat rose quickly. Once that sun broke the horizon around 7am, the temps started to rise once again. Let's just say that after two days with Nick and I sleeping in there, the van smelled like a locker room. So much in fact, Dawn said it took a couple of weeks for it to finally air out properly! Lesson learned. We know now to always spend the extra money and stay in a hotel. It's for everyone's safety, really.

I think since 2014, we've made it an annual trip every August to head down to Shelbyville for another great weekend of classic movies, keeping company with great friends, and having some amazing food. During those times, we've got to see such classics as the original *King Kong* (1933), Hammer's *Curse of the Werewolf* (1961), the original *Tarantula* (1955), *Horror Express* (1972), and so many more. It is something that I look forward to every year.

With vinyl making a comeback, and VHS tapes still being collected, maybe there's a chance that drive-ins can rise up again from the smoldering ashes and paved-over lots. Fans of vinyl and VHS state there is a certain charm, feel, and sound of those once-thought dead media. The same can be said with the drive-in. Try to help that by supporting a drive-in if you have one near you (and by near, I mean within a 1-to-5 hour driving distance). Head out there one weekend and give it a try and see if you don't have fun. Maybe it will bring back some good memories. Or, if you have kids, then the drive-in is the perfect place for you to create new memories with them.

We'll see you at the snack bar!

17

The Day of the Turkey

"I cannot - yet I must. How do you calculate that? At what point on the graph do 'must' and 'cannot' meet? Yet I must - but I cannot!"

Ro-Man, *Robot Monster*

Author Stephen Thrower once wrote, "The only truly bad film is a boring one." I couldn't agree with him more. The term "bad movie" sometimes gets thrown around by movie fans like pork chop bones at a Southern Baptist BBQ, but I don't think they are using the term correctly. A bad movie is where nothing happens, a movie so dull and boring that falling asleep instead of finishing it seems like the better alternative.

But how could one be bored watching Jeff Morrow trying to develop some sort of "anti-matter" weapon to destroy *The Giant Claw* (1957)? Or watch in bewilderment as our protagonist Herschell turns into a turkey-headed, blood-sucking monster in *Blood Freak* (1972)? Was it dull watching a music video being made as the ghost of Paganini goes on a killing spree in Luigi Cozzi's *Paganini Horror* (1989)? (Okay, maybe that one was a little dull.) But my point is that if you are entertained, find yourself laughing and enjoying the experience, then it can't be a bad movie, right? But it could be a Turkey.

What is a Turkey, you ask? Well, that's a whole different meal. According to Webster's dictionary, one definition is a "failure, flop, a theatrical production that has failed."

Failed, huh? I find that explanation very interesting because this is where the definition gets muddled and misunderstood. To me, a Turkey is a film that may have flaws, which could be due to a low-budget and/or the poor choices filmmakers might have made. In spite of those reasons, you, the viewer, are still having a grand old time with the end result. Granted, maybe the creators themselves weren't expecting their audiences to be laughing, pointing out the flaws and shaking their heads in disbelief at this cinematic nightmare. It was made with blood, sweat, and tears, by those who were honestly trying to make a decent film, but for some reason, they just missed the mark. Still, people are watching them and are being entertained. So how could they be considered failures?

Some might feel that a Turkey is generally one of those old black-and-white films from their parent's generation, but it really could be from any time period. A genuine Turkey is a movie that is not made poorly on purpose, meaning it was never meant to be cheesy from the very birth of the concept. For example, let's consider the slew of mutated monsters coming from the SyFy Channel over the last decade, such as *Mega Shark vs. Giant Octopus* (2009). Yes, they are cheesy. Yes, they are lame. And yes, they could even be entertaining. But I wouldn't consider them a Turkey. When you set out to make a "bad" film intentionally, you lose something in the translation. I liken it to an example I heard years ago that still applies today: When someone decides to start a punk band, they've already lost the concept. In the 1970s, musicians would just start a band and the kind of music they were playing became punk. If you set out to make a cult movie, there again, you've already failed in the delivery. It just feels synthetic and not genuine.

In the early 1990s, Comedy Central began airing 24 consecutive hours of *Mystery Science Theater 3000* on Black Friday, the day after Thanksgiving, dubbing the whole "event" their "Turkey Day Marathon." About ten years later, I decided to continue that tradition they started all those years ago. On Friday, November 28, 2003, while most others were either recovering from the Thanksgiving food coma, or facing the real-life horrors of holiday shopping, I decided to spend the day sitting in front of my TV watching as many cinematic shipwrecks as I could handle. Thus began my own Turkey Day Marathon, something that is now a tradition at the Kitley household.

Now granted, those first couple of years I was in the trenches all by myself, putting my eyes and brain through some torturous viewing, usually only getting through four or five titles. I learned very quickly that Turkeys are much more enjoyable with company. Trust me. Sitting alone and watching Ray Dennis Steckler's *The Incredible Strange Creatures Who Stopped Living and Became Mixed-Up Zombies* (1964) or Jess Franco's *Oasis of the Zombies* (1982) is not something I would recommend to anyone. Luckily for me, in 2005, my newfound friend Aaron Christensen joined me for this pursuit of movie madness, and has been my trusted co-pilot every year since. But it didn't stop with him. Soon after, we had other Chicago area friends coming to join, like Jason Coffman, Neil Calderone, and Brian Fukula, who are now staples of the event! Over the years, attendance has grown, with over a dozen crazy film fans in the same room, hungry to devour the lineup of Turkeys on the menu.

Now, there are those out there that don't get the whole concept of watching movies that are not, say, Oscar-worthy quality. If the acting isn't good, or the story is ridiculous, or you can plainly see the monster's costume coming apart at the seams, how could that be entertaining? It is easy to ridicule a movie as being crappy, stupid, or just plain inept. Seeing past all of that and still taking pleasure in what the filmmakers came up with is more than worth it. Sure, it may take a little getting used to, at least until the Turkey-Circuit pops in your brain.

What's the Turkey-Circuit, you ask? I have a theory that there is a little circuit in your brain that tells you when a movie is poorly made, with terrible acting, a cheesy looking monster, or any number of ludicrous attributes, and sends messages to your brain that this is a waste of time. But at some point, especially when you watch enough of these stellar cinematic achievements, that little circuit will pop, blow, or fizzle out, and those messages stop transmitting. After that happens, it's like looking at the films with a different pair of eyes. No longer are you getting those negative impulses, but you find yourself actually seeing past all of their shortcomings and start being entertained. As I said, it's just a theory. More tests need to be done for clarification.

Now, the important part to remember here is that we are not making fun of these movies. Yes, there are jokes made and usually a lot of laughing. But honestly, it is all done with respect for the filmmakers. We know that quite a few of these titles were made in a very different age than today. We understand the limits and challenges that these "artists" were under when creating these films, but they pressed on despite these limitations and got their movies made and released out into the world. And we celebrate them for that. So while we may shake our heads in disbelief, or snicker at the "science speak" that we hear in those early sci-fi monster flicks, at the end of the day, we still love the films and the people behind them.

Over the years, we have consumed a LOT of Turkeys, and we never seen to run out of candidates. In fact, Aaron and I were having a phone conversation one day where we were talking about what movies to add to the November roster and we complained that there were just too many Turkeys out there to be limited to only one event each year.

So, in 2015, we started doing Turkey Day in May!

At some point during this madness, something else started to happen. In the beginning, I would just have some snacks, or maybe order some food for Aaron and myself, and whoever else might have shown up. Then one year, my wife Dawn made a bunch of pizzas. Not just your normal pepperoni and sausage slices, but with exotic gourmet options and ingredients, like Dawn's Famous Crab Rangoon Pizza. Over the years, it has just exploded from there. So much now that I wonder if my friends are coming over to watch the movies or are just there for the pizzas! We go through over 15 or more each time. My son Nick joined in a few years later and each year they come up with some of the most incredible culinary creations. They start with Breakfast Pizzas, and move onto time-honored favorites like Chili Dog Pizza, Tikka Masala Pizza, or the infamous "Drunken Billy." Each time these two amaze me at the wonders they create for these crazy movie fiends that come over for this event.

In fact, in 2017, our 15th year of holding this event, we even had an Official Turkey Day cake with the turkey head from the film *Blood Freak* sitting on top, as well as T-shirts made with the same turkey head on the front and "The Power of Crap Compels You" emblazoned across the back! That's right. We take our Turkey Day Marathons pretty damn seriously around here.

We've had people drive several hours to attend our marathons, like fellow cinephiles Craig Clark (Bloomington, IN) and Alan Tromp (St. Louis, MO). Scott Bradley even flew out from California because he kept hearing stories of these marathons and wanted to see what it was all about. The first year Bryan Martinez attended, he quietly asked when he arrived, "Uh... we're not going to really just watch bad movies all day, are we?" By the end of the day, after hours and hours of laughing and cheering, his Turkey-Circuit popped and he understood everything. After hearing tales of our escapades, my friend Damien Glonek decided to start his own marathon in New Jersey, gathering local friends together to feast on some Turkeys!

That's the beauty of this whole thing. My challenge to everyone reading this is to start your own Turkey Day Marathon. It's pretty easy to do. Just send out an invite to a bunch of your fellow cinephiles to join you on the day after Thanksgiving to partake in a viewing party of some of the not-so-finer moments in movie history. The number of titles out there is so plentiful that it won't be hard finding a great selection. (If you're looking for suggestions, you can always head over to our website, kitleyskrypt.com, and look up our past Turkey Day celebrations to see what we've made it through. We've probably gotten close to a hundred titles listed by now, so there's plenty to choose from.) But no matter what you watch, the whole point is to watch and celebrate together as brother and sisters, united as horror fans. Remember, we are celebrating the triumphs of filmmakers rising to the challenge, getting their films made, and making cinematic history!

Love Live the Turkey!

18

And the Oscar Doesn't Go To... Wait? What? No Shit?!?!?!

"If horror pictures were taken seriously, he would surely be an Oscar contender next year."

The Los Angeles Times, discussing Vincent Price's performance in *Theater of Blood*

Why don't more horror films get Oscar nominations? Or more importantly, why don't more actors and actresses get nominations for their performances in horror films? Are they not working just as hard or as dedicated to their craft when working in these kinds of productions, compared to those working in a drama? Does the Academy think that since it is just some horror flick, the performances are simply phoned in? Do they even bother to look at these performances when judging the competition, or just automatically pass them by because they assume that these performances are not going to be as good as, say, the newest one from George Clooney?

I originally wrote this chapter around 2017 with the paragraph above leading into a whole long rant about how the Academy Awards always gave the horror genre the shaft. Then, in 2018, both *The Shape of Water* and *Get Out* not only nabbed a bunch of nominations in the top categories (17 between the two of them), they took home 5 Oscars, with *Shape* taking Best Picture and Best Director. That really changed the playing field. Or at least, I really hope it has changed, because traditionally, the Academy, and critics in general, seldom take what is happening in the genre seriously. While we did score a big win in 2018, as of this writing, we still have a ways to go for the proper people to get the proper recognition they deserve.

While I had had to go back and pretty much re-write this chapter, my thoughts and feelings haven't changed. We can still hope that we've made progress with the Academy being a little more open-minded, but only time will tell. Even with all the nominations that *Shape* received and won, one person that wasn't nominated was Doug Jones, the actor who portrayed the Amphibian Man. Why? Was it because he was completely covered in makeup? Gary Oldman won for *Darkest Hour* and he was probably under more makeup than Jones. Was it because Jones was playing something that wasn't human? Does that mean his acting prowess is any less impactful than someone playing a human? We'll come back to this in a little bit, but we can still take a look back at some of these shortcomings from not just the Academy, but from a lot of the mainstream critics as well.

Over the past century, actors in horror films have busted their asses to give stellar performances. They dig deep into their characters, placing their minds in very dark places to evoke a sense of the character and their character's motivations. They are often also spending long hours in the makeup chair, learning to emote under multiple layers of latex appliances so that their characters' performances can be felt, not just seen, on the screen. All that work takes place before they even step one foot on the set, spending hours under harsh lights and adverse conditions, only to repeat the process all over again the very next day. Do these actors get any recognition from the Academy for this hard work, or even the regular media for that matter? Sorry to say, not too often. Which is just a tragedy since these people are putting their heart and soul into their performance, just as hard as everyone who's regularly nominated for an Oscar. I'd like to see George Clooney give a performance that would amaze the audience while under a half-inch of rubber. Last time he did that was *Batman & Robin* (1997), and we all remember how great that performance was!

Even performances without makeup are usually overlooked. Since horror is and always will be the red-headed step-child of the movie world, we know that it is the rarest of occasions when one of our pictures is even nominated for an Academy Award, let alone winning one. The first Academy Awards took place in 1929 and it took over 40 years before a horror film was even nominated for Best Picture (*The Exorcist*, 1973). This story of the possessed little girl was actually nominated for nine other categories besides the top prize, including Best Film Editing, Best Art Direction, Best Cinematography, Best Director, Best Supporting Actress, Best Supporting Actor, Best Actress, and the two it actually won, Best Sound and Best Screenplay Based on Material from Another Medium. But was this just a fluke?

That is what I thought, at first. After doing a little research, I have to say that I was kind of surprised at the number of times that someone was nominated for an acting performance in a film that I would consider a horror film. Now granted, being nominated and winning are two different things, but even getting the nomination is pretty surprising because at least it shows the Academy was paying attention to the film, and the performances.

For example, did you know at the fifth Academy Awards, Fredric March won for Best Actor for his dual performance in the 1931 version of *Dr. Jekyll and Mr. Hyde*? (Well, you do if you read Chapter 15.) Or that Janet Leigh was actually nominated for Best Supporting Actress for her role in *Psycho*? For 1962's *What Ever Happened to Baby Jane*, Bette Davis got a nomination for Best Actress while her co-star Victor Buono got one for Best Supporting Actor. Kathy Bates won Best Actress for playing the psychotic "number one fan" in *Misery* (1990) while Anthony Hopkins and Jodie Foster both won the following year for *The Silence of the Lambs* (1991). Since then, there's been a spattering of other horror-related Oscar winners, including Natalie Portman winning Best Actress for her performance in *Black Swan* (2010).

Now, not to take anything away from those brilliant portrayals, but it is kind of strange how those last three films tend to be called "thrillers" now and not "horror." It's almost like the Academy of Motion Picture Arts and Sciences knew that if they had to give the highest kudos to these performances, they needed to refer to these films by the more marketable label of "dark thrillers" to avoid calling them what they actually are. Yes, it is great to be thrown a bone every now and then, but there are still so many more incredible performances, by such a wide range of talent almost every single year, that should have been given the credit and praise that they deserve.

My favorite actor of all time is Boris Karloff, without question. While his name is synonymous with the horror genre because of his role as Frankenstein's creature in both 1931's *Frankenstein* and its sequel *The Bride of Frankenstein* (1935), breathing life into a heartbreaking, tragic creature from under a ton of makeup and weighted clothes, no one but his most die-hard fans seem to be aware of his immense talent showcased in films, TV, and on the stage in a variety of other genres.

Take, for example, his role in Robert Wise's *The Body Snatcher* (1945), as the cab driver John Gray, who also happens to dabble in the "resurrection game." He is normal, outwardly friendly... at least to the people he likes, but underneath that smile is a dark and sinister soul. As I've mentioned in previous chapters, Karloff gives one of the best performances of his career here, with the scenes of he and co-star Henry Daniels throwing verbal jabs/threats at each other an amazing showcase. In his last great starring role, Karloff played a thinly disguised version of himself in Peter Bogdanovich's *Targets* (1968). As the aging horror film icon Byron Orlok, tired of his career in monster films, comes face-to-face with a real-life monster, the sincerity of Karloff's performance shows he could still deliver in his late 70s. There are plenty more roles that Karloff gave us over his long career that were more than worthy. Did he ever receive any Oscar nominations? Uh... no.

Vincent Price, another well-known creature-feature star, spent his early days on the stage before launching his career in movies that spanned over a half-century. He might have hammed it up in several campy horror flicks, but that doesn't mean he still couldn't give a great performance. In the films he made with Roger Corman, loosely based on the stories of Edgar Allan Poe, including *House of Usher* (1960) and *The Pit and the Pendulum* (1961), he presented audiences with two very different, and equally believable, examples of madness. During the 1960s and '70s Price found success in many British films. Two of his most acclaimed from this period are *Witchfinder General* (1968) and *Theater of Blood* (1973). In the former, he played the real-life character of Matthew Hopkins, a 17th-century inquisitor who roamed the English countryside torturing and killing people, especially young women, accused of being witches. As this powerful man who abused his authority by blackmailing, robbing, and doing whatever else he felt like, Price proved that he could leave the camp behind. In *Theater of Blood*, Price plays Edward Lionheart, a Shakespearian stage actor frequently panned by the critics for his performances. He decides to take revenge on his nay-sayers, knocking them off in twisted ways as referenced in the Bard's plays, complete with costume and makeup changes multiple times throughout the picture. It is a testament to Price's ability as an actor that he could move seamlessly from such a grounded and vile role as in *Witchfinder General* to an intentionally heightened dark comedy, rendering multiple stellar performances in one film! But did Mr. Price receive any nominations? Not a one.

Over a decade before he won an Oscar as Hannibal "the Cannibal" Lecter, actor Anthony Hopkins had blown my mind in a film simply called *Magic* (1978). Hopkins plays a ventriloquist whose grasp of sanity is slowly crumbling apart. He shows us the human side of this madness that is slowly breaking loose, creating a character that draws us in, feeling sorry for him as he slowly becomes the helpless puppet. The sequence where he is challenged to sit for five minutes and not have his dummy Fats do any of the talking is brilliant and heartbreaking. But again, it went unnoticed by the Academy.

There are two great performances that I always like to bring up that were performed by actors who had to work under an extensive amount of prosthetics makeup effects. The first is from one of my all-time favorite films, David Cronenberg's 1986 remake of *The Fly*, starring the incredibly underrated Jeff Goldblum. As the story unfolds, Goldblum's physical form is lost inside a mass of rubber, latex, and goo. While his outer appearance has disappeared, his performance still shines. Even under all of that makeup, when the only real part of Goldblum we see are his eyes, he is still able to emit such an incredible amount of sadness and anguish, even though we aren't looking at anything remotely human, strong and powerful emotions come pouring through all of that latex and paint into his performance. Chris Walas and Stephan Dupuis, who created the incredible makeup effects, received an Oscar for their hard work, but did Goldblum get a nomination? Nope!

Another Oscar-caliber performance comes from the human chameleon Doug Jones with his dual performances in Guillermo del Toro's dark fantasy tale *Pan's Labyrinth* (2006), where he played Fauno and the terrifying Pale Man. For both of these characters, Jones is completely covered under many layers of makeup, where he doesn't resemble anything human. For Fauno, not only is he trying to emit the personality of this character under all of it, but Jones also learned a completely different language! While the film received several nominations from the Academy and even won in three categories, there was no notice for Mr. Jones. I think a lot of people don't realize the hard work and effort that these underrated performers go through to bring these character to life, just as much as a normal actor without any makeup, but having to do with without their face lit up on the screen. Case in point again, Jones' role in *The Shape of Water*. (Jones has also led the cause to get actors that were normally just called "suit performers" to be credited as actual actors.)

But this isn't just men giving incredible performances. Not even close. In fact, in 2014 alone, there were four films where the performance by the lead actress left me emotionally drained. In alphabetical order:

Jennifer Kent's *The Babadook* stars Essie Davis as a troubled mother doing whatever she can to protect her small son from the title character. She shows us a mother who is the epitome of tired. I don't mean lack-of-sleep tired, but worn-down-to-the-soul tired. Trying to get over the tragic death of her husband while dealing with her emotionally charged son is hard enough… and now this storybook demon come to life. Watching her onscreen is just heart-wrenching. Kudos should also be given to 7-year-old Noah Wiseman who plays her son. It is simply unreal how good this youngster's performance is.

In Leigh Janiak's film *Honeymoon*, Harry Treadway and Rose Leslie play a young couple on their honeymoon at a cabin out by a lake. Shortly after their arrival, strange things start to happen as Leslie begins to show signs of changing. Subtle things like not using simple words the right way, or seemingly a little different than before. As Leslie brings this character to life on the screen in front of us, it is even more impressive because what she is becoming is something different than what we've seen before, so there is no standard for her to follow. She is just amazing.

Alex Essoe also makes an incredible and painful transformation in *Starry Eyes*, where she plays a young actress desperately trying to make it in the movie business. But her character Sarah has some issues, namely self-confidence, and goes into fits of anger and hair-pulling that will actually make you feel uncomfortable watching. She is an actress "willing to do whatever it takes" but doesn't realize exactly what that could mean. Watching her is sometimes hard to watch, but you can't your eyes away. I'm sure that "willing" quote refers both to her character in the film as well as Essoe herself and she more than proves it here.

Our last example is from an actress who had already spent more than forty years in the business, half of it on daytime soap operas. In *The Taking of Deborah Logan*, actress Jill Larson plays an elderly lady who has the beginning stages of Alzheimer's and has agreed to be the subject of a documentary on the disease. As the illness progresses and as we learn more about Logan, we find that there is much more going on. Larson's mind-blowing performance hooks into you and keeps you watching. What she puts herself through for this role is just amazing: wearing different kinds of makeup, dealing with some blood and guts issues, even appearing in different forms of nudity while in her mid-60s! There are times when her character will make you tear up and other times when the hairs on the back of your neck will stand on end just with a glance.

What do these four extremely talented actresses also have in common? Not one of them was nominated for an Academy Award. Shameful.

I guess the big question is this: What can we do to change this? Thankfully, Guillermo del Toro has already started it by opening the door with his film *The Shape of Water* and the accolades it received. We can argue all we want if it is a horror film or not until the tides come in and out, but there is no arguing that it is a creature feature that definitely has a terrifying monster in it. (Hint: the monster isn't the one in the water.) By winning both Best Director and Best Picture in 2018, this film shows that it can happen and there is hope.

At the end of the day, we want these artists, craftsmen, and filmmakers to know that we acknowledge and applaud their perseverance and dedication and to know that we think their work truly deserves notice. We, as fans, need to make sure we speak out and spread the word. When we see an awe-inspiring performance, let others know about it. This is where social media can be a great positive tool, when you can use it to spread praise for someone's hard work, as opposed to using it to beat someone down. So spread the word. Tell your friends about the recent movie that impressed the hell out of you. Post your thoughts and reviews. Get it out there. It may not get the film an Oscar nomination, but at least we are doing what we can to make sure more people know about it, are talking about it, and most importantly, seeing the film. If enough people do this, you never know what can happen.

19

Psycho-Babble

"Art is not meant to be cerebral or intellectual; it is supposed to be felt. And I think horror makes you feel it more than any other genre."

Professor Stephen Graham Jones

Just what is Psycho-Babble? It is a term that I've started applying to some theories that a few film professors and critics were coming up with that, while intelligently written and well thought-out, were garbage. Okay... maybe not garbage, but these theories were more opinion than what I would consider fact. And that is the part that irritates me most. That these intelligent and educated scholars were getting books published on their ideas, and even worse, teaching film students some of this drivel as FACT as opposed to recognizing it as their opinion.

The more I read some of these theories, the more I discovered that while these professors and critics would focus their intellect so intimately on a film searching for hidden subtext that no one else was picking up on, they were missing obvious basic plot points and character motivations. I'll give examples of all these in a bit so you'll have a better idea of what I'm talking about, and why I get so frustrated with these film scholars. But it made me feel that they weren't really watching the movie itself, trying instead to find evidence to prove a point they already had in mind, whether it was actually present in the film or not. If you tell someone to look for something, generally they will find it, even if it was never there to begin with. Like the old saying goes, tell someone to try not think of an elephant and they can't help but have that image pop in their head.

Again, I'm no expert in this field and never have claimed to be. Yes, I watch a lot of films and have been doing so for well over 40 years. I have no college degree or any advanced learning. Most of these authors have Bachelor's Degrees, some with Masters and Doctorates, so I am not trying to suggest that they are stupid by any means. These are very intelligent people articulate in their views with theories that are well thought-out and researched. Yet this is what baffles me so much. They can supposedly see such deeper meaning, but yet don't know (or are willfully ignoring) what is actually happening plot-wise in the film they are dissecting.

It could be something as simple as territorial jealousy. It irritates me that these people are getting paid to write and teach about these movies when, honestly, it would be something I would love to do as a career. But, alas, fate didn't deal me those cards. Instead, I've been working in the manufacturing industry most of my adult life, raising a small family, all the while keeping this passion of the horror genre alive doing what I can in my free time to help instill this same love I have for it into other people.

Or maybe it is because the horror genre, like heavy metal music, has always had to fight for its legitimacy even though its fans can be found in just about every age and profession out there. Maybe I just take a little offense at some educated know-it-all trying to partake in my little horror party, and I'm not having any of it! Well, maybe 20 years ago, I'd almost buy that argument, but not now. I'm all about education and having fans learn as much they can about this genre of film and the people behind it in order to get a better understanding and appreciation of the genre. I know that these professors and critics are fans of the genre too, but I think instead of just watching and enjoying the movies, they work too hard at trying to come up with some new and abstract idea to base their next book upon. Now, some of these theories they come up with are pretty fascinating and I applaud the author for doing that much research and study into the particular subject. But at the end of the day, it is still just theory. So please don't teach it as fact.

Ok, so back to the Psycho-Babble. Let me give you some examples of when and what started driving me crazy leading to this chapter. Keep in mind, if anything, maybe these examples will give you a little chuckle, make you smile or even laugh out loud. Or maybe, you will grind your teeth and have the same reaction that I had.

Back in 2003, at the Gene Siskel Film Center in Chicago, they were having a film study series titled *The Cinema of Horror*. It was a program that anybody could attend, even if you weren't enrolled in the film school. Each week, for a little over three months, they would hold a screening of a film on Tuesdays and Saturdays. After the screening on Tuesdays, Tom Gunning, a professor of Cinema and Media Studies at the University of Chicago would give a lecture. The series started at the beginning of the genre with the German silent film *Nosferatu* (1922) slowly making their way to more current films. Other titles in the series included *The Mummy* (1932), *The Bride of Frankenstein* (1935), *Invasion of the Body Snatchers* (1956), *The Texas Chain Saw Massacre* (1974), *Shivers* (1975), and so on. I thought this was an amazing idea and a great opportunity to get a little "professional" education with just the cost of a movie ticket. But it didn't take long before I started to realize what I had gotten myself into.

Again, I'm not in any way trying to claim Prof. Gunning has no idea what he's talking about. He is a very well-educated, well-spoken man. My problem is that what he was teaching he was presenting as fact, and that is where I disagree. If he would have started the lecture, "Some of the things I'll be saying here could be open for interpretation, but this is what I believe they mean," then I wouldn't have had a problem with it. In fact, I probably would have enjoyed the lectures a lot more. But when it is taught as "The director's point with this scene was _____", then I have an issue. Unless you heard that directly from the director himself, it's really only your opinion/theory and I'm not buying it.

It was during his lecture for James Whale's *The Bride of Frankenstein* that I really had the biggest disagreement with Prof. Gunning and from that point on I was admittedly on the attack. You have to remember, the horror genre is one of my great passions in life. It IS my life. So when confronted by a suggestion that goes against my feelings and thoughts on it, it tends to get under my skin. I think any film should be interpreted by each individual their own way; we can then discuss different theories and it might allow for different interpretations. I'm fine with someone having a difference of opinion about a movie and I don't expect everyone to have the same feelings towards the same films I do. Conversations would get very boring real quick if that were the case.

Okay... back to the story.

But wait... a warning first. I'm telling you right now that if you love the film *The Bride of Frankenstein*, you may want to skip the next few paragraphs because what I'm going to explain could possibly ruin your enjoyment of it and a certain sequence in particular. Though I have worked very hard to get rid of this thought in my brain, it is still hard for me to watch this particular scene and not have this stupid theory pop into my head. So if you cherish this movie, move on for your own good.

Still here? Well, to paraphrase Edward Van Sloane a bit as he stated to the audience at the beginning of *Frankenstein*, "Well... I warned you."

As I've mentioned earlier, Frankenstein's creature is one of my personal heroes and I feel quite a connection with him for a variety of reasons. In *Bride*, the creature is wandering the countryside and comes across an old hut on the outskirts of the woods. Inside is a blind hermit, living peacefully by himself, until the creature bursts into the small cottage. Of course, not being able to see this monstrosity, the hermit does not see the brute ugliness that others see, but instead welcomes a possible friend into his home to keep his lonely soul company. He "sees" past the obvious, what is at face value, what most people would be pointing, staring, jeering, screaming, and running in fear from. Even today, the resonance of that scene is something that is so lost in today's society. The creature realizes that this old man is not afraid of him and does not shriek in terror like most, but is instead kind, something he has never experienced before. During the scene after the creature and the blind man have become friends, he guides the tired creature to his bed and kneels down; with hands clasped together in prayer, he thanks God for bringing another lost soul to him to be his friend. The creature lays there, with tears of happiness streaming down his face. Right before the camera fades, when he is done giving thanks, the blind man lays his head down on the creature's body. Truly a heartbreaking and emotional sequence that has always pulled at my heart strings.

But this all came crashing down with Prof. Gunning's statements suggesting that the "obvious" thing that director James Whale was trying to sneak into his picture was the fact that the way the camera was positioned behind the old man kneeling down by the creatures waist was to imply that the hermit was performing oral sex on the creature. I mean... it is obvious, right? Since Whale was gay, along with several of the actors in the film, then it must be true, right? BULLSHIT! Not only did that stereotypical comment anger me, it took what I always considered one of the most beautifully poignant and heart-wrenching scenes in this film and dragged it through the mud, all for the sake of some cheap sexploitational headline. Now every single time I watch this film and that scene comes up, as much as I try to bury it, somewhere in the back of my brain, I'm thinking the creature is getting a hummer. And even worse... these students are thinking that this is the truth!

It's my opinion that some of these scholars try to put some sort of a sexual spin on these movies in order to gain the attention of a publisher, since that really seems what some of these guys are all about... getting published. Got to keep their jobs, right? So yes, if you dig deep enough and look hard enough, you will find whatever you're looking for, whether it is truly there or not. And once you point it out, of course, people are going to see it as well, but it still doesn't mean that it was the director's original intent or a point (if any) that he was trying to get across.

As I stated earlier, one of the things that I'll never understand is how some of these scholars are able to point out some hidden subtext underneath the surface of a film only to miss something so obvious, such as a character's arc, or journey through the film, what their motivations are, or even basic elements of the plot. Let me give you an example.

Carol J. Clover is a highly regarded American professor and author of the famous book *Men, Women, and Chainsaws: Gender in the Modern Horror Film*, published in 1992. In her book, Clover developed the "final girl" theory that is still being taught in film studies today. Now, once again, I'm not saying that Clover isn't educated. Obviously she is a very intelligent academic person. That being said, let us review an essay that would later become one of her most quoted works. In *Her Body, Himself: Gender in the Slasher Film*, an essay first published in 1987 in the No. 20 Autumn issue of *Representation* and later republished in 1996 in the book *The Dread of Difference: Gender and the Horror Film*, Clover, while discussing the 1986 film *Texas Chainsaw Massacre Part 2*, writes "Chop Top in *Texas Chainsaw Massacre Part 2*, is so called because of a metal plate implanted in his skull in repair of a head wound sustained in the truck accident in the earlier film."

Now you don't need to be a film school graduate to know this little tidbit is just simply wrong. I'd say that pretty much any horror fan worth their weight in BBQ can tell you that Chop Top is NOT the same character known as the Hitchhiker from the original 1974 film, since he was pretty much flattened by the semi truck at the end. In fact, the Hitchhiker character IS in the sequel, but as a stuffed puppet that they refer to as Nubbins, that the family apparently pieced back together and made into a human puppet. So they are two completely different characters.

How could Clover miss that, but see so much deeper context intertwined in these movies? Sorry... that tells me that she wasn't really paying attention to the actual movie as much as she was looking for ways to prove her point she'd already come up with. The interesting thing is that this little part was left out of her book *Men, Women and Chainsaws*. Was it left out because she noticed the error, or just to save space? But she allowed it to be published in 1996 in *Dread of Difference*. Who knows?

Later, when discussing David Cronenberg's *Videodrome* (1983), Clover writes that the main character of the movie, Max Renn, played wonderfully by James Woods, is a "producer of hardcore pornography." Sorry, but Renn runs the cable TV network, Civic TV. He doesn't produce any movies, let alone hardcore porn. Again, maybe the *Videodrome* signal was getting to her and making her hallucinate something that wasn't there... or again, maybe she just wasn't paying attention.

Okay... maybe that could have been something easy to miss. (I personally don't think so, but let's give her the benefit of the doubt.) But how about this next one? In the same book, in one of the footnotes accompanying the chapter *Opening Up*, in reference to the device that opens the door to nasty things, "In *The Evil Dead*, The Book is a videotape, in which a deceased man with knowledge of zombie-ism spells out the necessary incantations." A videotape, huh? Actually, it is called a "reel-to-reel tape recorder," Carol. Again, this may be a minute point, but how can she see all of this hidden subtext if she can't tell the difference between a videotape and a reel-to-reel tape recorder?

Then there was this huge tome that came out in 2014 called *A Companion to the Horror Film*, edited by Harry Benshoff. I went to add it to my "Want

List" on Amazon until I noticed the retail price was $180! Now granted, this was close to 600 pages, but that sure was a lot of money for a single book. We're not talking a volume like Tim Lucas' Mario Bava book either. There was no way I was going to fork over that kind of money. But I had another idea. Since I review books on my website, I wondered if I could get one for review? So after a quick little email to the publisher, telling them about my website and that I review these kind of books, lo and behold, I get a reply asking for my mailing address! Once the book arrived, I looked at the list of contributors and was impressed to see so many names with "Dr." or "Prof." in front of them, or followed by other letters attributing to their impressive background. I dove in head first because I had a feeling that it was going to take me a while to get through this tome. As I progressed, it wasn't long before I realized it would have made more sense to dive head first into a brick wall.

Once again, I was reading people's *theories* on certain films, not fact, even though they seemed pretty sure that it was all, indeed, facts. In Daniel Humphrey's essay "Gender and Sexuality Haunts the Horror Film," he wants to point out that the theme of homosexuality runs rampant throughout William Friedkin's *The Exorcist* (1973). His first example of this? Well, Rock Hudson's name is seen in a headline in a tabloid newspaper that one of the characters is reading. Uh... what? Could it maybe be just because Hudson was still a big name in the early '70s and it would have been very common for him to be mentioned on the cover? But what about the fact that Father Karras' friend, Father Dyer, likes show tunes? Surely that implies he is gay, right? I didn't write this, folks, but an Associate Professor of Film Studies did.

Here is one that really had me laughing. In their first encounter, Det. Kinderman asks Father Karras if he'd be interested in going to the movies with him because it is something that his wife doesn't like to do. Humphrey states that Kinderman "...pursues a curious, homosocial relationship with Karras." Couldn't it be that Kinderman just loves going to the movies? He even mentions that he loves to talk about film. Where is the author going with that angle?

These scholars love to point out the hidden sexual impulses that are secretly inserted into the picture. In Christopher Sharrett's essay, "The Horror Film as Social Allegory," he makes a comment about Robert Wise's *The Haunting* (1963). He makes the point that the character of Theo is obviously gay because she "rebuffs the advances of Luke, thus making evident (to the group) her lesbianism." So let me get this straight. If I was to try and pick up some women at a bar and she turns me down, that means she must be a lesbian? Damn. I wish I would have known that in my youth. It would have saved me a lot of heartache! Honestly it boggles my mind when such educated people come up with such drivel. Yes, I understand there are *other* elements that potentially lead some to see Theo's character as gay. But Sharrett's explanation is not only just ridiculous, but downright sexist.

Sharrett goes on to discuss "torture porn" films, stating that the character of Jigsaw from the *Saw* films is a descendent of vigilantes like Dirty Harry, mentioning some newer films of that ilk, like *Death Sentence* (2007), the *Walking Tall* remakes, and then says "...and *The Brave One* (2007), with the vigilante now a woman (played, astoundingly, by lesbian actor Jodie Foster) avenging her murdered spouse." What the fuck does Foster being a lesbian have ANYTHING to do with her role, character, the movie or what he's talking about? Not a damn thing! But let's throw it in there because he's a Professor of Communication and Film, so he must know what he's talking about. If you ask me, it seems that Sharrett is more fascinated with lesbians than anything else.

Now we all know the vampire genre has been around long before the days of Bram Stoker, probably one of the oldest of the "famous monsters." It is also probably the one subgenre that scholars love to tear apart, dissect, and explain all the hidden implications, meanings, and subtext within. Now for me, sort of going on the philosophy of Anne Rice, vampires are predators. They can see the beauty (and blood) in both sexes. Sort of the same when a lioness chases down an elk, it doesn't check to see if its prey is male or female first. If it was a female elk, that doesn't now mean the lioness is bisexual. The elk is just food, plain and simple. A vampire might take notice of the beauty in the life of the human, regardless of the sex of it. But these scholars... they just love to pull out all the stops when it comes to vampires, with phallic symbolism running rampant.

In his essay "The Gothic Revival (1957-1974)," Rick Worland discusses some Hammer vampire films. In *Dracula: Prince of Darkness* (1966), when Helen (Barbara Shelley), now a vampire, confronts her sister-in-law Diana, telling her, "You don't need Charles," Worland informs us "vampirism's often uninhibited bisexual lust manifests itself." Couldn't Helen be the lioness, stalking her prey, not really caring whether Diana is male or female, only to sate the hunger growing inside her?

If you think I'm reading too much into this, then how about another example where he loves to imply all sorts of silly meanings. When Charles breaks into the scene with a sword to defend himself and his wife, "Dracula seizes it and snaps it in front of him, a clear demonstration of who wields the greater sexual power." Uh... so the swords are really their dicks? And Dracula just snapped Charles' dick in half? Give me a break.

But the crazy theories about vampires go back way before this book came out. Here's another entertaining tidbit from an article in *Mosaic: An*

Interdisciplinary Critical Journal, published in 1983, entitled "Burying the Undead: The Use and Obsolescence of Count Dracula" by Robin Wood: "Dracula's attraction to blood, although generally focused on women, crosses the boundary of gender: when Stoker's Jonathan cuts himself shaving, Dracula wants to 'suck' him. This homosexual element is played up strongly in Murnau's film – not surprising, giving the director's homosexuality – in Dracula's nocturnal visit to Jonathan's bedchamber." So let me get this straight... just because Murnau was gay, that means everything he does is going to have reference to that fact? Once again, I think these people are reading way too much into and between the lines, when in reality, there is nothing there, or at least surely not what the author is implying.

Then there are some books where the author looks way too hard at something so simple, trying to explain all the economic and social breakdowns. In David Roche's book, *Making and Remaking Horror in the 1970s and 2000s* (2014), he discusses the ending of Tobe Hooper's *Texas Chain Saw Massacre*, where the truck driver, who happens to be black, stops his vehicle after running down the Hitchhiker. After getting out of the truck and realizing he is being chased by some nutter with a chainsaw, he grabs a wrench from his truck and throws it at the maniac. According to Roche, "Leatherface's parody of white corporate power might provide some symbolic outlet for racial, class, sexual, and economic tensions, namely by giving a black truck driver the opportunity to throw a manual tool at a white-collar maniac wielding a machine that, like the truck, needs oil to run. On this reading, the black truck driver is thereby enacting a fantasy that unties the exploited working class and the oppressed racial minority against the white capitalist."

Seriously?

Aren't we thinking a little too hard on this one? Couldn't it be as simple as the truck driver was throwing a wrench at Leatherface because he was being chased by a guy with a freaking chainsaw? Do you really think that was Hooper's conceit from the beginning? If I had to make a guess, I'd say that Ed Quinn, who played the truck driver in question, was probably the first guy that Hooper and company could find that may have his own truck and agreed to be in the movie.

Later in the essay, Roche is mentions the part in the 2004 remake of *Dawn of the Dead* when one of the security guards calls Ving Rhames' character "Shaq." But instead of thinking that the security guard did that because Rhames is a very large black man, a la famous basketball player Shaquille O'Neal, apparently there is a deeper social meaning behind it. Roche writes, "The use of the name draws attention to the historical opposition between basketball as a presumably African-American working-class sport and baseball as a presumably white working-class sport, an opposition suggested by the fact that the white security guards are all wearing baseball hats." Do we really think that James Gunn was sitting at his computer while writing this movie, trying to figure out the deeper connections to come up with a name for Rhames to be called?

My whole point of this chapter isn't to point and laugh at these film scholars and their perceptions and theories. Okay... maybe a little. Some seem like they dug real deep looking for something interesting and when they can't find it, they figure out a way to make their theory fit. (Did you know the shark in *Jaws* represents the infamous *vagina dentata*? Me neither.) I mean, they do need to come up with something to publish, right? Can't be an academic if you're not always publishing some profound writings, can you? Yes, this is coming from a 50-year-old horror fan that is admittedly jealous that these people have made a career out of writing about the genre that I love. But, as the old saying goes, sometimes a duck is just a duck, and I do think that is the case here. Plain and simple.

Halloween 1993

20

This is Halloween

*"Boys and girls of every age,
Wouldn't you like to see something strange?"*

The Residents of Halloweentown, *The Nightmare Before Christmas*

Halloween was always a special holiday for me. You get to dress up as someone (or something) else and go out and ask for free candy! Growing up with very little money in our household, free candy was almost like Christmas! I don't have a lot of memories of different costumes in my youth, though I do remember going as the Hunchback, having a pillow worn like a backpack under a sweatshirt. When I moved to Illinois, that first Halloween I went as a vampire, with very generic white-face paint makeup (almost Joker-like) and the usual plastic teeth, with a cape made from a black garbage bag!

Things changed when I reached my teenage years. While most other kids my age would be out causing havoc, I would be more content just staying home and watching movies on TV. That all changed again around the mid-to-late '80s when I started to dress up for Halloween again. This time it was for the trick-or-treaters at my future in-laws. The first year was 1986. I had started getting into special makeup effects, the basic beginner-type stuff from magazines and what books I could find. It was mostly me playing around with liquid latex and learning very quickly what not to get that stuff on, such as hair or clothing. Liquid latex is just what it sounds like, a liquid form of rubber that will harden as it dries. I lost part of an eyebrow the hard way in those beginning lessons, folks. The first year I dressed up for Halloween for the kids, my makeup was basically a bunch of latex, cotton, and tissue paper with fake blood thrown in. Nothing great, but it was a start.

By the next year, I was getting a little more daring. I had gotten some pre-made makeup appliances, which were just cheap pieces of pre-painted rubber/plastic like open wounds, an exposed rib cage, stuff like that. I decided to do a more advanced zombie design, covering my entire face in latex with my eyeball hanging out for an even better look. To achieve this dangling eyeball effect, my future wife Dawn took a fake eye, and with a combination of latex and yarn, made some nerves and stuff attaching the eyeball to my own covered eye. I had put on a bald cap (back when I needed one) and had a black wig that looked like something a Motley Crue wannabe would have. In the back of the wig, there was a huge hole where I had an appliance that showed some brains hanging out. I also had a pre-made piece of a rib cage that I glued to my chest and had a ripped shirt exposing the wound, finally covering the whole thing with fake blood. A LOT of fake blood.

Looking back on it now, I am impressed I didn't lose more than part of an eyebrow to the latex, or the other stuff I tried. Once I was all done and ready to go, I found I was unable to talk because the latex mask I had made had pretty much hardened. The more I tried to move my face, the more the latex would start to come off my skin. As a bonus, the fake blood had started to drip down places I didn't expect.

Sure, it was cheap and cheezy, but I did manage to scare more than a few kids that year and that got me hooked. The payoff for all the hard work was right there... getting to see the reaction on those kids' faces. Again, not that I wanted to do the makeup thing for a living, but I couldn't wait until next year to see what else I could come up with to scare the little buggers coming up for free candy. Each year, my Halloween designs and plans got bigger and bigger, becoming more elaborate. Eventually, we were drawing a pretty good crowd of people into my future in-laws' neighborhood, with some folks driving to the sub-division just to come to our display. By the time I threw in the bloody towel, we had done it for about seven years and probably had a half dozen or so people helping me out on Halloween night.

How cool was it that Dawn's parents would let their crazy future son-in-law pretty much take over their house every year on Halloween? Darlene, her mom, was one of the craftiest people I knew, so no matter what crazy idea I came up with, she would either figure out how we could do it, or if I already did, she knew how to make it better. While I was working on my own effects, she and Dawn were making three-dimensional tombstones for their front yard. Not too many parents would have put up with this every year, but not only did they put up with it, they joined right along. It became a yearly neighborhood gathering, where the friends and neighbors would come over to see what we had done that year, sit and stand around and chat, while watching all the kids walk up to the house, laughing when we scared the crap out of some teenager who was trying keep his cool. It also might have had something to do with the huge pot of chili that Dar would make every year.

The second year, I designed a full-size mask that I made with some air bladders (aka condoms) in the forehead with tubes running into my mouth inside the mask. That way I could blow into them and the head would pulse.

Pretty fancy, huh? Sure, the mask itself looked pretty goofy, but I was still working out the kinks.

But it was the next year when we started to take it to the next level. I convinced a friend of ours to "volunteer" to be our victim. All he would have to do is lay down the whole night. No big deal, right? The concept would be that he would be laying down on a piece of plywood and have his leg cut off below the knee, while his right arm would be cut off by the shoulder, with the severed arm laying next to his body, complete with a still-moving hand!

This was the point where I started to really learn about magic and the concept of misdirection and how I could apply it to Halloween displays. Brian, our lucky volunteer, had his leg bent at the knee with his real leg going down a hole cut in the piece of plywood that he was laying on. Then I had made an appliance with a fake bone sticking out of it that attached to his bent knee. Add in a lot of blood and some real livers and guts bought at the grocery store and it looked pretty damn good. For his severed arm, Brian's real arm went down through a hole by his shoulder and then his hand would come back up through another hole attached to a severed prop arm laying there, so the hand on the arm could still move, making for a pretty convincing effect.

Okay, so it wasn't the most comfortable position, laying there like that, but he did volunteer! Except, we probably didn't mention that once he got into this set up, with all the blood and stuff on him... he was pretty much stuck there until Trick-or-Treating was over. Oh yeah... and it got down to about 50 degrees that night too, so all that fake blood that we had poured all over his severed leg had dripped down through the hole in the table, down his real leg, into his sock. Here's a fun fact. Once Karo syrup blood gets really cold, it starts to pretty much solidify. Like glue. So at the end of the night, Brian's sock was glued solid to his foot until it warmed up enough where he could get it off. In the process, we also managed to stain his foot red from the food coloring we put in the syrup.

Putting all of Brian's pain and suffering aside, the effects looked amazing and we got a lot of great responses from it. People hadn't seen gory effects like this around the neighborhood and the word was starting to get out. Needless to say, after this was all over and done with, we didn't see Brian again for a whole year, until the very next Halloween when he showed up to see what other dummy... I mean, volunteer I had gotten to take his place! We put him through hell, so I didn't blame him a bit.

One year, we cut a hole in the bottom of a candy dish and placed it on a large box. We then had another of our volunteers inside the box with his hand coming up through the candy dish. We then placed a strobe light right behind the dish, making it hard for the kids to see it, so when they reached into the dish for a prize, the hand would grab them. Cue screaming!

The following year was probably the best layout we ever did. It was also where the whole misdirection thing worked like a charm. There were several young kids that we scared so badly they dropped their candy and took off running. I consider that a big win, wouldn't you?

My plan for that year was to have someone cut completely in half, with the upper half of their body staked upright to a board. In reality, our volunteer would be standing, with a 7-foot plywood plank standing up at a slight angle with his body going through a hole. I then made an appliance for the bottom half of his torso with intestines hanging out. The "intestines" were just pantyhose sewn and stuffed with cotton, another great idea that came from my mother-in-law. Once we soaked them with fake blood, they looked pretty good.

At the bottom, I had a box where the "severed legs" were sticking out. They were connected to a piece of wood that our volunteer, standing there cut in half, could step on with his real leg to make the fake legs move.

I had dressed up kind of like Leatherface from *The Texas Chain Saw Massacre*, with a "face" mask made again from latex that I had cut into pieces, painted different colors then sewn back together. Walking around with a large machete, it was pretty easy to intimidate the kids.

But the real beauty of the set up was where and how we had that candy dish. Since it worked so well the year before with the hand in the dish, I decided to take it a step further. We had made a scarecrow-like dummy and had it sitting on a bench with the candy dish placed in its lap. Behind the bench was a wall we made out of a sheet of corrugated paper. There was a hole inside the dummy's chest so a volunteer behind the wall could stick their hand through the chest and grab at the kids reaching for candy. Then another friend was also dressed up like a scarecrow sitting next to the fake one. It played out like this… when a group of kids would come up, you'd let the first one take their candy. But when the second one came up, the hand would come shooting out of the dummy's chest reaching for them. This would get the first set of screams and jumps. Then, when the next kid came up, they would be coming up so slowly, eyes completely focused on that candy dish waiting for that hand to come out again… and that's when the real scarecrow next to the fake one would quickly sit up and scream, reaching for the kid! I can't tell you how many times I was laughing so hard when these teenagers were trying to keep their cool in front of their friends and would just lose it, and then quickly try to act like it didn't scare them. Cruel? Sure. Fun? Damn skippy!

The following year, instead of having a guy cut in half, we had him laying on the table again, but his stomach was cut open with his ribs and guts hanging out all over the place, with some medical instruments lying on the table next to the patient, sort of a like an operation gone bad. For added shock, the patient's real arm would come out of the chest, holding his own guts!

That year I actually dressed as a clown, granted, with big pointed teeth, really long fingers, and blood and spit drooling out of my mouth the whole time. Nothing scarier than a clown, right?

Here's another little makeup tip for you kiddies out there. The fangs that I was using were more like a set of plastic dentures, covering both the uppers and lowers of my real teeth. To help them stay in place, it said to use denture cream. Well, I was in my early 20s. I had never used denture cream before. But I wanted to make sure these things didn't come loose, so I probably used a little more than I should have. Not only did they not come loose over the next few hours, but when I finally did take them out, the cream had oozed out and had covered my gums and the roof of my mouth, where I could feel the stuff there every time I closed my mouth. I sat in the bathroom with a toothbrush, brushing and scraping the roof of my mouth over and over, trying to get all of this crap out of my mouth. It was so bad that even when typing this little story, it is making me want to gag. So that was the first and LAST time, I've ever worn dentures for a costume. Live and learn, my friends. Live and learn.

The final year of our little Halloween set up, which I think was in 1993, we went with a zombie theme. I had a new volunteer and we decided to cut him in half again, only this time we would amp up the fake gore guts. I had gotten a couple of 55-gallon drums from work and had painted them to look like the barrels from *The Return of the Living Dead*. Funny how I went to all that trouble to put the name and phone number of the company in the film on both barrels with probably not a single person knowing where it was from. Oh well. Once a fan, always a fan.

I was going to be a zombie, but figured it would be even better if I had a victim. I had managed to get my hands on some mannequins, including a young boy model. I cut off one of the mannequin's legs just below the knee and made a fake bone sticking out of the stump with fake latex skin around where it was cut off, so I could grab some of the latex in my mouth, pulling on it like it was real skin. I then cut a large hole in the side of the kid's head, lined the inside with a plastic bag, and then put cooked pasta with a lot of red sauce in there. So as the kids were coming up to get candy, I was sitting there with this "kid" lying across my lap. I would then proceed to reach inside his head and pull out his "brains" and eat them. It made for quite an impressive effect, especially from an amateur just having fun. So impressive that this would be the first and only time that I ever had an adult come up and say that was all a bit too much. Usually the parents would be walking up the driveway, a beer in one hand dragging their kid along with the other, telling them, "Oh, come on. Don't be scared. It's fun!" I'm sure there were a few kids that we traumatized over the years. But after putting on these productions for all of these years, and only getting one complaint I guess that was a good record. As it turned out though, that was our last year of doing this.

The main reason I stopped doing it was that it just becoming too much work. Trying to come up with different things each year, not repeating myself, was becoming challenging, especially when bigger meant it was going to take more time, more money and more people involved to not only help you get it made, but also to help out on Halloween night. That really was the hard part. Sure, people liked coming over and watching the festivities, but try and get one of them to be cut in half for the night? FORGET IT! Spending most evenings in October building the sets, getting the props made, finding out who's going to do what... It just got to be too much work and stress, almost making me dread the Halloween season because it was becoming more work than fun.

I still remember some of the plans that I had come up with for the next year that never came to be. One plan I had figured out was centered on a torture chamber theme. I would have a guy lying on a rack that would bust in half at the right time. I had also designed an electric chair that would be part dummy and part real person, where the dummy part would make people think the arms weren't going to reach out and grab you... until they did! But these plans never got farther than just the design stage.

I will say, that even with all the hard work, the cold weather, and all the other mishaps, there are times when I really miss those days. We did have a lot of fun. Years later, after we had stopped our annual productions, as I was taking my own son trick-or-treating through that same neighborhood, we were behind a large group of people that started talking about this house in the neighborhood that used to go all out and have "people cut up and stuff." This brought a smile to my face, but made me sad all at the same time. I thought about bringing it back when my son and his friends were young and naive enough to volunteer to help, not having a clue what was in store for them. But it just never happened. Plus, with all the conventions and movie marathons usually going on around that time of year, it would be even harder to get stuff done.

Where we live now, which is still in a good neighborhood, we'll be lucky if we get two or three kids coming to the door on Halloween. Not sure why. Even when we would have plenty of decorations out in front, it still wouldn't attract any kids. It's a shame really. I miss those days of that constant stream of kids making their way up and down the driveway, looking for goodies. For those few years though, we really made the neighborhood a fun place on Halloween night.

Just because kids stopped haunting the neighborhood streets in search of candy, it didn't mean we should give up celebrating our favorite holiday all together. Not a chance. Halloween is one of the few times during the year where we can really let it all hang out. Granted, every day is already Halloween for us, but those October days should be celebrated in a special way. So we got a group of friends together and took our party indoors to celebrate horror!

Of course, it is a costume party and over the years, I have been amazed at some of the creativity our friends have shown with their costumes. From the Blind Dead to *Creepshow*'s Jordy Verrill and the green stuff to Asa from *Black Sunday*, it's exciting to see what they have come up with. This is the time to celebrate these movies and our friends go out of their way to do just that. If you make the poor decision of not showing up in a costume, we *will* revel in ridiculing you. So the pressure's on, even for yours truly, the host! Coming up with a costume can be a real challenge. I seem to take forever, trying to come up with an idea for a character, and then twice as long trying to find the appropriate costume. It can be a real nightmare. Then there are the ones like my son Nick, who decides one year he wants to go as Darkman, makes one trip to the thrift store and finds a black trench coat and hat, and he's done. Yeah... cheers for him.

There are two reasons that people show up for our Halloween party. The first is definitely the food. To say that Dawn goes overboard is like saying Stephen King has written a few books. Dawn came from a family that, when planning parties, would take the number of guests you think you'll have, triple the amount of food needed, and then make even more, just in case someone might show up hungry. She amazes me each and every year at all that she does for our little get-togethers. Yes, every now and then I might help, but she goes above and beyond to fuel our celebrations.

The second reason people show up? The games.

Since a majority of the guests coming over are huge horror fans, why not celebrate the genre with some horror movie-themed party games? Over the years, I've used, taken, borrowed, or flat-out stole these ideas from game shows, board games, or other ideas I came up with, putting a little horror twist on them. Please feel free to use these ideas for your next Halloween party. I will warn you that some require a bit of planning and time to get things ready. Don't start planning this stuff the day before your party, because you won't finish in time. Start *weeks* ahead of time. Trust me, I know.

Audio Movie Trailers - Get a selection of movie trailers (YouTube is a great place for this, just copy the links) and play them one and a time on your TV, or somewhere where everyone will be able to hear them, but with no picture. The first person to guess which movie it is *just from the sound* wins! When selecting the trailers, make sure the title isn't mentioned or stated right in the beginning. Yes, it takes some time finding the right ones, but it is a lot of fun. You can also just use different movie clips and have them guess the title, but those can be a little trickier to figure out.

Name the Quote - A movie quote is read off and the first person to guess the correct movie wins. You can also give bonus points if the person can name the character who said it and the actor who played them. You can either have the host read the quote or divide the people into teams and have a person from the team read the quote, but all teams can guess. This makes it more fun because each person gets to read the different quotes, maybe even getting into the character a little. Have fun with it!

The Pyramid Game - No, this isn't a scam to get money from your guests. The name comes from the old game show *$10,000 Pyramid*. The game is simple. Find a category, like "Things You'd Find in a Vampire Film," and write ten different things on an index card, one card for each word. Such as a cross, a coffin, a stake, etc. This has to be done way before the party. Then you divide into teams, with two people from one team playing at a time. The two from the other team that are going to play for that same category have to leave the room, so they don't hear the clues or the answers. For example, if you have three teams of six people each, you'll have one team playing with two people from each of the other two teams leaving the room while the first team goes.

For the first two playing, one will be reading the clues, while the other is guessing. Have them face each other. Once you start the timer, the one reading the clues can say anything except the word on the card. For example, keeping with the vampire movie theme, if the word is "stake", the person could say "This is what is used to kill a vampire!" Or "It's the long wooden thing they stab the vampire in the heart with." They keep going until the person guesses the correct answer. Once you get through all 10 cards, note the time on the timer and then the next team comes in and goes through the same cards. The team with the fastest time wins! If someone is struggling with a particular word, you can say "PASS" and go to the next card. But you have to go back to it before you're done.

Be creative with the subjects, such as "Things You'd Find in a Slasher Movie," or "Things You'd Find in a Hammer Movie," or "Things You'd Find in a Zombie Movie," Again, have fun with it, but make sure you find that balance between too hard or too easy. If it is too hard and nobody is getting it, it's not fun anymore.

Tag Lines - Read out tag lines from different movies for people to guess. You can get these from movie posters, ad mats, or many other places. Once again, the Internet is a wonderful place to find this stuff. Maybe give them a bonus point if they can guess the year the movie came out!

A to Z Game - Give everyone a pen or pencil and a sheet of paper that has A through Z listed on it going down the page, like A on the first line, B on the second, and so on. Once everyone is ready, tell them they have to write down a horror movie title that starts with each of those letters. The first one that gets all the way through wins!

Title Game - Everyone gets another piece of paper, this time blank, with something to write with. You also need someone with a timer. When everyone is ready, give them a word, like "Night" and then they have 30 seconds to write down as many horror movie titles they can think of that has "Night" in the title. Whoever has the most wins! You can use words like Blood, Revenge, Return, etc.

The Continuous Title Game - This one is for smaller groups, maybe five people or under. Once again, you start with a common word like "Night," and then the first person has to name a film out loud with that word in the title. Then it goes to the next person and they have to name a different movie that has "Night" in the title. Then it goes the next person, and the next, and so on. Each time, a new title must be named. If you can't think of a title, then you are out, and it goes to the next person. Once you're out, you're out of that game. It keeps going until there is only one person left, and then they win.

Horror Pictionary - Out of all the games that I have come up with over the years, this one still seems to be the favorite. If you've played Pictionary before, then you'll know how to play. The only difference is that what you'll be drawing are horror movie titles. Divide into teams. One person will come up to the board, pull a title from the bowl, and then have 60 seconds to draw *something* that will make their team guess the movie. You can try to draw out the exact title, such as if the movie is *House on Haunted Hill*, you could try drawing the house up on top of a hill. Or, if the title is a little more difficult, you can try and draw a scene from the movie. The only rules here is that you can't use numbers or letters in your drawing.

Here is the important part of the game. It is not about winning or losing. It's not about being creative in your drawing. It is simply about laughing at your friends' limited artistic ability when they try to draw something simple, like a frog, that no one else can figure out what the hell it is supposed to be! Okay, maybe making fun of them is not the right thing to do. But it will probably happen anyway!

Here, the prep work is once again the time-consuming part. First, you need a dry-erase board and some dry-erase markers. (Using permanent markers will make for a very short game.) The board needs to be big enough for everyone to be able to see. Having an easel or stand for it would be even better. The host will also need to spend time gathering movie titles, writing them down on little individual pieces of paper that will be folded up and put in a bowl to be drawn from. You will want to make sure that no one can see the movie titles as they reach in the bowl.

Now a quick word on the titles. You'll want to have a wide variety. Some easy, some hard, and some that are downright impossible, like... maybe Jess Franco's *The Sadist from Notre-Dame* (1979). Number one, this will show just how smart and creative your friends are, and number two, it will also give more horrible sketches to laugh and point at. Seriously though, you'll want to use a wide range of titles, from the classics to newer ones. If they don't know the title they picked, they are not allowed to draw another one. They'll just have to try and draw it on the title alone. Again, good times.

As the host, this will take a *very* long time to prepare, especially finding all the right titles, so again, don't wait until the last day before the party.

All of these games are meant to be fun with your horror friends. Sure, there will be some jesting and joking made at each other's expense, but it is all about having fun, while you are celebrating the genre that we all love. At the end of the day, having fellow horror friends to rejoice at this time of year is the best part of this. Halloween is our time to be the "normal," so let's make sure we do it right!

Halloween 1975

21

Science Fiction Isn't Really a Genre

"Fiction dealing principally with the impact of actual or imagined science on society or individuals or having a scientific factor as an essential orienting component."

Definition of "science fiction," *Webster's Dictionary*

Okay, before all you Trekkies and sci-fi fans get your panties in a wad and start sending me hate mail, let me explain. First of all, I'm not totally serious in this chapter's title statement. Well... maybe a bit, but hear me out before passing judgment.

Let me preface this by being completely up front on why I have a little chip on my shoulder about this whole thing. Obviously the horror genre is a huge passion of mine, and has been most of my life. So when I go into a retail store, such as a book store, or video store back in the day, and see there is no "Horror" section, only to have horror-related titles lumped in under the "Sci-fi" section, I get irritated. Why couldn't horror have its own section? Too embarrassed to separate these genres for fear of the kind of cretins that may come in and browse it? Okay... maybe a little overdramatic, but hopefully you see my point.

In the 1950s, all these movies with mutated bugs growing to enormous sizes due to radiation or atomic energy, or those fun end-of-the-world type pictures, for some strange reason they are generally referred to as "science fiction" films. Why? Why science fiction? Was it because there was some sort of scientific explanation as to why these creatures have grown to this enormous size? Or that some scientist had to try and discover a way to stop this monstrous menace before it destroyed the world? So therefore they are in the science fiction genre? Why weren't these called horror films? I'm sorry but when your story consists of a giant insect terrorizing a city, that sure sounds like horror to me!

It may have something to do with the fact that after WWII, horror pictures weren't as popular as they were in the 1930s leading up to the war. Times were looking up in the world so there was no need for monsters to scare the public. Or at least that was what movie studios perceived, since the old Universal monster standards had been slowly dying off at the box office. Maybe this had more to do with the quality of the pictures they were cranking out as opposed diminishing audiences. But once the film *Them!* came out in 1954 which had sales at the box office as big as the ants on the screen, the other studios rushed in to cash in on this new subgenre. Of course, not wanting the negative connotations that the horror genre typically gets, these films were now referred to as science fiction pictures!

Maybe this is just me being a little protective of the genre I love so much and want to stand up proudly to defend it, but you don't have to be a genius to know that at its core, these films were meant to scare and terrify their audiences. Even if we were to go with more of a modern-day title, such as *Alien*, which is a title that is always brought up as being a science fiction story... Sorry guys... that's horror. A creature stalking a crew on a spaceship, brutally killing them one by one? That sure sounds like a horror film to me. Why not call it what it really is?

That is when I started to think about the intent of the filmmaker when they make their picture. A "comedy" is supposed to make you laugh. "Horror" is supposed to scare or terrify you. "Dramas" will likely contemplate the human condition in a serious manner, bringing up feelings of sadness, anger, and/or catharsis. An "action/adventure" should give the audience thrills and excitement. Now, there are films that combine genres, such as horror/comedies or comedy/dramas. But what about science fiction? What is the intent of the filmmaker there? What would a sci-fi movie be that isn't part of another genre?

I guess that is how I would define a film genre: What is the intent of the filmmaker? What are they trying to make you feel? According to the dictionary, "science fiction" is "a genre of speculative fiction, typically dealing with imaginative concepts such as futuristic science and technology, space travel, time travel, faster than light travel, parallel universes, and extraterrestrial life." Okay...I get all that. So the intent of the film is to make you think about things that don't exist yet? Can that be the only thing that genre is supposed to do?

The more this topic was kicked around, usually after-hours at a convention, I started to put some more thought into this theory. For me, sci-fi is more of a *setting* than it is a genre. Mel Brooks' *Spaceballs* is a comedy within a sci-fi setting. *Close Encounters of the Third Kind* is a drama. *Star Wars* is an action/adventure saga. Name me a sci-fi movie that isn't also a comedy, drama, action, or horror film as well. But science fiction all by itself? Hard to think of one.

According to Filmsite.org, sci-fi films are classified as "often quasi-scientific, visionary and imaginative –complete with heroes, aliens, distant planets, impossible quests, improbable settings, fantastic places, great dark and shadowy villains, futuristic technology, unknown and unknowable forces, and extraordinary monsters ('things or creatures from space'), either created by mad scientists or by nuclear havoc." To me, that sure sounds like they are explaining a setting: "Distant planets", "improbable settings," "fantastic places." The rest of the explanation could be used in several different genres. The "great, dark and shadowy villains" and "futuristic technology" sound like they could be part of any number of James Bond films. The "extraordinary monsters ('things or creatures from space'), either created by mad scientists or by nuclear havoc," covers a lot of those flicks from the 1950s. But again, the main intent of those movies is to scare the audience, regardless if the monster came from under your bed or from a Petri dish.

So put yourself to the test. Name a film that you'd consider a science fiction film and see if it doesn't have any other elements from other genres. Try and name a film that doesn't fit into anything else. *Blade Runner*? Sorry. Film noir, set in the future. *The Terminator*? Action/horror. Keep trying. Let me know when you come up with one.

One genre that sort of goes against my theory is "the western." Originally I also considered it a setting, same as sci-fi and not a real genre. But the more I thought about it, these films go beyond a setting and really have a style unto themselves, with the way they are filmed, their look and feel, their tropes and themes, the archetypal characters found within, etc. Sure, there are westerns with comedy and westerns with action and westerns with drama, so maybe it really comes down to having that particular style. Look at "film noir," for example. The dictionary defines it as "a style or genre of cinematographic film marked by a mood of pessimism, fatalism, and menace." So maybe there are genres that are just defined by having a certain style to them. Could be. And would sci-fi be part of that?

Please don't think I'm trying to do away with the science fiction genre. It really came up as a topic to get some discussion going, and yeah, maybe there's a bit of deep-rooted anger in there where I was trying to stir the pot. But it really does get you thinking, doesn't it?

If you do come with a suggestion of a sci-fi movie that doesn't fit into any other subgenre, let me know. I'll be waiting.

Tom Sullivan, Nick, and the head from Evil Dead

Flashback family!

22

Tales from the Road

"It was the best of times, it was the worst of times..."

A Tale of Two Cities by Charles Dickens

Quoting Charles Dickens might seem a little lofty for a humble horror fan, but it fits so well in describing my feelings about movie conventions. Some of the best moments of my life have happened throughout my 30+ years of going to these conventions, collecting many incredible and unforgettable memories along the way. I have met literally hundreds of people over the years, more than a few of which I now consider to be my closest friends. I have also met quite a few celebrities during that time, some of them leaving me speechless and star-struck, while others were so friendly and down-to-earth that the whole experience doesn't even seem to be real.

Of course, there were also plenty of times where it was the flipside of that, such as when a convention is poorly run or advertised, or when you go up to a celebrity to tell them you've enjoyed their work and their response is to ask you if you're going to buy something. You're always going to have both sides of the coin. Sure, my feelings towards these events have changed over the years. You can't be doing this for over 30 years and not see some changes along the way. Sadly, not all of these changes have been positive. This is why I had to go back through this chapter and re-write a lot of it. I had started this chapter quite a few years ago, but when I got close to being actually done with it, upon reading through it again, I found more negative comments than I wanted.

The main issue that kept coming up was the whole autograph thing at shows these days. As you'll read in some of my early convention reports on my site, I started when autographs were always free. Now they are not. I used to bitch about people paying for autographs because it was reinforcing a bad policy. Then it hit me. As much as I don't agree with giving a currently working actor $50 for a signature, if the fan wants to spend that money, then so be it. How different is that from me spending $50 for a movie poster or reference book that someone else might think was a waste of money?

Whatever makes the fan happy. Who are we to judge? We have enough non-fans out there judging us; we shouldn't be doing it to each other. If you are like me and have a problem with autograph pricing, then do what I do and just don't pay. Skip it. Just go say hello to the guest, let them know that you enjoyed their work, and then walk away.

Since I have been fortunate enough to attend well over a hundred conventions during these past three decades, covering each and every one of these shows would be tedious, repetitive, and probably boring for you, the reader. Instead, what I'd like to do is go over some of the highlights as sort of a "Best of" episode. Some memories will be longer and more in-depth, while others might just be a story or two. Really depends on how interesting the show was. Or in some cases, when the trip to and from was just as interesting as the show itself. To begin with, let's go back to the very beginning, to my very first real horror convention.

Fangoria Weekend of Horrors 1988

Back in the late 1980s, I had been going to a few local movie memorabilia shows in my area and even a couple of Star Trek cons. Granted, most of the merchandise and memorabilia at these shows wasn't what I was looking for, but at least it was some sort of a con. There were also movie memorabilia shows that didn't have celebrity guests, focusing instead on dealers selling everything from posters, stills, books, and just about anything else you can think of. But the only real horror convention around that I knew of at the time was Fangoria's Weekend of Horrors. I'd been an avid fan of *Fangoria* magazine for a few years by then, and would see their yearly ad for their cons. They looked amazing, but were always out in California or New York. I decided that I was going to take the plunge and make a trip out to their next show in April of 1988. This happened to be a month before my upcoming marriage. I didn't know anybody that was interested (or crazy) enough to go out there with me, so I was going on my own. This was my first solo trip on an airplane, as well as my first trip out to California. People had often asked me where I went sightseeing while I was out there. They didn't seem to understand that I was there for the show and nothing else. It also might be because I just didn't know any better. I went right from the airport to the hotel where the convention was at, stayed there the entire weekend, and then left late Sunday afternoon, back to the airport. In the three days that I was at this gathering of demented, degenerate, and twisted horror film-fiends, what I saw, what I *experienced*, simply changed my life.

Before this show, I had never met anyone famous. Granted, most of "normal" society wouldn't have considered the people I met that weekend famous either. But to me, or any horror fan, these celebrities were definitely at the top; some even icons. Names like Robert Englund, Christopher Lee, Tom Savini, Tobe Hooper, and many more. Up until then, these were just names on the movies that I'd been watching since my childhood and read about in books and magazines. But now, I would actually get to see them in person. Needless to say, I was more than a little excited, not to mention a bit nervous.

Being my first convention, I really didn't know what to expect. It opened at 11am on Saturday and I figured there might be a line in the morning. Since I really didn't have anything else to do that morning, I wanted to make sure I got in right away when it opened. So I got up early and went down to find out where the show was actually at in the hotel and to see if there was a line yet. This was at 6am. That's right... 6am. And at 6am that morning, there were already a few people in line. Granted, it was only three, but it was still a line and I knew it was only going to get longer. As more and more people started to filter down to the area, I knew my choice of timing was a good one. Eventually, the people working the show separated the lines into one for people that had advance tickets (like me) and one for those that needed to buy tickets. Both of these were huge by the time the show opened.

While we were waiting, I was chatting with a couple people in line around me. One of them was a kid in his mid-teens wearing a Metallica t-shirt. The funny thing was, as we were talking, I noticed that Kirk Hammett, guitarist for Metallica, was standing by the door talking to one of the convention workers. He was pretty easy to spot, with his long, black, curly hair. So I point over to Kirk and started to tell this kid who that is. "No, it isn't," he replied. "Yes, it is. I guarantee it," I stated again. So he grabs a piece of paper and pen and walks over there to find out. He stands there for a second until Kirk looks at him, and I see the kid ask him something, Kirk smiles and nods his head. He then hands him the paper to autograph, and then while Kirk is signing it, the kid turns back to me with a huge smile on his face pointing to Hammett. I can still remember the look of pure happiness on that kid's face.

The show had a schedule of events and the full list of guests that were scheduled to be on hand. I quickly scanned over the lineup and got even more excited. For some reason, Christopher Lee was not on the list anymore and must have cancelled at the last minute. But there were plenty of other names listed that made up for that, such as Clive Barker, Roddy McDowall, Anthony Perkins, and George Romero.

At 11:00am, the doors opened and they started to let the people with advance tickets into the dealer room. There were two separate rooms for the convention: the dealer room and the auditorium, where the Q&A sessions were going to be held. Once we got into the dealer room, it was a mad dash to scope out the different tables to see what offerings they might have that

I knew I would have to go home with. This was a horror fan's dream come true. There were poster dealers, magazine dealers, makeup supplies, bootleg movies, t-shirts, soundtracks (on LP no less), and tons more. Remember kiddies, this was years before eBay and Amazon. Finding items like these was next to impossible in my hometown, so I was in horror heaven.

I don't recall everything I bought that weekend, but here are a few highlights: I picked up a few soundtrack LPs like *Near Dark* and *Creepshow*. I also remember getting a *Creepshow* one-sheet, with the ticket booth artwork, for $10. Yes, I still remember the price, especially since they now go for a few dollars more. There was also someone selling 8x10 stills, which at the time I collected. I found a great 8x10 lobby card from *The Legend of Hell House*, which I was thrilled to find since it gave me something to have McDowall sign. More on him later.

One of the displays in the dealer room featured props from the upcoming *Fright Night 2*, which is why McDowall was there. Spread out over several tables were different hand/arm appliances and armatures, the bat creature, and several busts of some of the characters. They even had the bust of Julie Carmen's character in the burn/melting stage from the end of the movie. Granted, this was before the movie was even out, so we really didn't know what we were looking at, but these were the first real movie props that I had ever seen in person and it was just incredible to get to see them up close.

I spent about 90 minutes in the dealer room wandering around, taking it all in before I decided to check out the auditorium area for the Q&As. As I left the dealer room, they were still letting people in line with advance tickets in, and hadn't even started with the people without tickets. The non-ticket holders were not too happy. I quickly made a mental note for future shows, especially ones run by convention organizers Creation, to always have my ticket ahead of time and to get in line early!

As I was walking towards the auditorium, I saw a few people gathering around a rather tall man standing there, who had a big smile on his face. It was none other than George Romero. I immediately dug out my copy of Tom Savini's how-to makeup book, *Grande Illusions*, to see if he would sign it, since he wrote the introduction. He was signing a few different things that people were handing him so I patiently waited my turn. He finally took my book, signed his name, and handed it back, again with that enormous Romero grin. This was my first autograph. Even though I would meet Romero quite a few times in the future, getting a few other things signed, I still have that book in my collection and it remains very special to me for that very reason.

The auditorium was huge but I knew it would fill up pretty fast the more people had time to get into the show. I found a spot in the front row, near the center, and planted myself down. The only problem was that once you got up, you lost your spot. So I made sure that I was going to be there most of the day, to see most of the great guests they had lined up. I also planned on taking plenty of pictures with my little Kodak camera. I had brought plenty of film and plenty of flashcubes. Anybody remember those? Little did I know that the range of those things wasn't the greatest, but at the time that was all I had.

I don't recall the exact schedule of guests, who was on first and so on, but I do remember a couple of them who were on the stage early on one of the two days. Writer/director Frank LaLoggia was there promoting his new film, *Lady in White*. They screened the trailer for it, which looked really good, with lots of spooky atmosphere. When I finally got to see it in the theater, I just loved it. Such a beautiful, truly timeless movie. Years later, LaLoggia would be my first interview I did for my little fanzine *Visions of Darkness*. Another early guest was Bob Keen, the makeup effects artist for Clive Barker's *Hellraiser*. He was there to promote his latest film, *The Unholy*. We got to see some shots of the creature and even some makeup props that he had brought along, including one fake head where a person got their eyeballs slit open! Good stuff! The creature looked really twisted and cool. Unfortunately, by the time the film came out, this design had been replaced by something that looked more like a mutated Muppet. Very disappointing.

Another icon that I got to see was the immortal Dick Miller, who had some great stories. Even back in 1988, Miller was still considered an icon. From his days working with Roger Corman, cranking out films like *Bucket of Blood*, *It Conquered the World*, and *The Terror*, to his days working with Joe Dante, he was always memorable, even in the smallest roles.

Speaking of which, Joe Dante was at the show as well, though honestly I can't remember what he was promoting. He might have just been there to chat. Other celebs were there, such as Mick Garris, who was promoting his directorial debut, *Critters 2*, bringing along a very large Krite with him on stage. Frank Darabont and Chuck Russell talked about their new remake of *The Blob*, even telling stories of battling the studios who didn't want them to kill any kids. They didn't listen.

Another panel that was pretty impressive consisted of George Romero, John Russo, Tobe Hooper, and author Gary Brandner. I don't recall the exact subject of the panel, but having Romero and Hooper about 20 feet in front of me was pretty damn unreal. Think about it... here were two directors that each made a small independent film that changed cinema history! I did get to shake hands with Hooper a little later, but the only thing I had for him to sign at the time was a book of short stories that he wrote the introduction for. In all my future years of conventions, I never had the chance to meet Hooper again.

Makeup effects wizard Tom Savini was a god among horror fans back in the late '80s, but he was also a big horror fan, just like the rest of us. He genuinely loved meeting and talking to his fans. It was very common to see him walking around the dealer room and buying different things from vendors. He had recently done *Texas Chainsaw Massacre 2*, as well as finishing up with Romero's *Monkey Shines*. He brought along a bunch of props from his films and also gave a demonstration on bullet squibs, where one lucky member of the audience got the chance to get shot by Savini! I went up to him later, when I saw him in the dealer room, and asked to get a photo with him and a couple of things signed. He welcomed the opportunity and was so gracious. This was a man that I considered to be an icon of the industry. He wasn't just a guy working in the movies, but a huge fan of them as well. And it seemed that he never forgot what it was like to be that younger fan, maybe because at that time, he still was.

Speaking of icons, there were two people attending that show that truly deserved that title. The first one was Anthony Perkins. While he was up on stage, talking about his career and answering questions, I sat there just a few feet away, watching the real Norman Bates pacing nervously back and forth on stage. He acted like Norman, sounded like Norman, and looked like Norman. Now, this isn't a criticism in any way. It was just that that really was what Anthony Perkins sounded like and his mannerisms weren't too far off from those of the character of Norman.

But when the second of these icons, Roddy McDowall, took the stage, I discovered something that day. As he walked back and forth on stage, answering questions from the audience, I looked upon this man that I had been watching on screens, both big and small, for most of my life. From his many appearances on a multitude of TV series, even in his younger days, to the countless movies that I've seen, and I did not see any those characters on there on the stage. Instead, I saw this incredibly talented actor, who seemed to be able to really transform himself into a different person for those roles. So while I watched and listened to him, I was looking for Peter Vincent from *Fright Night*, or Benjamin Fischer from *Legend of Hell House*, or even Cornelius from the *Planet of the Apes* series, but they were not there. I was amazed and in awe of this actor. I was thrilled later to have him sign the 8x10 I found earlier from *Hell House*. I was so excited that I even took a picture of him signing my photo! Calling an actor a legend is something that shouldn't be thrown around on a whim. McDowall truly deserved that title, and I defy anyone to convince me otherwise.

Clive Barker made a surprise appearance at the show, which was a mixed blessing; had I known, I would had brought a few of his books to sign! Granted, I would have the opportunity many times in the future. Nonetheless, I was able to meet him, shake his hand, and have him sign a book of short stories I brought with me that he had contributed to. He was there to talk about *Hellbound: Hellraiser 2*, which was still in production. In over three decades of attending cons, I have never witnessed someone as entertaining, funny, and engaging with the audience than Clive Barker. He is such an extremely talented man, in so many areas, and one that seems to have never lost touch with his fans.

Robert Englund was there at the show as well, but I missed most of his Q&A because I was in line getting an autograph from Mr. McDowall. I was able to make it back into the auditorium to catch the last part of his talk though and snap a couple of quick pictures. While I was a little bummed that he wasn't signing autographs that weekend, it wasn't that big of a deal. Especially if I would have known that some years later, I would be driving him to a movie screening in Chicago. But let's not jump ahead.

Before I knew it, the weekend was over and I had survived my very first horror convention. It is so funny as I look back on it and how things have changed since then, with the shows, the guests, and even with me. I flew out to California for this event, by myself. Once I arrived there on Friday, I checked into the hotel and spent the rest of the night in my room, by myself, only stepping out to the hotel restaurant to eat, again, by myself. After the show on Saturday, I pretty much did the same thing, except this time I had all the stuff I bought in the dealer room earlier in the day to occupy my time. There was no socializing for me. I didn't know anybody and I wasn't the most talkative person either, especially with strangers. My, how things are different now. Some 30-odd years later, my favorite thing about going to shows is having the chance to talk to different people, those that I already know or complete strangers. I've learned that we all have this same bond or kinship with the horror genre. No matter what, you always have that connection with them and can (and should) treat them like family.

To quote Mary Shelley, *"It is true, we shall be monsters, cut off from all the world; but on that account we shall be more attached to one another."*

Okay, so it took me a few more years to learn that… but I finally did.

Looking back at this, my first real convention, I am eternally grateful that I had the chance to experience a show when the guests were there to talk about their past projects, promote new ones, or just there to meet their fans and show their gratitude for the support over the years. The shows were a celebration of the genre and all those involved, from the fans all the way up to the people that worked in and on the films. Maybe this is why I'm a little bitter about what conventions have become these days, money-making cattle-drives, where it seems the guests are not there to meet their fans, but to collect cash from customers. I guess that is just the way things have progressed, like it or not.

Victoria Price, daughter of icon Vincent Price, posted something on her website a few years ago that always stuck with me and is something that I think is lost on modern celebrities. She said that he father told her that when he started on Broadway, starring in the play *Victoria Regina* with Helen Hayes (who was considered to be the First Lady of American Theatre), she gave him a piece of wisdom that he always tried to live by: "An actor is a public servant. Never forget that: Without your audience, you will not get to continue doing what you love." It's a shame more of today's talent weren't given that advice.

Okay... complaining is over. Let's get to our next convention!

Fangoria Weekend in New York City

My next convention adventure took place two years later in 1990, at another one of Fangoria's Weekend of Horrors. This time, we weren't heading to the sunny beaches of California, but to the dark and scary East Coast... New York City. And this time, I wasn't going alone. A neighbor kid, who wasn't even out of high school, was a pretty big horror fan and was dying to go along with me. He asked one of his friends to join us, who in turn brought one of his friends. So the four of us flew out to the Big Apple on a Friday evening in, I believe, January of 1990. This was supposed to be another big show, with guests like the one and only Christopher Lee (once again), Sam Raimi and Bruce Campbell there to promote their newest film, *Darkman*, along with Clive Baker, Gale Anne Hurd, Tom Savini, Linnea Quigley, members of KNB EFX Group, and more.

After we landed in the Big Apple, we walked out of the airport, looking for a cab to take us to the hotel. A man seemed to step out of nowhere, asking if we needed a cab. I replied yes, and he pointed around the corner to where his car was supposedly waiting. Now, since I was the elder of the group (at the ripe old age of 25), the rest in my group quickly looked at me as if we were about to be murdered the second we turned that corner. But being naive (and/or stupid), I figured, "What could go wrong?" As we walked around the corner, there sat a huge Lincoln Town Car with the guy holding the door open. I gave my group a stern authoritative look, as if I knew we were safe. That was until we got into the car and started moving. I think the driver averaged about 70 miles an hour. And I do mean, *averaged* that speed. I could deal with that for most of the time, but once we hit the Queens Midtown Tunnel, I thought we were going to die in a fiery car crash. As we were whipping through that tunnel like a bullet, the driver would turn around, leaning back over the seat asking (in a thick Jamaican accent) if we'd like to go to the Village and see his sister and to party. This tunnel had barely enough room for two cars to pass by each other, giving very little wiggle room. As we sped down this certain death trap, all I could think was that we were going to swerve into the oncoming lane and collide head on with another car. If we were lucky, it would be a large truck because then death would be instantaneous, as opposed to stuck in a burning car, roasting to death in the tunnel. At least part of me was hoping for death, because if I did survive, I'd have to explain to my neighbor's parents why their 14-year-old son's body was spread out over about 10 miles of a New York tunnel. Okay, maybe it wasn't that bad, but for a kid making his first trip to the Big Apple, and never seeing anybody drive that fast down a long, narrow path without paying attention, it really was enough to etch that bit of terror into my brain.

Before I knew it, the car was pulling up in front of the hotel, where we all stumbled out of the car like we had just been on a three-day bender. We walked on shaky legs into the lobby and got checked in. We tried to find a place to eat, but quickly realized that for some reason the cost of living seemed to be much higher in New York than back in Illinois. Finding a shabby looking hamburger was going to set us back about $13. Remember, this is 1990. So we said no thanks to that. We'll wait.

We decided to get to bed early because we wanted to be in line early the next morning. Since my past experience, I figured there would be another huge line and I didn't want to spend most of the afternoon waiting in it. So instead, we got down there at 6am and spent the next five hours ... waiting in line! As my young convention companions complained the whole way down from the room about having to get up so early only to see there were already about a dozen people in line, they realized that I might have been right. By the time the 11am opening came, the line went out the hotel and down the block, straight out into the New York January winter! From what I heard, it took several hours for those people just to get inside the building, let alone the show. So again, getting up that early didn't seem like such a bad idea after all. Once the show opened, we were off and running.

Compared to the California show, this one was gigantic. There were three different dealer rooms and one huge auditorium for the Q&As. As young fans wandering through these rooms, looking at all the amazing memorabilia pleading to get our money, it was almost a collector's overload. There were stills, posters, magazines, model kits, videos, and so much more. It was a challenge to try and scope out the whole place, checking out all the different vendors to see what was available before dropping any of that dwindling wad of cash that we had all brought.

Here's a little lesson for all you collectors out there: Never take that first plunge on buying something before really thinking about it, and even more important, before doing some research. You never know when you might come across it later at a much cheaper price. Let me give you an example.

Around that time, there was a magazine called *The Horror Fan*, which I first learned about it when I picked up issue #2 a year or so before this show, but I had never come across the premier issue, which came out in December of 1988. Well, there was a dealer at this show selling a copy of it for $100. That's right... for an issue that originally cost $3.50 not even two years ago. Apparently that issue had skyrocketed in value. Now, I am a completist, and really wanted to add this issue to my collection, but there was no way I could justify dropping a C-note on one little magazine. Well, two weeks after this show, while at a local comic book shop, browsing through their $1 magazine box, not only did I find this same issue, they had about 3 or 4 copies in there. Just imagine the sinking feeling in my gut (not to mention my wallet) imagining if I had forked over that $100 only to find it a couple of weeks later for a buck? So take a lesson from this, kiddies. If the price seems too high... it probably is. In my 30 years of collecting, I've usually found items much, much cheaper than when I first came across them. You just have to wait and be patient.

Anyway, back to the show.

One of the highlights of the weekend was the Q&As, with Clive Barker once again stealing the show. He always was a riot, making lewd comments, cracking jokes, and showing that his wild imagination is not just for his writing. He always seemed to be able to captivate the audience with his wonderful stories. He was there talking about his upcoming film project, *Nightbreed*. That weekend, I didn't get anything signed by Barker, due to the massive amount of people that were standing in his line, as well as the unorganized way the show was managed. Maybe Creation didn't realize the number of people attending. Maybe they didn't care.

Bruce Campbell was there, talking about the early days with him and Sam Raimi, which was pretty funny. Raimi was funny as well as we heard terror tales of what they had to go through to get *Evil Dead* made and distributed. And the best part? After their Q&As, they were in the back of the auditorium signing for FREE! That's right, folks. Free. Whatever you were putting in front of them, they were signing. Ahh... such wonderful memories.

One of the biggest high points of the weekend was the opportunity to see a true horror icon, even though he fought for years to be rid of that title. This would be Dracula himself, Christopher Lee. Unfortunately, he was not signing autographs that weekend, but honestly, just getting to see him in person, up on the stage, with the audience so captivated and eating out of his hand, really was amazing. I know that I've openly bitched about Lee and his attitude towards the horror genre over the years, but there was no hint of that during his time on the stage. Well played, Mr. Lee. Well played, indeed. He spoke of his days with Hammer, *The Wicker Man* (and a possible sequel), James Bond, and more. It really was an honor to see one of the last great Masters of the Macabre!

The rest of the show really was a blur. The time went by so fast, much like our spending money. But at the end of the weekend, I knew I was coming back with a ton of autographs, lots of stuff for the collection, and some great memories. As we were leaving the hotel, there was a cab parked directly in front of us. The doorman asked if we needed a cab, to which I nodded yes. He then reached out and opened the cab door as we all piled in. I was the last one to get in and tried to close the door but the doorman was still holding on to it. He asked me if everything was okay, which I replied with a puzzled "yeah." Then he said in a little louder voice, "Is everything okay with ME?" Then I got it. He expected a tip for reaching his hand out and opening a door to a cab that was already parked there. Sorry guy. Not today. So I responded in the same stern voice he gave me, "YES," and pulled the door shut. As we pulled away from the curb, I could still hear this guy cussing not only myself, but my parents as well. This would be the first of many trips I would make to New York for a Fango show, but it would be several years before I would make that journey east again. The reason for this return would be because of one simple name they announced as a guest for their 1996 show. Before that though, there were a few other shows to attend!

Fango Comes to Detroit!

By the summer of 1990, Fangoria had started to branch out with their conventions. In addition to New York and California, shows were also starting to pop up in other areas. That August, they were coming to Detroit. Well, actually it was Dearborn, Michigan, a suburb. Guests announced for this show included Sam Raimi, Bruce Campbell, Kane Hodder, Greg Nicotero, and others.

Michigan wasn't that far of a drive, a hell of a lot closer than New York. Plus, my family lived in Michigan, and this was only an hour or so past them. My friend Dave, who I had met when we went to that first trip to New York, was going, along with my wife Dawn. We also planned to pick up my niece Angel and nephew Jeremy (who were around 18 and 15 at the time), since they wanted to go as well. We left Illinois in the middle of Friday night, drove the four hours to Eaton Rapids, picked up our two passengers in the wee hours of the morning, and made the rest of the trip to Dearborn. We wanted to make sure we got there early enough to get in line. I didn't want to be stuck outside waiting to get in like I'd seen at the other shows. Of course, this was years before we would have a van, so fitting 5 people in a car... Well, let's just say it wasn't the most comfortable for those in the back seat. But we were all still young and carefree (or stupid), right?

We finally made to the hotel and checked in, then made our way to the show, around 7-8am, explaining to my group why we needed to be there early. Of course, there was barely a line when we got there. Even when the show finally opened, the line was nowhere near the sizes of the two previous two shows I'd gone to. So much for that theory. Not only was the line much shorter, but the size of the show was also a lot smaller. I barely remember the dealer room, other than some dealers with masks, some with posters, and some model kits; drastically different, both in size and scope, when compared to the shows on the East and West coasts.

Before we got into the convention, I had given some helpful tips to my young relatives Angel and Jeremy. I reminded them that we were going to be there for the whole weekend, so they should pace themselves on their spending. If they saw something they liked right away, make sure they browsed through the whole dealer room first before spending their money. You never know what you might see next. It could be something better, or at a cheaper price than what you just saw at the previous table. They seemed to understand. Or at least they *seemed* to. Within 30 minutes of getting into the dealer room, my nephew Jeremy walked up to me, toys, model kits, and other goodies, piled up in his arms and said, "I spent all my money. Can we go home now?" Ah, to be young again. After explaining that since he didn't do what I had suggested, he was going to now have to wait for the rest of us, not to mention the show to finish, he was going to be in for a long day and weekend.

It was at this show that I started to realize not to trust Creation, the convention organizers that ran the Fango shows or the people higher up in the organization. One of the things that they would have at some point during the show was an auction. In the same room where the Q&As were held, they would auction items off to those sitting in the audience. The guy on stage running the auction was one of the top guys for Creation. On Saturday's auction, one of the items was a model kit of Lon Chaney's *Phantom of the Opera*. This guy states that he actually owns this kit because he is a HUGE fan of Chaney and loves all of his work, and that this kit was one of his favorites. Now cut to Sunday's auction. He's up there again, this time auctioning off a Screamin' model kit of "The Vampire" which was actually Lon Chaney from *London After Midnight*, the vampire character from the lost 1927 silent film. Our buddy running the auction, who just stated yesterday that he was one of the biggest Lon Chaney fans, holds up the model kit and says, "This is some kind of... vampire figure." This may sound a bit petty, but you are such a huge Chaney fan and you didn't know which movie that was from? I call bullshit! It was little things like that, which I started to pick up on more and more, that made me start to question how much honesty was going on behind the curtain. At least with this particular person.

Besides all of that BS, it actually was a pretty fantastic show. Getting to see Sam Raimi and Bruce Campbell for the second time and hear them talk about the two *Evil Dead* films (this was a couple of years before *Army of Darkness* came out) was very cool. Raimi was there in a suit and tie, being all professional, still promoting *Darkman*, which looked really cool. (I still think it is a fun comic-book style movie, filled with great camerawork and definitely some Raimi-esque style.) Campbell was still hamming it up for the audience and even did his famous hand-flipping-himself stunt that he did in *Evil Dead II*, which brought on a huge round of applause.

It was also at that show that I started to collect model kits. I ended up bringing home a few that weekend, including a Billiken's Frankenstein and Creature from the Black Lagoon. Billiken was a Japanese company that put out some amazing kits with some incredible likenesses. I also picked up the Pinhead kit from Screamin'. At first, I had a friend of mine paint these for me, but eventually, as I bought more and more of them, I started to paint them on my own. I never felt that I was really that great, but they usually turned out okay. Plus, I just really enjoyed it. Well... maybe. My problem with painting these things was that once I started, I would work on it every chance I could until it was done. Not that I would rush it, but just never took my time. After awhile, I realized that I just didn't want to spend the time doing that when there were other more important tasks at hand. So I stopped. There are times I regret it, especially when I see a really cool kit for sale. But at the same time, I do realize how much money I've saved over the years!

We made the trip back home after an exciting weekend and were really worn out. I'm pretty sure everyone had a great time though. I know I did. It's kind of funny, looking back on these smaller shows and how quickly they go by, with really nothing going on besides the dealer room and Q&As. But still, it was a good time.

World Horror Con

In 1991, while I was still reading a lot of horror fiction, a fellow avid reader friend and I decided to venture down to Nashville, Tennessee, for the first-ever World Horror Con. This was different from the shows that I had been attending the last few years. It was still a horror convention, but one that dealt with horror fiction. Pretty much all the vendors were different book dealers or publishers and the guests that were appearing at the show were all authors. And there were a lot of them! Once you pre-bought your ticket, they sent you a list of all the authors that were going to be appearing at the show. I quickly made a list of the authors and what books that I had of the ones attending, including anthologies that might include one or more authors appearing that weekend. Kind of like a little cheat sheet. That way, if I happened to see a particular author, I would find their name on the list and all the books that I had brought with me to the convention. Seemed like a pretty simple idea, right? The only problem was that I had a ton of file boxes with books that I was bringing. I honestly don't remember how many file boxes I had filled with books, but I just know that both the trunk and the backseat of my car were packed full of boxes.

The Grand Master Guest for this first show was none other than Robert Bloch, the man responsible for penning *Psycho*, not to mention many other novels and countless short stories. In the literary world, this man is a God. But even in the movie world, much of his work had been adapted, especially in the Amicus anthology films. So it really was a true honor to be able to meet and shake this man's hand. They gave him an award on Saturday night and his sense of humor was just awesome. He was full of dark sarcastic wit, all said with that little gleam in his eye. It made for a very memorable evening.

But the best part of this show, besides spending a stupid amount of money in the dealer room, was the signing party after the show ended on Saturday. They had all the writers in one huge room, all sitting at tables along the outside wall, like a big square, with little name cards there so you knew who was who. Then you would just walk up to them and they would sign whatever books you put in front on them. Some authors might have a little bit of a line, which you could either wait in or just go to another author. It was very casual and all the authors were very friendly to talk to. The reason that this was the best part of the show was that not a single penny was spent on autographs. The authors signed however many books you brought to their table with a smile, just thrilled that you liked their work, or even had spent money on one of their books.

This was the first and last time I've ever made it out to one of these shows, since they keep changing the city where they hold the show every year. Even when they were in Chicago, I never made it, which I regretted afterwards. I'm not sure if they still do that autograph party, but I've met up with authors at other shows and they have never charged me to sign something. It just makes me wonder why authors are more than happy to sign copies of their books for free but those in the movie business feel the need to charge you. Personally, I think the authors are just more appreciative of their audience and don't feel the need to nickel-and-dime their fans every second they get. But that's just me.

Fanex and Hammer Horror!

While the Fango shows continued, I became aware of other shows that were going on in different parts of the country. There was one in particular that was in Baltimore simply called Fanex, which had started back in

1987. It was run by Gary and Sue Svehla, editors and publishers of the long-running magazine *Midnight Marquee*. I really regret not attending their shows sooner because they had some amazing guests at their previous shows. Names like Jeff Morrow, Ray Harryhausen, John Agar, Yvette Vickers, Robert Wise, Robert Clarke, Beverly Garland, and even William K. Everson, author of *Classics of the Horror Film*. So much talent, with I'm sure so many stories to tell. If I could only have a time machine!

The particular Fanex show that got my attention was going to take place in the summer of 1994. Before I get into the details, let me explain my love of Hammer Films. These films were not only filled with beautiful women, but all sorts of monsters, usually in glorious color, and engaging stories that made them so much fun to watch. Sure, they were a little dated when compared to what was coming out in the '80s and '90s, but they had a look about them that very few could ever replicate; not just the look, an essence. Hammer films had style! From the striking colors to their original makeup effects to the multitude of highly underrated actors, the stories, the sets, the locations, and everything in between, there just wasn't anything like a Hammer film. One of my all-time favorite titles from The Studio That Dripped Blood was 1970's *The Vampire Lovers*, starring the alluring Ingrid Pitt. While she only made a handful of films, she made quite the impact on me back then, and still does to this day.

When I came across an ad for the Fanex #8 show, taking place later that summer, I saw that it was a Hammer-themed show. This certainly caught my interests. Then I saw the guest line-up, which included James Bernard, Martine Beswick, Veronica Carlson, Val Guest, and the one and only Ingrid Pitt! I knew I was going to be at that show. There was no way I was going to pass up the opportunity to be able to meet this lovely woman. So once again, plans started to form in my little brain.

I immediately called up my friend Jon Stone. I knew he was as big of a Hammer fan as I was, and he'd never been to a convention before. He loved the idea and we made our plans. I would fly out to Baltimore while he would drive up from Ohio and pick me up at the airport. Pretty strange since even though I'd known Stone for about two years by then, we'd never met in person before. But our mutual love for all things horror had made us fast friends. Not to mention that to meet Ingrid Pitt, I'd get a ride from Satan himself if I had to! I bet he'd have a killer ride too.

This show was much different than the Fango ones that I'd been going to. While it was much smaller, with more of an adult crowd, one thing that remained the same was the passion for these movies. During that weekend, I got to meet some of the lovely Hammer Glamour that I'd watched on TV over the years, and they couldn't have been nicer. And yes, I got to meet

Ingrid Pitt, who was just as full of life and energy as she was on screen. On Saturday night, they were screening *Horror of Dracula* at one of the local theaters, which we knew we weren't going to miss. Not only was the theater one of those old classic ones, it was pretty big. By the time we got there, the only seats left were right up front. So yeah, it may have killed my neck a bit by the end of the movie, but it was still a very unforgettable experience.

The Q&As were just as much fun. It was so cool hearing stories first-hand from the people actually involved in them. These weren't interviews that we were reading in a book or magazine, but being told directly to us in the audience. I have so many great stories and memories from this show.

Ingrid Pitt was another one that I could check off my celebrity bucket list. When I first got into Hammer films, I just was in awe of her. I'm sure it helped that she was usually in some form of undress, but I also thought she was as talented as she was beautiful. Over the years since that show, when she did more and more appearances, mostly at events across the pond, when I would see footage of her on those or on UK newscasts and interviews, she seemed to be a bit... full of herself. With talk of how gorgeous she was back in the day, she was definitely a personality not to be kept quiet. After a while, that seemed to be what I focused on and not the talent that once had me under her spell. But that would change years later.

Fanex Part 2

I didn't make it out to another Fanex show until three years later, in July of 1997, when oddly enough, they were doing another Hammer-themed show. This time, along with returning guests Veronica Carlson and Val Guest, they also had Freddie Francis, Caroline Munro, Virginia Wetherell, and Jimmy Sangster! I knew, once again, I'd be making the trip out there. And once again, I called up my buddy Mr. Stone, and we made plans to attend.

In between those two shows, I had made it out to my one and only Chiller Theatre show in New Jersey. I believe this was around 1995. Honestly, I'm not sure why I made the journey out to that show, but Mr. Stone was ready to go along as well. I do remember the show did have a pretty impressive guest list, such as Reggie Bannister and James Karen, who have to be two of the friendliest celebrities I have ever met. You walked away from their table thinking you have a new best friend. That is how they make you feel. Just two down-to-earth and genuine individuals.

At that time, I dabbled in the "gray market" (not-quite-black market), selling movies on VHS that were not available through normal means. This was years before DVDs, so finding rare films or ones that weren't released here in the States was something that all movie fans were looking for. One of my customers was going to be at this show so we had planned to meet up in the evening. Mark McConnaughey, later to be known simply as Monster Mark, was from Baltimore and even though he was a bit older than myself, he talked as fast as a little kid who had just eaten about five bowls of sugar-laced cereal and soda! He was one ball of furious energy, talking a mile a minute. It was obvious his passion for old horror and sci-fi movies was just as powerful as mine and Mr. Stone's. Once he and Stone began talking about some old obscure movies, I would just sit there in awe. These guys were popping off titles that I had never heard of before, getting a wide-eyed look from the other as soon as another rarely seen film was mentioned, only to promptly reply with a "Yeah! What about..." This went on for what seemed like hours.

Ok, back to our second Fanex show. Since Mark lived in Baltimore, he said we should meet up and go to the show together. The plan that Stone and I came up with was crazy as hell, but we were still young and stupid, so we didn't think anything of it. I would leave Aurora, IL, Thursday afternoon and drive the five hours to Dayton, OH, to pick Stone up. Then we would drive all night to Baltimore, where the show was at, meeting up with Mark Friday morning. He worked the 3rd shift at a 24-hour grocery store and would be getting off work about the time we would arrive. Perfect plan! Now, I have to say, the drive TO a show is always a breeze. The adrenaline is pumping and the excitement for the show has me wired, so driving through the night was easy. It also helped having another crazy horror fan riding with me, as we went through movie after movie after movie, telling stories about the first time one of us saw a particular title, or a story about one of our favorite actors, and on and on. We not only talked about movies, but life in general. It was one of the best road trips I ever made, and a lot of that had to do with Mr. Stone.

We finally arrived in Baltimore around 6am or so. This was before GPS, so the fact that we found this grocery story with just a map and some rudimentary directions was pretty amazing. We start wandering through the store looking for Mark. Now remember, we've both been up for over 24 hours and it's starting to catch up with us. We stumble around for what seemed like hours before we finally go back to the front of the store and ask if Mark is there. "Oh no... he went home already." Great. Now we have to try and find his house.

But, as we started to walk away, we heard someone say, "Are you those guys from out of town?"

"Yes... that would be us."

"Mark said he'd be right back up and meet you guys here."

So we go back to the van and wait. Within minutes, Monster Mark shows up and is still as fired up as the last time we saw each other. We follow him back to his house so he can start us on the tour. Now, any serious fan or collector knows that when someone comes to your home, you have to show them your collection. The reason for this is simply because being a fellow collector, you know they will appreciate it, be in complete awe, or at the very least, understand why and what you are doing. If you were to bring someone into that domain that wasn't a collector, it wouldn't mean squat to them. They just wouldn't understand.

Mark starts to show us different movie posters, comic books, and all sorts of things that he's picked up over the years. Mark used to run a comic book store in town for years so he's been in the business for quite some time, and has a pretty impressive collection. As we were talking, he pulls out issue #9 of *Fangoria*, with the pig-faced killer from *Motel Hell* on the cover. Now, back then, for some strange reason, this issue was pricey as hell. If you could find a copy, it would set you back easily $100 or more. I had started buying *Fangoria* at issue #51 and had since ordered copies of all the back issues. Except #9. There was no way in hell I was going to pay that much for a single issue and it remained an open wound in my collection. As a fellow collector, Mark knew and understood what certain things can mean to someone, sometimes meaning more to others than even yourself. As Mark pulls out this rare issue, he sees my eyes light up as I start to tell him that is the only issue I don't have in my collection, which he already knew because I'm pretty sure we talked about it before. He then hands it to me and says "Here... it's yours. It would mean more to you in your collection than it does here in mine." That is the kind of guy that Mark was. I have never forgotten that and still have that issue. His generosity and passion for these movies didn't stop there. He had asked me at one point if I had ever seen any of the Mexican horror films from the '50s. At the time, the last thing I needed was another subgenre to get into, so I told him no, but didn't care to start just yet. Within a week, I had about a half dozen videotapes show up on my door from Mark, all Mexican horror titles. Again, this was just another example of the kind of person Mark was. He knew he had found another person that shared his passion for these kinds of movies and felt the need to pass copies of these movies along to another kindred spirit.

Anyway, Mark let Stone and me crash for a few hours of much-needed sleep before we headed over to the hotel for the Fanex show. And, once again, it was an unbelievable time. Sitting in on the Q&A with writer/director/producer (not to mention just about every other job at Hammer) Jimmy Sangster was just unreal. Here's the guy, sitting not ten feet in front of me, that was responsible for writing Hammer's *Curse of Frankenstein* and *Horror of Dracula*, not to mention being involved in countless other Hammer classics. I had picked up a copy of his recently published autobiography, humorously titled *Do You Want it Good or Tuesday?* and had him sign it. It was a real honor to meet this man.

Same goes for Freddie Francis. Not only had he directed some great titles, like *Dracula Has Risen from the Grave*, but he is also an Oscar-winning cinematographer, and worked on *The Innocents*, one of my favorites. I had him sign a still from *Tales from the Crypt*, which is another prized piece in my collection, as well as the one-sheet for Hammer's *Paranoiac*. This would also be the first of many times I'd get to meet the lovely Caroline Munro, who was another real treat. Like all the guests at this show, she was just so friendly.

I had such a memorable time at this Fanex show. I really wished I could have made it to more of these. I'm sure it didn't help since it was way out on the East Coast, but they had a great run while they lasted.

It's strange how this friendship thing can work. I've only seen Mark maybe five or six times since we've known each other, and maybe talked on the phone twice as many times. But, for some reason, I consider him a very close and personal friend. Like Stone and me, we just connected. Even though Mark was more into comic books and sci-fi, it didn't matter. We still shared that same passion for this kind of stuff and related well with each other. If we would have lived closer, I know we would have spent a lot more time together, and probably gotten into a lot of trouble as well!

Fulci Comes to New York

Now I have to backtrack a bit, to sometime at the end of 1995. It had been several years since I'd been back to New York or California for a Fangoria Weekend of Horrors. They were already starting to get a sour reputation amongst some fans, mainly due to Creation, the company that ran the shows. At some point, they announced that the one and only Lucio Fulci, director of some of my favorite films, would be a guest at their upcoming show in January of 1996, and once again, I knew I was going to be there. I knew there was a very big chance that something would happen and he would be a no-show, but I didn't care. I had to take that chance.

One of the things that most young horror fans are attracted to when first getting into these movies is the gore. This was especially true in the '80s, when gore and makeup effects were sometimes the only reason we'd seek out a particular flicks. And if you were a gorehound, you most likely had discovered the Italian films of that period, specifically the work of Lucio Fulci. Having a career that spanned more than three decades encompassing just about every film genre out there, he was best known for his gore films of the late 1970s and early 1980s, titles like *Zombie, City of the Living Dead, The Beyond, The House by the Cemetery, The New York Ripper*, and so on. Fans of his work knew that he was much more than just a director of gruesome features, but a skilled technician that could create amazing films... if he had the budget. No matter the genre, Fulci is a major deity and still should be recognized as such, even today.

Once I started looking into it, flying to New York seemed to be a bit expensive. After talking with a mutual friend, he seemed pretty excited about going to the show as well and mentioned the idea of driving out there. Since he offered to drive, I was more than happy to go along for the ride. Now, riding in a car for the 16-18 hour drive, well, let's just say there's no way to describe it other than it can seem like an eternity. Driving through Pennsylvania on I-80 seems like it goes on for days. Sure, the first couple of hours are pretty cool since you are driving through mountains and the view is amazing. After that, it just goes on and on and on. We didn't care though. We were going to meet Lucio Fulci!

After what seemed like forever, we finally made it to the hotel where the convention was being held. As I'm standing in line to check in, I glance over to my left and I see an older bearded gentleman standing there, wearing a big wool coat and a strange red hat who, for some reason, looked familiar. Then it hit me. Not only was that Lucio Fulci standing right there, but he was wearing the same hat that he wore in his 1990 film *Cat in the Brain*! All my fears of him not making it to the show were gone. I knew it was going to be an incredible weekend. I vaguely remember some of other guests that were there that weekend, including John Saxon, Matt Frewer, Clint Howard, and Jennifer Rubin, who was there promoting her new film *Screamers*. But, no offense to any of these guests, I was there to see Fulci.

During his Q&A, Fulci spoke very little English, with a translator there to help out. There were a lot of people in the auditorium for this, as it should have been. It was great that he was able to see such an appreciative crowd where those films he made all those years ago not only made an impact at the time, they were still doing so today, decades after they were made. You could tell that he was very humbled by the crowd.

He answered questions about the ending of *City of the Living Dead*, how much he said he was actually involved with *Zombi 3*, as well as his upcoming project, *Wax Mask*, which was to be produced by Dario Argento. Even though he was speaking through a translator, it was an unbelievable experience. I had grown up in a time when most of the older icons, like Karloff, had either passed away, or were generally too old to do many, if any, appearances. Being able to see Lucio Fulci, who I consider an icon, is a memory I will always hold in the highest regard.

Any time there is a guest at a Fango show, you can only hope they are going to sign autographs. Sometimes, depending on the guest, they will just be there for a Q&A and then quickly depart the show, which is understandable if they are on a tight schedule. But most of the attending guests agree to sign after their talk. Honestly, if Fulci left right after his Q&A, I still would have been fine with it. At least I got to see him in person. But as it turns out, he WAS going to sign. So right after the panel ended, I quickly rushed out in the hall to find the line for him, which was already getting pretty big. Remember, this was back in 1996 and my collection was still growing, so I had only brought a few things to get signed if the opportunity was there. I had an 8x10 color still of the worm-faced zombie (actor/stuntman Ottaviano Dell'Acqua) that was used on the American one-sheet of *Zombie*, as well as the actual one-sheet. I also brought a copy of a little book from the UK called *Fantasy Film Memories*. As I was waiting in line, getting closer to the Maestro, there was an announcement making its way down the line. "Don't tell him where to sign!" Not sure what the fuss was about, but I really didn't care where he was going to sign my stuff as long as it was signed. When I got close enough to see him signing though, I completely understood. A guy set down a one-sheet for *Zombie* and pointed off to the side where he wanted it signed. Fulci looked up at him with this glare and then turned the poster over and signed the back of it, and then handed it back to him. There were items where he would start to sign his name on one part, then either finish it or start over at another part. So let's just say some of the signatures were not in the best possible spots. So when I got up there, I quietly handed my items over, shook his hand, and quietly nodded. He signed all three of my items, and signed all three dead square in the middle of the zombie's face. But again, this was Lucio Fulci and I didn't care. I was able to meet the man, shake his hand, and walk away with an experience I'll never forget.

Sadly, our hope of the Godfather of Gore making any sort of a comeback was not to be. Only two months after this show, his one and only convention appearance in the States, Lucio Fulci passed away on March 13th, 1996, due to complications with diabetes. It was a real blow to fans, especially since we had been hoping for another film from him. But as with any movie icon that we hold in high regards, we know that the fans will never let his memory be forgotten or fade away. We will keep his memory alive by watching and re-watching his films, and continue talking about their merits, what we love about them, from the gore to just how talented a craftsman Fulci truly was. He may be gone, but he will never be forgotten.

But our convention story doesn't end there. Around early afternoon on that Sunday, it started to snow. And snow. We figured it might be a good idea to get on the road and start our journey back before the roads got too bad. So we quickly gathered our stuff, said our goodbyes, and hit the road.

Now, I had made a comment early on our return trip that I had gotten to meet Fulci, so I could die a happy man. It was a kind of a joke that we've all made at some point in our lives. But shortly after our trip home started, I had to make sure I clarified to anybody that might be listening that it was, in fact, *just a joke*. As the snow continued to fall and pile up, we were having difficulties even getting out of the city. The roads were becoming very slippery, with cars starting to slide backwards down entrance ramps. I figured if we could at least get out of the city and on the highway, we'd be okay. So we pressed on. Very slowly.

Over the next five hours, we traveled less than a hundred miles. The snow continued to plummet from the sky, making it very difficult to see the road we were on, let alone that far in front of us. All we could do is keep an eye on the taillights of the car ahead and hope that it stayed on the road. We had made it out of New York and through Jersey, now slowly making it into Pennsylvania. I kept thinking that at some point the snow would taper off, and as we made it past the storm, we'd start to get a little relief in the terrible road conditions. But that was not meant to be. The storm was either following us, or it was just that big. We found out later that area we were in had been hit with 30-inches of snow before it was over.

The part of I-80 that we were on has two lanes of traffic going west and then another two lanes going east, but they are not connected. There are times you can see the opposite lanes but because of the mountainous terrain, sometimes you couldn't. I don't remember the time, but the sun had gone down some time ago. It would have been much darker but the snow tends to brighten things up a bit, so even though it was later in the evening, you could still see the sides of the road. As we were creeping down the road, probably averaging about 15 miles an hour, every now and then the car would swerve a little bit. Not enough where we lost control, but it was still slippery. The plan was to keep moving, no matter how slow, but not to stop. As the roads started to become a little more "challenging," we started to question that plan. Then we came across a semi-trailer that was on the side of the road, completely facing the opposite direction. This didn't come from one of the oncoming lanes. Instead the truck driver had managed to completely turn his tractor and trailer a full 180 degrees, ending up in the ditch. It was at that moment, when I turned to my friend who was driving and said, "We're getting off at the very next exit. I'm not dying in a ditch or over the mountainside somewhere." Once we did take the first exit, we had to do a bit of driving through the small town that we came into, eventually finding a little dive of a motel. It was a two story little thing that had about 10 units. The prices were cheap enough and at that point, it didn't matter. Of course, the interesting thing was that during the night, we noticed the guy running the place go out to the sign and raised the prices three different times. Supply and demand, I guess. It wasn't the greatest room, but much better than the ditch.

We got up the next morning to find our cars buried in the snow, along with everyone else that had ended up there during the night. As my buddies tried to dig out our car, I went to the manager's office to check out. The vending machine in there looked like it hadn't gotten a fresh supply of treats in over ten years. The motel clerk asked me where we were going, stating that we couldn't leave because of the roads. I told him in no uncertain terms that we would not be staying at his establishment another night.

As I went back out to help dig our car out, I noticed some of the other guests that were also in the same predicament, trying to get back on the road. Ken and Pam Kish from Video Wasteland (soon to be Cinema Wasteland) were doing their best to exhume their van. I'd known Ken from seeing him at nearly every convention I had been to, since he was a staple when it came to horror cons. Also digging out was Mike Pierce from Monsters Among Us, another longtime dealer. Once we all got our cars dug out, we made a little convoy down the road trying to make it to the interstate. Some of the roads leading to it were still very slippery, making it a very bad thing to come to a complete stop. There are a lot of hills in that area of Pennsylvania and if you stopped while going up one of the hills, you would end up sliding backwards. So at a slow and steady pace, we made our way closer to the interstate. As we got close to the entrance, we all pulled into the gas station there to fill up before we hit the road. Of course, while we're in there, we hear that I-80 has been completely shut down by the State Police and a state of emergency has been initiated. No one is allowed on the interstate until further notice! What. The. Fuck? Lucky us, huh?

This was now Monday morning, in case you had been keeping track. I had the day off from work, but was supposed to be back by Tuesday. Since we were being told that the earliest that we "might" be able to get back on the road would be tomorrow, that was going to put me home sometime late Tuesday. So I had to call my work and tell them that I was stuck in PA for a day or possibly more. Of course, our first order of business was to find a place where we could stay the night since we all knew we were not going back to that dive we left that morning.

There was a Ramada Inn down the road a bit so we headed that way. Lucky for us, they had plenty of rooms… unlike the amount of staff they had working there. In fact, most of the staff had been stuck there since the day before, because they were also stranded. We made the best of our stay there, getting together in Ken and Pam's room and talking about movies, conventions, music, and just about everything in between. It was one of those highlights of an otherwise bad situation. All in all, we could have been stuck in a ditch on the side of a mountain with no hope of being discovered until next spring! Bright and early Tuesday morning, we were back on the road, starting the long drive home. Yes, it was one hell of a journey.

In the end, I got to meet Lucio Fulci. So yeah, it was more than worth it.

A Spanish Werewolf in New York

When I heard that Spanish horror legend Paul Naschy would be appearing at the New York Fango show in January 1998, I knew once again, just like when they announced Fulci two years earlier, I wasn't going to miss this opportunity to meet one of my idols.

Airline tickets were once again too expensive at the time, so the only other choice was to drive. Being that I didn't drive on my last trip out to NY, I wanted to make sure I was in more control this time. I figured that if I could find enough people that were crazy enough to make the trip with me, it would much cheaper. The first person I called would be the guy that introduced me to Naschy's work all those years ago, the one and only Jon Stone. He was just as excited about meeting Naschy as I was and immediately joined the trip. Eric Ott and another friend (who shall remain nameless, for reasons which will become apparent) decided to make the trip as well. I think the main reason they were excited was because of the *Phantasm* reunion the show was planning, with director Don Coscarelli appearing alongside actors Angus Scrimm, Michael Baldwin, Bill Thornbury, and the one and only Reggie Bannister. So each of us had enough reasons to make this long journey from Chicago to New York. There is an excitement and anxiousness when going to a convention, anticipation of seeing certain guests, seeing your friends, and browsing the dealer room. Therefore the thought of a 16+ hour drive, straight through to New York, didn't seem like a big deal. It would be fun. Right?

After my last escapade to NY and running into a bit of snow, I was a little worried. But what are the odds of that happening again? Of course, Buffalo, NY, had just been hit with a severe ice/snow storm the day before we were set to leave. In fact, my mother-in-law informed me that, "New York is completely shut down," which I highly doubted. So I called the hotel where the convention was going to be held and asked what the weather was like. "It's about 72 out now," the voice on the other end of the phone said. I paused, making sure that I had dialed the correct number. I asked if they were kidding, since this was January and this was New York. She confirmed that was correct and that they were having a warm streak coming through the city for the next few days. Strange how things happen.

The plan was to leave town late Thursday evening… okay actually Friday morning, around 2am. Eric was literally just getting back from a family vacation, meaning he would be pulling into his driveway, dropping off his family, then turning around and driving another 90 minutes down to Aurora to meet up with us at 2am at our other riding companion's house, which was the designated meeting place. So I get to our friend's house around 1:30am and ring the doorbell. No answer. I ring it again. No answer. Bang on the door. No answer again. I start to think to myself, "What a great way to start out the trip." I get back in the van and call him on my cell phone. After about the fifth ring, he picks up, and the conversation went sort of like this:

"Kitley! What's going on?"

"Where the hell are you?"

"Uh... I'm at home."

"THEN ANSWER YOUR FUCKING DOOR!"

"Oh... Sorry... I was sleeping."

This was to be an omen of things to come. This mutual friend was one of those kind of people that somehow you were friends with, but not really sure why. He wasn't a bad person and didn't mean any harm or ill will towards anyone. Basically he was annoying. Careless. And would just drive you nuts. But somehow, he was going along with us on our journey. So he opens the front door and I go inside to wait for Eric to show up. As I'm sitting on his couch, where he had apparently been sleeping, I look down and start to count the cigarette burns in the carpeting. I lost count after 100. Seriously. Another omen. Eric finally gets there a little after 2am. We all pile in the van and hit the road. The plan is to pick up Jon Stone on the way at his mother's in Indiana, right off I-80. Stone tells us, once we get off at the designated exit and turn down the road she lives on, to look for a big star made from Christmas lights. No problem. About 90 minutes later, we were pulling off the I-80 tollway. We roll up to the toll booth, which was about 4am maybe... to find this old man sound asleep. So we're sitting in the van, all looking at this guy, who is just snoozing away. I finally honk my horn, which woke him up. But the fact that he was sound asleep didn't seem to faze him one bit as he opened his window and asked for my toll ticket and the appropriate fee. And so we were off, searching for a star in the sky.

As we strolled down this deserted road, it was still dark enough that we couldn't see anything. No house numbers. Nothing. For a moment, it didn't look like we were going to find this place! Then, off in the distance, like a sign from a higher power, we spot this glowing star ahead on the horizon. We pull on up to find Stone anxiously awaiting our arrival. After a brief break to stretch our legs and use the facilities, we pile back in the van and head out once again, with still a long, long way to go to our destination.

Traveling on I-80 through Indiana and Ohio is a straight shot and pretty much the same. Boring. Once we hit the Pennsylvania border however, all of that changed. The sun had come up by then and we could start to see the mountainous terrain we were traveling through. It was just beautiful. Coming from the Midwest, we don't get to see views like this on a regular basis so it was pretty impressive to see. That feeling of wonderment, with John Denver singing in our heads (yes, I know... different area of mountains... just trying to set the mood), lasted about an hour or two. After that, we just wanted the trip to be over. It just seemed to go on and on forever. Years before anybody ever heard of GPS, when you'd use an actual atlas (aka road map) in the car, you were always excited to get to the side of the map, which mean the end of the state. Not so for Pennsylvania. Once you get through to the side and turn the page, you realize you are only halfway and have to travel through another whole page all over again! But still, the anticipation of being able to meet someone I considered an icon was keeping me wide awake and very excited. So we journeyed on.

We finally pulled into the Big Apple, which driving around for my first time, felt much like being in Chicago. A ton of cars everywhere, but all going in the appointed directions. Once we were on the island of Manhattan, it didn't take long for us to find our hotel. We left the keys with the valet, unloaded our luggage, and made our way into the hotel.

Sure, it was going to be very cool seeing the *Phantasm* reunion and footage from the upcoming *Phantasm IV: Oblivion*, and even getting to hang out with Reggie Bannister in the bar later on in the evening. As cool as all of that was, I was here was to see Paul Naschy. And just like the last time I was at a Fango show, as I was checking in, I spotted him in the lobby, so I knew he was here and that was all that mattered. My excitement level was just as high as with Fulci. Here is a guy from a different country that made so many incredible horror films that the very thought of ever having the chance of meeting him was all but a dream. Now, here he was, a mere few feet away.

Ever since Stone had introduced me to Naschy's work, I just loved this guy's movies for some reason. It could have been the countless different monster-rama style movies that he made, filling them with vampires, mummies, zombies, and of course, werewolves. But I think the main reason was because of his own personal passion for these movies. Naschy made horror movies not because they were popular, or made a lot of money, or was the "in" thing to do at the time, but because he loved the "cinema fantasique" and those were the films he wanted to make. But around this time, Naschy's career wasn't doing that great. While he was continued to make movies, his reputation in Spain was not what you would have expected, even though he had appeared in over 70 films by that time.

During his Q&A, it was obvious that he was inspired by the number of fans there to see him. He could see that all of his hard work and dedication on those movies he made all those years ago did have an impact on this enthusiastic crowd of fans that had gathered there for the weekend. He even spoke of bringing back his most famous character of Waldemar Daninsky back, especially after going to the theater the night before and seeing the disappointing *An American Werewolf in Paris*. See that? Something good did come out of that debacle after all!

Once I found where Naschy was going to sign, Stone and I got in line. Now, even though there were a lot of people in attendance at the Q&A, it didn't seem like there were that many fans in line to get stuff signed; maybe because his posters are not that easy to find. Remember, eBay had only been around for a couple of years at that point, so it was only crazy collectors like myself, Stone, and a few others there, that had been accumulating posters and stuff from his films over the years. I think I ended up getting probably about a dozen or so posters signed, pretty much bringing any and all that I had. It was a real joy to see Naschy's face light up at some of the different items, especially when he had never seen some of them before. It wasn't just about getting these items signed, but being able to shake his hand and tell him (through his interpreter) just how much his movies meant to me. To see a genuine gleam in his eye, when I told him this, meant more to me than any poster or any signature. Sam Sherman, from Independent-International Pictures, was also there with Naschy. Sherman was the man that was really behind bringing Naschy to the States when they picked up his first werewolf movie, *La Marca del Hombre Lobo*, re-titling it under the infamous moniker *Frankenstein's Bloody Terror* and unleashing it and Naschy upon unsuspecting drive-in crowds across the USA.

In the English version of his autobiography, *Memoirs of a Wolf Man* (Midnight Marquee, 2000), near the end, Naschy had questioned whether he had made the right decision earlier in his life, going into movies as opposed to a safer career route as an architect, since he probably would have been better off financially than he was at that point. He took some solace though in the realization of just what his accomplishments meant to the world, going on to write, "*The only deep-rooted consolation I have is the knowledge that a lot of people around the world have been happy and forgotten their troubles watching my movies. I hope that all you fans in the United States will always have a place for me in your hearts and that you will continue to cherish the memory of Waldemar Daninsky howling at the full moon.*"

Years later, Naschy's popularity in his home country started to pick up, which included him receiving lifetime achievement awards at different film festivals, and even getting a street named after him, so at least he was able to see the impact his contributions had made to the genre. Naschy continued to work, making another 20+ films since that appearance in New York before his death in 2009. He still remains an icon of the horror genre, right up there with names like Karloff, Lugosi, Chaney, Cushing, Price, and Lee. I still make it part of my quest to make more people aware of this man's incredible body of work.

Another great moment of the weekend was the panel on the new movie *Dark City* that was soon to be released. In attendance were director Alex Proyas and actor Richard O'Brien (from *The Rocky Horror Picture Show* fame) giving away promotional mini posters that they were signing. I had loved Proyas' film *The Crow* and this new one looked like it was once again filled with some incredible style.

As I mentioned before, the other big draw for this show was the reunion from the original *Phantasm*. While I had met Reggie Bannister a few years before, this was the first time getting to meet the entire cast. Angus Scrimm is one of those gentlemen, much like Boris Karloff, who appears in films as a variety of evil characters, but in real life couldn't be nicer. Such a gracious smile he had. When they were doing their Q&A and someone was talking, he would be looking out into the audience. I had my camera with the big telephoto lens hoping to catch some good shots. When he would notice me with the camera, his expression would change from this unbelievable kind and gentle smile, in an instant, twisting into the famous Tall Man grimace! Don Coscarelli is one who has stayed out of the Hollywood system and you can tell when you talk to him. The word "genuine" doesn't even come close to defining this man. I have met him several more times over the years and have met very few that were more open and friendly than him.

Of course, then there is Reggie. I had met him the for first time at the Chiller Theatre show in 1995 and later that year he came to Aurora to record an album called *Fool's Paradise*. During the recording, Reggie spent well over six months in the area, so I had the opportunity to hang out with him more than a few times, including one evening where I went to just drop by and pick up my laserdisc player that I had loaned them, along with my *Phantasm* laserdisc. I stopped by after work, somewhere around 6pm, and didn't end up leaving until about 4am, with most of that time spent standing in the kitchen chatting about movies, music, and life. I have never met a more down-to-earth soul than Reggie, who would give the shirt off his back for a friend. There was no "Hollywood actor" here, but a guy that after talking to for a few minutes, you'd think he was your best friend. That is how Reggie treated everyone. If you've ever seen Reggie at a convention, you'll notice the line of people waiting to see him. Every single one of those fans leaves that line with a new best friend. That is the beauty of Reggie. He just connects with everyone and is so damn sincere. I can't praise this man enough. The world needs more quadruple-shotgun-toting dwarf-killing Ice Cream Men like Reggie.

After an amazing weekend, I gathered the troops and we hit the road sometime late Sunday afternoon, with a long drive awaiting us. Thankfully, the gods were looking favorably on us and there was no snow this time. The adrenaline that we felt on the way out was nowhere to be found on our way back home. Could it be because we now had to travel back to the real world?

Or could it be that, for some strange reason, I think I only had about eight hours sleep since Friday?

Let's do the math. We got to the hotel Friday evening, after being on the road since 2am. We checked into our room, and then quickly headed down to the bar to meet up with other convention friends, where we promptly stayed up until 2am when the bar shut down. We hit the bed for a few hours of sleep before getting up around 7am to get some breakfast before getting in line for the show. Then on Saturday night, the pattern repeated itself, except, after the bar closed at 2am, we decided it would be the perfect time to go to a 24-hour diner connected to the hotel for some food, staying there another hour or so. Then we stumbled off to bed somewhere before the sun came up, only to be back up at 8am to get moving once again.

Now, there is something to be said about getting sleep at a con. In the early days, when money was at a premium, the cheaper the costs were the better. So if you could get four to six people in your room, it just meant the rates would be cheaper for everyone, right? Sure, sleeping on the floor isn't the most comfortable, but we're not here for comfort anyway! Granted, as you get older, you start to realize how important sleep is, especially on the drive back. Or at least, that's what I've been told. But all I needed was a few hours of sleep and I'm good.

Another thing you have to be very careful of is WHO you're letting into your room for the weekend. Since there is going to be very little time for sleep, when the time comes, you need to take advantage of it and not worry if you'll be dead when you wake up! Our nameless buddy that rode out with Eric, Stone, and me smoked. A lot. He also snored. A lot. In fact, the only time he wasn't snoring was when he would wake himself up, light a cigarette, and quickly fall back asleep, with the cigarette still smoking in his hand. We'd yell at him to put it out, which would bring him to some form of consciousness, only to put it out, and then quickly fall back into ear-shattering snoring slumber. But then a short time later, you'd see the flash of a lighter as he fired up another cigarette. This went on... ALL NIGHT LONG! As I was laying there on the floor, a decision was going through my mind: which was more important? Getting a couple of hours sleep, or worry about burning to death in a New York hotel? I mean, I had already gotten to meet Lucio Fulci two years ago and just met Paul Naschy, so I could die a happy horror fan, right?

Fortunately, we didn't die in a blaze of glory after all and managed to survive the weekend. Now it was time to drive home. Needless to say, starting a drive that you know is going to take you until the next morning to reach home is kind of a daunting task. And of course, you assume that your faithful traveling companions would stay awake to keep their driver awake and alert, with many conversations about the weekend, or movies in general. Well, not so much. I don't think we were even out of Manhattan before most of them were already snoozing away.

An interesting thing that happens on these long, sleep-deprived trips is that strange things seem to happen. When you make stops for gas or to take a break from driving and stretch your legs, you come across some very unusual places. For instance, one gas station we stopped at in the wee hours of the night. As we walked into this little place in the middle of nowhere, the fact that there were no other cars around didn't seem to mean anything to us at the time. But as we entered, you could tell just by the smell that this wasn't a nationwide chain, just a little mom 'n' pop place trying to stay in business. The place had a cement floor that looked like it hadn't been swept in quite some time. One part of the counter had some ice cream in it, in three large five-gallon containers, like they had years ago. But the odd part wasn't really the ice cream, but the several large jars on top of the ice cream counter, containing an assortment of items floating in liquid. They had regular pickles, but also other... things. Pigs' feet were the only thing that I could make out in the strange, somewhat clear liquid. These were not coming from some mass-marketed supply house, but looked like they were made in someone's basement. What made it even stranger (and downright creepy) was the fact that right behind the counter was a large wooden sliding door. This massive thing looked like it could keep a tank from busting through. As we entered this fine establishment, this enormous wooden barrier slides open, but only enough to let this man slip sideways through, sliding it quickly shut to greet us. While I wasn't staring at the guy, it sure seemed as if he didn't want us to see what was behind that door. Of course, he was wearing a red flannel shirt and overalls. Honestly, I know it sounds like I am making this up and, honest to god, I wish I was. The guy wasn't intimidating looking or even scary, more like a busy man whom we had interrupted, wanting to get back to whatever he was doing behind that as quickly as possible. I had never felt as uneasy as I was walking into that place. I'd been to gas stations on the South side of Chicago and never felt like my life could be ending at any second, like I was feeling then. Maybe I had just watched *Texas Chain Saw Massacre* one too many times. All I knew was that I wanted to get out of that place as quickly as possible. So as tempting as it was to get some pickled... things, we got what we needed, got back in the van, and hit the road. All in one piece.

Further on, there was another pit stop we took that really had us scratching our heads. It might have had something to do with the fact that we all were going on very little sleep, but as we pulled off the interstate to get gas and stretch our legs, it was still dark enough that we couldn't see anything around... except this little building surrounded by lights, and encased in some sort of fog or mist. There were no lights in the distance. No buildings that you could see down the road. Nothing at all but this small, little shack. As we walked into the place, it was if we had stepped back in time. Eric Ott had walked over to the candy aisle, soon calling us over to look at what they had. There was candy that I hadn't seen since I was a kid, including candy cigarettes, which were no longer being made due to the negative connotations cigarettes now had. All the candy was priced from 5 cents to 10 cents, like it would have been decades earlier. Luckily for us, the proprietor of this establishment wasn't nearly as devious looking as the other guy. Just a quiet older man sitting behind the counter. As we all marveled at how this place looked like something from long ago, we just figured that the modern era hadn't caught up with this part of the country yet. Eric quickly picked up every single box of the candy cigarettes, as well as some other novelty items, and we were back on the road. We joked as we drove away, that if we were to come back here during the day, this place would be an abandoned little shack that had been closed for 30 years, as if we had stepped into an episode of *The Twilight Zone*. Stranger things have happened.

That really is one of the best things about convention road trips, something that I've always loved. You get to see the country. You find these little places that are off the grid that haven't been swallowed up by the national chains yet. Stopping to get something to eat, and trying to find a place that looks interesting and unique, can be a fun challenge.

Goin' (Back) to California

In 2003, I returned to L.A. for another Fango show, 15 years after my first trip out there. But this time, I was not alone. Joining me on this trip was by good friend Phil Meenan, or "Tattooed Phil" as I refer to him as he's pretty much covered with horror tattoos. Phil is not only a huge horror fan but probably has the biggest Frankenstein memorabilia collection I've ever seen. (If you ever got to see Shout Factory's *Horror Hunters* show, that was Phil and I showing off our collections!)

Just like the first time, the guest list was huge. I knew I was going to spend more time taking photos this time around than spending money. I had a purchased a Gold Seating Pass, which gave me an assigned seat in the auditorium for the Q&As and also allowed me one free autograph from each of the celebs that were attending.

On Saturday morning, we were standing in line outside waiting to get in. As always, a huge number of people were there too. As we were waiting, someone walked by asking if there was a line for people with tickets and one for those fans that still needed to buy tickets. I said that I wasn't sure, "but since this is a Creation show, I'm sure they have that all worked out and under control." Well, as I said that, one of Creation's "line nazis" walked by and heard my comment.

She stopped and shouted, "Who said that?"

I raised my hand proudly and said, "That would be me."

"Was that supposed to be sarcastic?" she asked.

"Well... is there a line for people with tickets and one without tickets?" I asked.

"Uh... I don't know," she stammered out.

"Then I guess that would have been sarcasm," I replied.

In a huff, she walked away. There also a couple of times when we were standing in line for an autograph session only to be told to move to a different area by one of Creation's personnel. Then two seconds later get yelled at because we were in the wrong line. Some things never change.

One of the main reasons for me wanting to come to this show was that Blue Underground was putting out Jose Larraz's 1974 classic *Vampyres* on DVD, and to promote the release they were going to have Marianne Morris and Anulka Dziubinska, the film's two stars, there. All those years ago, when I was entranced while watching one of the most erotic and brutal entries in the vampire genre, to think that I was now going to be able to meet the two female leads was beyond belief. Although, while sitting through the Q&A with them, I did get a little depressed and irritated when it seemed most of the audience had never even heard of the film, let alone seen it before. It was one of those times when I discovered I was becoming "old." But the two ladies were wonderful to meet and so thankful that someone had come out to meet them. I was able to get a couple of things signed but unfortunately had no real posters or anything special for their signatures. Of course now I have more than a few different posters I could bust out. If I only had a time machine...

I felt the same way when I passed a dealer table where David Durston and Lynn Lowry, director and star of the 1970 cult film *I Drink Your Blood*, were sitting. They were sitting alone with very few people approaching their table. It showed me that newer fans still had yet to embrace the older and lesser-known films, and it really made me want to step up my efforts to educate these "young 'uns" on their horror history. *IDYB* is one of the films that really defines cult and exploitation cinema. Whether you actually like the film or not doesn't change the fact, the status, or the simple importance of this particular title. But the kids were more interested in seeing the cast from Rob Zombie's new film than the classics. That said, if it wasn't for *House of 1000 Corpses*, a lot of these newer fans never would have known great talents like Karen Black or Sid Haig. So for that, I'll be forever grateful to Zombie for reinvigorating these journeymen actors' careers, especially Mr. Haig.

Speaking of Ms. Black and Mr. Haig, one of the Q&As was for the cast of Zombie's *Corpses*, which they both attended. I had never met Ms. Black before, but I had grown up watching her on so many different TV movies and shows, and EVERYONE my age knew her from the classic 1975 TV-movie

Trilogy of Terror. Earlier that day, while I was in line to get her autograph, I was standing a little to the left side of the line, taking some pictures of her while she was signing at her table. At one point she looks up at me with a stern face and told me this was her "bad side" and to take photos from her "good" side, pointing to the right side of the line. At first I thought she was joking, but from the look on her face, I realized quickly that she wasn't. When I did get up to her though, she was very friendly as she signed my *Trilogy* still.

When it came time for the Q&A, I made sure I was in the audience for that. One of the perks of Gold Seating was that I had an assigned seat, which was a little left-of-center stage, a good angle for more photos of the entire cast. That is, except that I had forgotten which side of the audience I was on, especially in regards to where Karen Black was sitting. In fact, it didn't even hit me until I was looking through my telephoto lens, taking close-ups of each of the cast. When I got to Ms. Black, she was staring straight at me, right down the barrel of my lens, with those devilish eyes and crossed brow, pointing to the right and mouthing the words "other side." I'm not sure she understood that since these were assigned seats, I couldn't move, even if I wanted to! So I tried to avoid her deadly gaze, thinking that my camera lens might shatter and only took a few shots here and there, very quickly.

Speaking of *Corpses*, one of the guests was Gregg Gibbs, the production designer for the film, who had brought a bunch of props from the movie and was actually selling them in the dealer room. My friend Phil, being a huge fan of the movie, was going nuts and buying more and more props from Gibbs. I don't even want to know what kind of cash Phil was dropping on this guy, but he kept coming back with more and more stuff. I love Phil to death, but there is something special about him. He never seems to plan ahead and somehow it always works out for him anyway. I don't know how he does it. At one point during the show, we had gotten separated and I was just wandering the dealer room. I was in the area that looked out over the parking lot and I saw this guy walking across the lot with his arms holding up something over his head. Something big. Damn... that kind of looks like Phil. Wait... it IS Phil. And he was carrying what looked like this large piece of plywood. I go outside to meet him and, with a huge smile on his face, he puts down what he is carrying and shows me what it is. He had just purchased the sandwich board from Captain Spaulding's Murder Ride from *House of 1000 Corpses*! This thing was about 3 feet wide and 4 feet tall and was made up of 2x4's and thick plywood. Then it hit me.

"Uh... Phil? How are you going to get that home?"

"I'll just take it on the plane."

"Phil, they are not going to let you take that on the plane! It's too freaking big!"

"Eh... I'll figure something out."

Now this whole time, Phil still has a smile on his face. He is not worried at all about getting this home, knowing that something will work out. Which it did. Our friend Jill from Lix just so happened to be vending at this show. Jill would always drive to these shows, packing everything in her van. So I went inside to explain the situation and to see if she would have room in her van for it. She was gracious enough to do just that. Later, Phil drove down to her store and picked it up. But again, it still boggles my mind how it just all works out for him. That is the beauty of this guy.

Even with the slight run-ins with the Creation staff, it really did feel like one of those old Fango shows. The only difference was there were plenty of celebrities that were now really vendors, just selling their autographs. But other guests, celebrities that were not dealers, were there as well, doing Q&A sessions and signing, which was pretty cool. I did get to meet both Stan Winston and Wes Craven at this show, which now that both have passed away, I feel very honored to have had such an opportunity. When I busted out my Turkish poster for *Pumpkinhead* for Winston to sign, it blew his mind, mainly because the images on it had *nothing* to do with his movie. Another two genre icons checked off the list.

Like all shows, the two days just flew by and the next thing I knew, Phil and I were packing up and ready to head to the airport. Now, John Kassir, the voice of the Crypt Keeper from the *Tales from the Crypt* series was also at this show, and Phil had brought the head from his full size Crypt Keeper for Kassir to sign. As we were packing to leave, Phil discovered he no longer had room in his bag because of all the *House of 1000 Corpses* stuff he had bought. I had room in my bag, so I told him I could take it. Yeah... big mistake.

We get to the airport and are going through check-in and security. Phil goes up, gives them his bag, and he's on his way. I go up, hand over my bag, and then hear a loud beeping sound, and then am told to go to the side and wait while they go through my bag. I was told in a very strict voice not to move from this spot as they go through my luggage. So I'm standing there about two feet from my bag when the security guy slowly unzips the bag's zipper. And then it hits me what is in there. That's when I hear Phil laughing off to the side, because he remembered too. As I look back at the guy, he slowly opens the bag to see the severed head of the Crypt Keeper looking back up at him. This guy quickly looks up at me as I began patiently waiting to be jumped by the rest of security. I started to tell him that it was a movie prop and we were at a movie convention when he told me to shut up and just stand there. With plastic gloves on, he takes the head out and rubs it with some sort of cloth or something, looks at the cloth, and then puts it back in my bag and shoves it to the side and tells me to move along. Anytime I tell this story now, if Phil is within hearing distance, he starts laughing all over again.

For Fango shows in general, I will admit that we usually had a great time. It is just a shame that they couldn't get someone else to run the actual convention besides Creation. Plus, by this time, conventions in general were changing and the Fango shows like they put on in the '80s were just no longer possible in this decade. Damn shame too.

Before I continue with more convention stories, here's a quick detour with a little tale from the road that once again shows Phil's unique sense of humor. The Gene Siskel Film Center is located in downtown Chicago that has movie screenings for both the film school located next door to it and for the public as well. They'll have film fests and occasionally have guests appearing there. In 2005, I read that they were going to be screening the new movie from Spanish director Álex de la Iglesia, *Crimen ferpecto*, and that the director was actually going to be there! I have been a fan of Iglesia since 1993 with his first film *Acción mutante*, which is about a group of handicapped terrorists! So I was thrilled to have the chance to be able to meet him. Phil was going to meet me there, since he was also a fan, especially of Iglesia's second film, 1995's *The Day of the Beast*. Phil even brought a shirt from that movie to give to him.

When we arrived at the Film Center, there was a sign on the door informing us that the screening was sold out. Needless to say, I was more than a little pissed. Even more so when, while we're standing there, we see different people, sophisticated types, entering the theater dressed in suits and ties. It made me wonder if any of these people had ever even seen one of his films before or even knew who he was! Yes, I was still fuming at this lost chance to meet one of my favorite directors. I was going to just take off and head home but Phil said he was just going to stick around to see if he can see Iglesia when he shows up, that way Phil could at least give him his t-shirt. By the way, to stand out like the fanboys we are, Phil is wearing his own *Day of the Beast* shirt and I have an *Acción mutante* shirt on.

Once again, proving that things just work out when Phil is around, we decide to go inside and wait for him there. As you first walk into the Center, you go up a huge flight of stairs where the theaters are located. We walk up and wait at the top, figuring we'd be able to see him as he comes up. And we wait. And wait. Finally, Phil sees him walking up. As he comes up the stairs, he notices our T-shirts and starts laughing and pointing. When he gets up to the top, he asks us if he could get a photo with us, which we promptly obliged. So friendly and nice, but then he is quickly taken away to introduce the film. I try to snap a photo, but realize that my flash battery is completely dead. Great. Another reason to get me fuming again. But at least I got to shake his hand, even if I didn't get anything signed or even a picture with him. Before I start to leave, Phil says he's going to stick around a little longer, just in case he comes out during the movie. Okay, I thought,

I'll hang around with him. What else do I have to lose?

We find a table in the lounge area and sit down. There are other people in the lounge as well, standing around chatting. A young woman asks if she could sit at the table with us since it was pretty crowded. We start chatting and find out that she is actually from Russia and is going to film school here. We start talking about movies a little bit and then Phil says something out of the blue, with a completely straight face.

"So, were you upset when Rocky beat Drago?"

"Excuse me?" she said with a puzzled look on her face. I buried my face in my hands, because I could not believe what Phil had just asked.

Thinking that she didn't hear him the first time, Phil asked again.

With a slight pause, she responded with a quick "Um... No."

The whole time Phil barely had a smile on his face, except when I looked at him and then he had that same evil grin that he gets.

Around that time, they announce to the crowded lounge that the screening had officially sold out. People started to make their way out and down the stairs. We stayed sitting there, me still in bewilderment at what Phil had asked her.

Then a guy from the film center comes up and asks if we're together. He said that they did have a few tickets left, but not enough for that big crowd. But if we were still interested, we could still get tickets. We might not be able to sit together, but at least we could get in. I looked at Phil and he had that same grin, except now it was even wider.

"Told you!" was all he said. We got our tickets and went inside for the screening.

Crimen ferpecto is a dark comedy and was damn funny. Afterwards, Iglesia got up and did a Q&A, which was even funnier than the movie. He was now wearing the *Day of the Beast* shirt Phil gave him and even pointed to Phil in the audience to thank him. When it was over, we rushed out to the lobby to see if we could get some stuff signed, which when he came out, he did so graciously. The Russian girl was out there now as well with her phone taking photos. I asked her if she could take a photo of Phil and me with him, which she did, emailing it to me later.

For an event that would have been such a disappointment if I was left on my own, thanks to Phil and just the way things work out for this guy, I was not only able to meet this great director, but I got some lobby cards signed, and a great photo of the three of us together. I'm forever grateful to Phil for that day. Not to mention the countless other times Phil is just being himself.

Next up, more convention stories! But, with one very important difference....

23

Becoming a Dealer

"We keep odd hours."

Severen (Bill Paxton), *Near Dark*

When I was growing up, the term "dealer" usually meant drug dealer. Not that I ever met one, but from '70s TV shows, they never look like the nicest members of society. Later on, through the education of the movies, you would learn that dealers tended to become dealers to support their own habit. I can say for a fact that reasoning also works in other trades as well, especially in the movie memorabilia trade!

Way before guests, it was just about the merchandise. You could find posters, stills, lobby cards, soundtracks, promo items, and so much more. We would get there early, sometimes two or three hours before the show opened, because the line would start to grow. By the time it opened, there could be over a hundred people in line and you wanted to make sure you were in there early to get any quick cheap deals from some of the dealers.

At one of the first memorabilia shows I went to, there was one poster dealer that had a lot of foreign posters on display. As I walked by, my mouth dropped open when I saw the Spanish one-sheet for *La noche del terror ciego*, better known as *Tombs of the Blind Dead*. The artwork featured two of the titular creatures in the top part of the poster with another two in the front starting to chomp down on a woman. I quickly went over to the dealer and asked how much the poster was. He told me it was $40, but he had brought it for someone else that was supposed to be coming to the show. When he told me that, I was both glad and depressed at the same time. Depressed because I really wanted that poster, but also happy because I was still in the beginning stages of being a collector and spending that much for one poster was quite a lot. When he saw my depressed look, the dealer told me to come back tomorrow because if the guy hadn't shown up by then, he'd sell it to me. Sure enough, I was back there the next day and the poster was still there. And $40 later, I walked away with my very first (of soon to be many) Spanish posters, which I still have to this day. I wish I could say this was the most expensive poster I ever bought.

This is something that very few younger fans will ever experience at these modern shows. You could go up to a dealer who would have stacks and stacks of movie posters, sometimes a foot high off the table, and you'd have to go through each poster of each stack, slowly and carefully opening up the poster to see if it was something you wanted. You could find some great deals in there... if you took the time to look. By about 15 minutes or so into that first batch, your back would start to ache, sending up pain signals to your brain telling you to stop. But you would keep going because if you stopped, what if that very next poster was something rare, the Holy Grail that you'd been looking for? Thoughts like that popping in your brain would keep you moving through each and every stack. More times than not, you would come up with some interesting finds. Or there would be the other poster dealer that would have a couple dozen boxes of mixed one-sheets that would start as $5 posters on Friday and go down a $1 each day. I've found many great titles in those boxes that I still have in my collection today.

A couple of years later at one of these shows, there was one dealer who just had posters, but they were from Spain. Now being a fan of Paul Naschy, the odds of finding one of his posters was pretty good. But you had to be even more careful because the paper stock for Spanish posters was a lot thinner and much easier to rip than American one-sheets. So off I went, slowly picking up each poster and being careful opening it up just enough to see what movie it was for. A frown usually followed as you once again carefully folded it back up and set it down, moving to the next one in the stack. Over and over and over again. Then I came to one that as I started to open it, a smile started to break across my face. Making sure I didn't speed up the process and therefore increasing the chance of it ripping, I slowly opened it. And then there it was... right in front of me... a Spanish one-sheet for Naschy's very first werewolf movie, 1968's *La marca del Hombre Lobo*. I quickly asked the price, trying my best not to show my excitement. There's another tip for you beginner collectors. Never show that you're interested. Some of these less-scrupulous dealers will adjust the price according to how much you want it. But when he shrugged his shoulders and said $10, I couldn't get my money out quick enough. Even though I still had plenty of posters to go through, I wasn't going to take a chance not buying this. I think that was the only Naschy poster I found that day, but I did manage to find a couple of other good ones in there. But again, it was a lot of work!

There was another poster dealer that we always made sure to hit up at this show. His name was Josh and he had a huge selection of posters, divided by genre, so it was very easier for customers to go right to a particular section. He kind of looked like Roger Corman and even had that big grin, especially when we'd pull out some schlocky title and be so excited that he actually had a poster for it. He would just laugh and say, "You guys are something else!"

His prices were very reasonable, if not damn cheap, and as a result I picked up many classic posters from him over the years, such as $25 for *Shock Waves* or $20 for *Slave of the Cannibal God*. I believe he later retired from his real job and moved out to California to sell posters full time. Damn, do I miss him. My wallet doesn't though.

I think they held these shows about once every six months or so and I was back there each and every time. I would always try to make a list of different things I was looking for, but by the time spent roaming around the different tables, it all became a blur.

I was going to these shows pretty regularly for a couple of years before I started to think about making the move to the other side of the table. At some point, probably somewhere in the mid-'90s, I made the official jump to becoming an actual dealer. I started setting up at some smaller shows like these, back when a vendor table would run you like $35. Ah... those were the days.

I officially got my start as a dealer at these little movie memorabilia shows that were held at the Holiday Inn in Skokie, Illinois. They were called Hollywood Fest or something like that, but we always called them "Vito shows," since that was the guy's name that ran them. These were small shows consisting of all types of movie goods, from posters and stills, to movies and whatever else movie-related to be found in that kind of market place. There were no guests, but plenty of merchandise for sale. And, man, were those shows fun. Whatever money I made just meant I had more spending money.

As I mentioned in the last chapter, I began, like a lot of people back then, by selling VHS tapes that were in the "gray market" area. I know this is frowned upon by some people, but I feel that if it wasn't for the bootleg market then, we wouldn't have special edition DVDs and Blu-rays of our favorite cult classics today. We never would have had companies like Anchor Bay, Synapse Films, Scream Factory, Dark Sky, or Severin. When these distributors saw how much people were willing to pay to own a copy, no matter the quality, of a rare or hard-to-find movie, they knew if they put it out legitimately, they would get that money. Once they started, they did just that.

Another aspect of it, especially for me, was that since I loved these films so much, I was thrilled to be able to introduce them to other fans that were looking for them as well. I made many new friends those first few years, hooking them up with some rare titles. We shared a connection, like a lot of horror fans, and I was thrilled to be able to help them. Plus, for me it was great because whatever money I made, I would usually spend at the same convention on different memorabilia. I used to buy a lot of posters back then. I'm glad I did too, since the prices of those have skyrocketed to something crazy these days.

As I mentioned before, you become a dealer to support your own habit! Plus, it was easier to convince yourself to spend $40 on a poster when you just made $20, so it *really* only cost you $20! Funny how the brain works, isn't it? I found a lot of great deals back then, before eBay came along, before there were more serious collectors out there like there are now. I am still amazed at some of the prices I see on certain things these days, like particular movie posters that I found in a $2 box that are now going for hundreds of dollars. At one show, an older lady, who was also a dealer, always amazed me at the types of films she'd buy from me, the gorier the better. While looking through the stuff on her table during the show, I saw she had a one-sheet for William Castle's *Homicidal*, for only $20. As I was looking at it, I noticed it was signed at the bottom... by William Castle! At the time, I had no idea how much his signature was worth, but know now it can go for over $2000. Needless to say, I quickly handed over my $20 and took it home, where it still resides today. I know those days are long gone, but I still consider myself damn lucky to have gotten to experience them when I did.

It was at one of these shows where I first met Eric Ott. He was selling 16mm films and other little curious things, which seemed to be Eric's specialty. After chatting about movies and such over a few shows, we became good friends and remain so to this day, setting up at dozens and dozens of shows together over the years. It was also at this show that we became friends with another vendor there named Phil Satterley. Phil would usually deal in videos of mainly British TV series and whatnot.

There was the famous "Elvis Guy" that would come to each and every one of these movie shows, going up to each and every table and ask, "Got any Elvis stuff?" Even if it was pretty apparent by what was on your table that you DIDN'T have any Elvis merch, he would still ask. EVERY. SINGLE. TIME. So, at one of these shows, Eric and I are chatting with Phil, who is set up next to us, and we see the "Elvis Guy" making his way down our aisle. But when he stops at Phil's table, we were not ready for the exchange that was about to happen.

"Got any Elvis stuff?"

With a completely straight face, Phil replied with a quizzical look on his face, "Elvis...?"

A puzzled look comes over the Elvis Guy's face. "Elvis Presley."

"Uh... is he an American actor? I mainly sell British shows," Phil followed, playing it straight.

"Elvis Presley! The singer!" The man says loudly, clearly getting irritated by this point. It is all Eric and I could do to keep quiet and hold back our laughing as we watched this exchange unfold.

Phil then politely tells him, "Oh. Is he a local guy? Sorry. I'm not from this area."

I thought the guy was going to lose it, actually shouting at Phil now, "ELVIS PRESLEY! THE SINGER! How could you have never heard of him?!?!" He quickly storms off, walking right past our tables, never even stopping. At that point, we all burst out laughing. I couldn't believe the control Phil had to be able to sit there with a straight face and make this guy think he's never heard of Elvis before. This is a Convention Story that I have told countless times during the after-hours chat sessions over the years, and it is still one of my favorites.

These were still the days when these little shows were just about memorabilia. There weren't any celebrity guests in the beginning, or if there were, it would only be one or two, someone like Spanky McFarland from *Little Rascals* or the kid from the *Lassie* TV show. But things slowly started to change. Shows would start to get a couple celebrity guests. Then a couple more. Which was all fine at first because we figured it would draw more people to the show. But what we didn't see coming was that these guests were starting to charge money for their autographs. Back then, it was only $5 or maybe $10, but as we all know now, prices would slowly start to rise.

Now, while on the subject of autographs, if you ever plan on buying an item that is already autographed from a dealer, keep this in mind. Most of these come with a "certificate of authenticity." Now I'm sure there are a few legitimate autograph dealers out there, but if you are forging a signature, couldn't you just forge a "certificate" as well? The reason I bring this up is because at one of these early memorabilia shows I was attending as a dealer, there was an autograph dealer set up as well. A buddy of mine, a fan of '70s-era porn stars, was looking through a stack of this dealer's autographed photos. After a little while he gets my attention and calls me over. My friend then proceeds to show me an autograph photo where the signature doesn't match the person depicted in the photo. Meaning, whoever "authenticated" the signature, somehow didn't realize it wasn't the person in the photo. I started to look through the stack as well and found a photo of Ingrid Pitt which was labeled as someone else. So we called the guy over and told him that this was Pitt in the photo, not who was labeled and "authenticated." He quickly grabbed it and said, "Oh, thanks!" and put the photo under his table without even looking twice at it. This tells me that he wasn't even concerned about it being labeled wrong, which made me feel that he knew some of these were not legit. So, the moral of the story is I tend not to trust anybody selling autographs, unless I personally know and trust them... not a little piece of paper that can be printed on your computer.

Back to our story. I did the gray market thing a year or two before I decided to explore a new career path for my little business. For a while, I switched to selling "legit" VHS tapes, or pre-recorded movies as they were called then. This was around the time that a lot of Mom and Pop video stores were closing due to the influx of Blockbuster Video stores coming in and putting them out of business. So there were quite a few shops where I would go in and buy a shitload of movies to resell. I was lucky enough to have a couple of opportunities when looking through "for sale" bins at a video store, picking up quite a few tapes, only to have the owner tell me, "I've got a few more boxes in back that I haven't put out, if you want to go through them." These "few" boxes were more like 18 large boxes of old rental tapes. Needless to say, $1500 later, I drove home, car loaded to the brim with tapes, all the while trying to figure out the best way to tell my wife that we might be a little short on the house payment this month. Lucky for me, she completely understood my reasoning. Or at least she said she did. Either way, she didn't kill me or kick me out, so I consider that a win! (It is times like that when I realized just how lucky I am to have a wife this understanding.)

So hunting for tapes became a quest. I'd drive around looking for video stores and asking them if they were interested in selling any of their old tapes, specifically any from the horror genre. Usually I'd be told "no" flat out, or if they were willing to sell, they usually wanted way too much for me to try and resell and make a profit. But every now and then they would be willing to get rid of some, or they already had a section of tapes for sale. Or you'd find a store that was going out of business and selling everything. Those times were a blessing and a curse.

Eventually, as that market started to die out, I knew I had to find something else to sell at conventions. I had started to pick up a few horror reference books here and there and have them on the table for sale as well. I had noticed that there were very few, if any, people selling these kinds of books at the shows. Since I had a huge passion for them myself, I thought this might be a great niche in the market to get into. It would be something that I could not only sell, but stand behind too. Just like getting that thrill I used to get when I would hand over a long sought-after movie title to a fan, I would get the same when seeing someone's eyes light up as they paged through a book that they had been either looking for or didn't even know had existed. And even more so, knowing that I just might be helping a fan learn more about the genre, well, that was a whole new kind of awesome!

For those out there that think it is pretty easy being a vendor, let me say that as fun it may seem, there is a lot of work and stress involved. First of all, there are the finances. You have to pay for your table, which could be anywhere from $50 to $350, and then add in the cost of the hotel room and food for the weekend. You could be looking at having to make $500 to $600 before you even start making a profit. And that doesn't even include the cost of your merchandise. Which means if you only made $500 at a show, you pretty much just gave away $500 worth of merchandise... for free. It's things like that you have to think of when getting into "the business."

Back in the day, getting a table at one of the New York Fango shows was a real crap shoot. There were some shows where they would oversell the dealer room, so while most of the dealers were in the main vendor area, there would be some tables... somewhere else. That could be in another smaller room, if you were lucky. I remember at one show, the "other vendor room" was on the 12th floor, right where you came out of the elevator. That's right. In the little lobby part, there were like 3-4 vendors set up there. This basically means that you are getting a very small percentage of the public even coming up to your table, let alone buying anything.

There was another New York Fango show where we ran into an issue with our tables. My buddy Tom and I had ordered and paid for our usual three tables, one for me and two for him. On the Wednesday before the show, less than 48 hours before we were set to start our 16-hour drive out to the Big Apple, a rep from Creation called me up to tell me that there was a slight problem with our tables. They were just getting around to laying out the dealer room (that's right kiddies... mere days before the show, and NOW they start to look at the dealer room) only to discover that they had oversold the dealer room and don't have enough tables. So instead of getting our three tables, we're only getting one. Now, it doesn't take a Physics major to realize that you can't fit three tables worth of merchandise onto one table. So I started to explain to them that I had already rented a van to bring out three tables worth of merchandise and that one table was not going to work. Not to mention the fact that I had already paid for the three tables months ago. The person on the phone really couldn't care less and just asked me if I wanted the table or not. I told them yes, but I needed to talk to someone else that can explain how a company that does these conventions for a living can screw something like this up. But I realized that Creation really didn't care squat about horror shows, and only cared about their real meal ticket, the Star Trek cons. After hanging up with them, I started to call my buddy to explain to him what was going on, when Creation called me back. Apparently the next dealer they called to break the news that his number of tables has been decreased told Creation to piss off and that he wasn't going to bother coming. (I might be paraphrasing that a bit.) Since this guy decided not to come, we would now have two tables. As pissed as I still was, two was better than one, so I could work with that. We did get a refund for that third table, but it still sucked. This was not uncommon practice for Creation back then.

And then there are those little things in life you learn... sometimes the hard way. Remember to never leave food in your car while you're at the show, especially in the summer. One fine August, we had set up at the

Wizard World Comic Book convention in Rosemont, IL. I believe these have changed names, merged, or something since then. Back then, it was a huge comic book show, with a few elements of horror in there as well. With like 30,000 people coming through the door, we had the potential to still make some good money. On the way there on Saturday, we thought it would be a good idea to stop and get some White Castle cheeseburgers to eat on the way in, which we did. What I didn't realize when we got there was that some of us left some of their uneaten sliders in the car. In the parking lot. Outside. In the August summer heat. At the end of the day, we come strolling back to the van, all happy and jolly from the money we made throughout that afternoon, until we opened the door to the van. The smell hit us like a ton of bricks. The stench immediately assaulted our noses, making our eyes water, and causing our gag reflexes to go into overdrive. I think I know what those people feel like when they come across a dead body that has been decomposing for weeks. We had to open all the doors in the van and sit there for about thirty minutes waiting for it to air out enough until we could handle sitting inside again. This is another very important lesson here. Be warned.

See what fun being a dealer can be?

Then, there are some shows that are just poorly run. Either they didn't do enough planning, or promotion, or just failed to draw in the crowds. People think that putting on a convention is easy as well, but it is amazing how much work can go into one and have it come off successfully. In my 20+ years as a vendor, I've done plenty of shows that I wished I had never bothered with and just stayed home. But unlike being a paying fan where you can just walk away and eat the cost of admission, a vendor has a lot more money and time involved. Here are a few fond memories I have of some of the… lesser quality shows I've had the pleasure of enduring.

Again, I won't mention any names of these shows for obvious reasons. One show wasn't really a convention but a good old-fashioned movie memorabilia show. Or at least, that is what the promoter told us it was going to be. As we entered the parking lot of the hotel where the show was held, we see a sign on the hotel's marquee that read: "Beanie Baby Show." Hmmm… Maybe there is another show going on at the same time. Uh… No. Besides us, selling our horror movie merchandise, there was a guy selling autographs, one selling T-shirts, another guy selling movies. The rest were dealers selling, you guessed it, Beanie Babies. I immediately found the promoter and (in a very polite and courteous manner, of course), asked him what the hell was going on and what was up with all the Beanie Baby dealers. He said he didn't realize that this many were going to be selling the same kind of merchandise. I then asked him why then did he have a sign outside stating that it was a Beanie Baby show? He said that he had to promote it as a movie memorabilia show so those customers would still show up. I should have just turned around and left, but we set up anyway. You just never know. It was a local show so I knew we could just pack up and go home at any point. Which is exactly what we did about two hours after the show opened. Not only did we not sell a damn thing, we didn't even have a single soul stop by our table to even browse. So after that brief period of time, we started packing up. The promoter walked by and never even said a word to us, but turned his head and walked away. Lucky for me, the table was pretty cheap so I wasn't out too much. I could have bitched about selling me the table under false pretenses, but I know I wouldn't have gotten my money back.

There was another show that wasn't so close to home that I made the mistake of attending. It was in Michigan, about a four-hour drive for us. The only reason I decided to do it was because, since it was only a one-day show, on a Sunday, I could go up and visit my family that lived in Michigan on Saturday, hit the show on Sunday, and drive home. Like the previous show, I was told how big the show was going to be because the promoter spent a lot of money on advertising. He even had a celebrity guest, Tom Sullivan, makeup and special effects wizard who worked on the original *Evil Dead*. But once we got there, we realized that we were probably in for another dud. And it was.

The show held about ten or fifteen dealers. There were a couple of comic book dealers, a few artists, a poster dealer, and a few other guys, but nothing major. I made only one sale at that show and that was to Mr. Sullivan. I think they may have gotten... twenty people through the door... maybe? And just imagine if the promoter hadn't spent all that money on advertising!

There was another show that we did which promised to be a much bigger show, with celebrity guests, but this was a prime example of not knowing what the hell you're doing. The main guests were three actors from the original *Friday the 13th* and Stephen Geoffreys from *Fright Night*. I believe there were a couple of other guests, possibly one or two from a sci-fi TV show, but not sure. It was a first-time show, so you can always assume there were going to be some growing pains. But then you wonder if any of these guys really put any thought at all into what they are doing. Since most of your guests were known for being in a horror film, you'd think you would maybe play up that angle? Nope. In all the advertisements, banners, badges, and everything else printed with the show's name, it just had Sci-Fi and Fantasy convention. So any horror fan that might come across any advertisements for the show isn't going to bother looking further. Why wouldn't you put the word horror in there? Afraid of the dregs of society it might bring in? Then why have those guests there at all?

Anyway, the tables were pretty cheap so we got three of them, figuring we could really spread out. It was a normal three-day show from Friday to

Sunday with a pretty decent-sized dealer room. Once we got set up and walked around, I figured we might be in for a little trouble. Every one of the dealers was selling sci-fi and fantasy stuff. I don't recall seeing another dealer that was strictly horror merch besides me. So the doors open Friday evening and the crowd comes filing in. No, wait! That was in my dream at the time. Because when they did open the doors, not a single person was there waiting to come in! It might have been because the admission price was just too damn high, even for a single day. Or maybe it wasn't advertised enough. Or maybe no horror fans came out because they figured it was a sci-fi show. I think maybe twenty people came through the door Friday. I had a couple of browsers, but no sales, other than selling one book to another dealer. A buddy of mine had gotten a table as well and was set up next to me. He didn't sell much of anything either. I told him that when we left for the night on Friday, that if I didn't sell something before noon on Saturday, I was leaving.

So Saturday comes, the doors open, and nobody is waiting to come in, once again. The promoter and the people working the show are trying to get people at the hotel to come in, even letting them in for FREE! I did end up selling something before noon. Another single book... to the same dealer that had bought one from me on Friday. But once noon came, I was more than done, and started packing up.

A couple of dealers close to me came over, with this bewildered look on their faces and asked me what I was doing. I simply said, "I'm going home."

"But... the show goes until 5pm tonight and it's still open tomorrow."

"Not for me," I replied, as I continued to pack up.

"Does the promoter know you're packing up?" he asked with a nervous look on his face.

"I don't care. I've sold two books so far this show and I'm not wasting my entire weekend here," and continued to pack up.

About ten minutes later, the promoter shows up. "What are you doing?"

"Uh... packing. I'm going home," I replied once again.

"You can't leave this early. We're still trying to get people to come to the show!"

I stopped packing and turned around to face him, about maybe a foot between us. Now I don't remember exactly what I said, but I'm pretty sure it came out something like...

"I've sold two books so far and that was to another dealer. I've counted maybe three people that have walked into this room so far today. I know that because I have sat here watching once the door opened. I'm not going to waste my entire weekend for a show that nobody is coming to."

Then I turned back around and continued to pack.

He keeps talking as I pack. "You know, I've spent a lot of money advertising this show. A lot of my own money and the least you could do is show some respect for all of us trying to put on a good show."

I stopped and asked "Why isn't horror mentioned in any of your ads? Especially when most of your guests are from a horror movie?"

"Uh..."

"Exactly!" I snapped. "How do you expect to draw horror fans when you don't even promote it as something besides a sci-fi and fantasy show? And I don't care how much money you spent promoting it... it didn't work. There is NOBODY HERE!" I turned and started packing again.

He stormed off and I couldn't help but notice about half a dozen other dealers standing around watching what just happened. I could tell by some of their faces that they wanted to do the same, but apparently lacked the balls to do it. I've been to more than a few shows that were just run like shit, unorganized, poorly advertised (if at all), and were just a waste of time. If I've paid to be there, which is part of a contract that you sign, then I also expect the promoter to honor his part of the bargain and spend the money to get people in the door. When Ken Kish planned his first Cinema Wasteland show, he was advertising it a YEAR IN ADVANCE! Same with Mike and Mia Kerz and their Flashback Weekend show, peddling flyers to their first show a year before too. Now their shows are even advertised on Svengoolie! That's how you do it.

So we packed up and were ready to leave a little after 1pm. Thankfully, the show was in a Chicago suburb so I didn't have a long drive home and still had most of my weekend. All I lost was one vacation day and a day of my time. Since then, it has be something really special for me to take a chance on a first-time show.

I've also seen over the years that sometimes it doesn't matter how big or small a show it is, sometimes you just can't trust them.

Back to the Creation/Fango shows, it was not uncommon for them to have a name on the guest list that they never had even contacted, especially in their later years. At one of their cons, they had announced H.G. Lewis as a guest, even putting him on the full-page ad in their magazine. I emailed Lewis about something else and mentioned to him about being at their upcoming show. "I am?" he replied. I emailed him a scan of the ad, to which he replied, "I guess I better contact the promoter and ask him when they were going to check with me." Nice, huh? Fango told me that the producers of some film that Lewis was involved with had told him that they would be bringing Lewis to the show. Sounds great, but you'd think that if you're going to be putting Lewis' face on the advertisement, maybe you should reach out to him to make sure? Just a thought.

There was a smaller show here in the Chicago area back in late 2000 that really was a textbook case on how to screw dealers and fans. When this show was first announced, they were advertising a ton of guests, some of them pretty big names in the horror genre, such as not only Dario Argento, but his daughter Asia as well! They had also announced Jess Franco and his wife Lina Romay, as well as cult names like Ron Jeremy and Traci Lords. Well, I was chatting later with a friend who knows Argento personally, and I mentioned that Argento was going to be coming to the States in September for a show. I got a quizzical response, saying that they had just talked to Dario and he said nothing about coming to the States. They promptly called him to double-check and made sure... Argento knew nothing about it.

So, about a month before this new convention was to take place, they were still advertising Argento being there. I was set up at another event when the promoter of this "new show" walks up to my booth. I knew this guy from a previous show and never really trusted him to begin with. He always seemed a bit shifty to me. Anyway, he comes in and asks me if I was setting up at his show next month.

"Uh... no." I quickly replied.

"Really? We have Argento coming", he said.

"No. No, you don't. Argento knows nothing about your show so how could he be coming?"

"Uh... uh... Well, we've talked to his secretary!"

"Well, great then. Maybe his secretary is coming, but he's not."

The Friday right before the show, I found out from someone else that Franco and Romay were in fact at the show, but pretty much the rest of the bigger names were no-shows. So, I went anyway, if only to meet Franco.

When I show up to the admissions booth to get my ticket, the conversation went kind of like this:

"So... Argento here?"

"Uhhh, sorry. He couldn't make it. He's working on a new film. But all the other guests are here."

"Oh, really? Asia is here?"

"Oh, no. She had to cancel."

"Traci Lords is here then?"

"Well ... Uuhhh... No."

"Ron Jeremy?"

"No."

Why would a promoter do something like this? Simple. To get people through the door. They probably have no intention of either putting on another show, or at least not using the same name, so they don't care about reputation. But when a promoter announces a guest lineup like that, it will get dealers to want a table because they think it will be a big draw. Fans will buy advance tickets because of that same reason. But then when all the guests "cancel" at the last minute, all those people that bought early tickets are now screwed. So it really comes down to being able to trust the promoters. The bigger shows these days, you can pretty much trust them, though maybe not the guests themselves, who might have a tendency to cancel, which really has nothing to do with the show.

I did my first official Fangoria show as a dealer back in January of 1999. This was just around the time when these shows started to change. Before, as I stated in my previous Fango reports, these shows were amazing, with tons of guests and so much fun. But things began to change. At least that was the way it seemed from a fan's point of view. The guest lists started to become smaller. Then Creation started getting a reputation for guests not being there when show time came around. Nonetheless, these shows in New York still drew the crowds. Once I started as a vendor there, we really didn't care about the show itself as much or the guests, as long as the fans were coming out and spending money, that was the important thing.

Now I know what you're thinking. That I had turned my back on the genre and was just there to make a buck, right? Partly right. I didn't turn my back on the genre, just these shows. Because of all the issues that we'd have, such as getting dealer tables, trying to find out when we could set up, and having to deal with Creation and their personnel, it really started to become a nightmare. But as I mentioned, the fans would still come out. So much so that it was not uncommon at these shows that you'd be so busy at your table, talking to customers, and making sales that you didn't have time to worry about anything else. Remember, those were the days when autographs were still free for the most part. There were some guests that had started to charge, usually $5 or $10. But the main guests at the show were usually free. So the money that the fans were bringing went straight to the dealers. Oh, such fond memories...

In 1999, the headliner was going to be Dario Argento, who was promoting his latest film, a remake of *Phantom of the Opera*. He actually was at the show, which drew a huge crowd. The line to get something signed was very long so I didn't bother because I had to be behind my table. But I was able to get some pics of him while he was signing. I believe H.G. Lewis was there, as well as Andrew Divoff who was there promoting *Wishmaster 2*. They still had a good crowd at the show, but it definitely had a different vibe than the big ones from just a few years before.

This was when the shows were still being held in Manhattan and we usually would have a great time there. Granted, the drive out there still sucked major balls, but I was younger and dumber, and was still trying to make these trips driving straight through. The whole weekend would end up like a fever dream, with little sleep to be had until we'd get home Monday morning. The routine would be something like this: Leave Thursday night, somewhere between 9pm and midnight. Drive straight through and get to Manhattan sometime Friday evening. We'd hopefully be able to find someone from Creation and be able to take all our merchandise for the show up to the dealer room and at least drop it off by our table. Then we'd find someplace to eat and then hit the bar in the hotel. There we'd meet up with other dealers and convention friends and hang out until they closed, usually around 2am. Since we'd been up for over 24 hours at that point, we would make the wise decision to get a few hours of sleep before we had to be down to set up, usually around 9am. Once the show closed for the evening, usually around 6 or 7pm, we'd do the same thing as the night before... eat... hit the bar... close the bar ... 4-5 hours of sleep. If I was a smarter man, since I knew I'd be driving pretty much all night long on Sunday night, I would go to bed early on Saturday night/Sunday morning so I could be well rested for that long drive. Yeah... right.

Speaking of bad decisions, one of them involved a 24-hour '50s style diner called the Tick Tock Diner that was connected to the hotel. They had something they called Disco Fries, which were basically American fries, covered in cheese and gravy. I know that might not sound too appetizing, but damn if they weren't pretty tasty. I believe this place is still around now and really hope to make a return there at some point. But at one of these trips, after the bar had closed, which would have been around 2am, we decided that we needed to get some food and shambled into the Tick Tock. For some unknown reason, I decided that I had to try their potato pancakes. When they arrived, I can remember cutting through one of them with my fork, only to have the grease start to ooze out and pool around the bottom of my plate, as if I'd just cut into a living thing, except instead of blood, it was grease. But they tasted incredible. Granted, this is around 3am at this point, with very little sleep, so I wasn't in the most clearest of mindsets. I finished off both the deliciously juicy pancakes and then we headed up to the room for some sleep a short time later. When I woke up the next morning, I felt like death. Not sure if it was the amount grease that I ingested in the few hours before, but my stomach was in sheer agony. The thought of putting anything else in there just made the pain even worse. In fact, I didn't eat the entire day. Later in the evening, when we were driving home and stopped for a late dinner, my stomach had eased up a bit and I was able to convince myself to eat a little something.

Since I don't drink alcohol, I think the monkey on my back is food. But not just any food. Food that isn't healthy for you. I guess it is one of those things that, in your youth, you might sample something that an older version of yourself would surely step in and say, "Ah... hold on there, son!

That is not the smartest thing to do right now and you will surely pay for it." Granted, I have a feeling that if my older self had shown up at that moment, he would have told me to double the order and sat down next to me, fork already in hand.

Fango held their NY shows in Manhattan for another two years. In 2000, their headliner was Udo Kier, and in 2001, it was going to be Rob Zombie, scheduled to be promoting his first feature film, *House of 1000 Corpses*. Zombie ended up being a no-show, with rumors flying that he never knew he was even scheduled to be there. I had even asked Fango (after Universal dropped *House*) if he would still be at that show, and they assured me it would happen. Right. Never was there. There were a lot of pissed-off fans that were showing up to find out when they got there that Zombie had cancelled. Of course, these pissed-off fans were still buying stuff, so I wasn't complaining.

The following year, they moved the show to Brooklyn for some reason. Robert Englund was the headliner for that show. They also were going to have a big *Return of the Living Dead* reunion, with several of the actors scheduled for the show. When the show came, I think their "reunion" was just two guests! Not really a reunion, you know? The number of people coming through the door was dramatically smaller than the usual NY shows. From what I was told by a local, you can't get to Brooklyn from Manhattan, which confused the hell out of me since I got there from Chicago. But apparently the trains don't run late or something like that. So it turned out to not be a good show. A real dud in fact. When they announced their next show, which would again be in Brooklyn again, we decided against it. Shame too since their headliner was David Cronenberg and I've never had the chance to meet him since that show. Italian director Luigi Cozzi was there as well, so it was a bummer that we didn't go. But after that last one, I just couldn't see doing it.

That was the last Fango show I did until they started back up in Chicago in 2006. And from the guest list they were announcing, it almost seemed like a return to the glory days. Originally, George Romero was the only guests that sounded like he would draw a crowd. But before long, they had announced a huge *Slither* panel, including the main cast and director. They were also having some guests from *Silent Hill*, and French director Alexandre Aja, who had recently remade *The Hills Have Eyes*. So it was a pretty good lineup and they did bring in the crowds.

Which leads us to some of the usual Creation screw-ups. Trying to find out what time the show opened and closed throughout the weekend was a challenge. Each Creation representative you'd ask would give you a different answer. On Friday, I had asked what time the dealer room opened the next day only to hear everything from 9am to 11am. We got there around 8am to make sure we had our table ready for the big crowd that had already started lining up down the hallway. I'm glad we got there when we did, because Creation decided to let people in early, around 8:30am since the line was so long. Now to all those dealers that were told the show wasn't open until 10am... guess they just had people wandering by their table with no one there. Nice, huh? Same old Creation... never really caring about the vendors that help pay for the show. But again, like the NY shows, we made out alright. Our table was in a great spot, just as you came through the door, and we did pretty well.

Fango did two more shows in Chicago over the next couple of years, and each time you could see the writing on the walls. There were a lot of changes going on in the Fango front office at the time, with tons of rumors swirling around, so you were never really sure what was going to happen. And then, before you knew it, it was all over. Fango just stopped doing them.

So, has being an "official" dealer changed me at all? Definitely, for better and for worse. As I mentioned earlier, when I see the same celebrity guests over and over again, they sometimes lose their sparkle. On the flipside, there are some that I have built a friendship with over the years and that has been priceless.

Also, in the past, I never had artwork displayed in the Krypt, other than regular movie posters and such. Over the years though, I have become good friends with many different artists who are also dealers. Getting to personally know them and their art opened my eyes to their talent and what they do. Like me, they have the same passion but the outlet is much different. It still blows my mind how they create such amazing pieces. Whether they work in paint like Dave Voigt, Steve Bejma, Chris Kuchta, Aaron Stockwell, and Mark Maddox, or pen and paper like Don England and Matt "Putrid" Carr, it knocks me out each and every time. These guys are putting their heart and soul into their work, so make sure you take a moment to appreciate it.

Most dealers are fans themselves, which is most likely why they decided to jump to the other side of the table. Of course, there are those that are strictly in it for the money, but I think they are in the minority since there are easier ways to make a buck. For me, personally, it is another way to help fans expand their knowledge. I'm not sure why, but fans tend to look up to dealers as some sort of authority. I know I did. And because of that, I always try to continue that thought process and help the fans in their quest.

Back when I was selling movies, I could start a conversation with someone about the classic Universal films of the 1930s and '40s, and then ask them if they've ever seen any of the Mexican horror films of the '60s? Or if they like Hammer Films, did they know who Paul Naschy is? Even though I mainly deal in horror reference books now, the conversations are still the same. It's a way to open the minds of the fans, like giving them a roadmap with a bunch of different trips laid out for them, offering them many different destinations, based on their individual passions. Turns out, my little mission statement for my website, the whole "Discover the Horror" tag line, I was already doing when I became a dealer. Because at the end of the day, that is still what it is all about for me.

Cinema Wasteland family, 2018

with Tom Savini, 1988

24

Further Adventures from the Kryptic World Tour

"After all, there is nothing real outside our perception of reality, is there?"

Brian O'Blivion (Jack Creley), *Videodrome*

The Gruesome Twosome and Other Fun Times at Flashback

When Mike and Mia Kerz started Flashback Weekend, they spent a lot of time and effort advertising their convention before it happened. They understood that you needed to get the word out, especially for a first-time show. When their event launched in August of 2002, we were there and have been at every Flashback Weekend since! We've made a lot of great memories at this show, and have met people that I now consider some of my closest friends. Mike, his wife Mia, and their whole family work hard each and every year to bring Chicago the longest-running Horror convention in town.

At this first show, the guest that I was most excited about was the Godfather of Gore himself, Herschell Gordon Lewis. I really hope that everyone reading this book knows who this man is and what he did for the cult, exploitation, and horror market. If not, you still have a lot of schooling to do. While having the Godfather there was thrilling in its own right, the big surprise was that his old partner-in-crime, the Sultan of Sleaze, David Friedman just happened to be in town and decided to stop by! Friedman is another very important name in the exploitation business and someone that you owe it to yourself to learn more about. To have this pair together really was a reunion beyond compare. They changed movie history in 1963 when they released *Blood Feast* – now, 40 years later, they had made the sequel, *Blood Feast 2: All U Can Eat*, which they were going to be screening that weekend at the Pickwick Theater.

One of the great things about this first show was that they had film screenings going on all weekend at the Pickwick Theater, which was only about ten minutes from the hotel. I had a tough decision to make when it came to the screening of this new *Blood Feast* sequel. I could either go in and watch the movie, or stand out in the lobby and listen to stories from Friedman about the good old days of his time as one of the Forty Thieves, who were film peddlers and promoters that walked a fine line between being salesmen or con artists. I eventually went into the theater once the movie started, and have regretted that decision ever since, especially now that Friedman has passed away.

The cool thing about these two guys is that they weren't charging a dime for their signatures, and were more than happy to sign whatever you put in front of them. Class acts, both of them. It really was an honor to meet them. Granted, I was lucky to meet both of them again a few more times over the years. I used to send Lewis a little email every year on his birthday and would always get a nice little response from him, thanking me.

Another feature making its debut was Don Coscarelli's *Bubba Ho-Tep*, starring Bruce Campbell, who also made an appearance. It was just awesome to have the chance to see the film in the theater like this, way before it finally was officially released to cinemas.

That first Flashback show was great. It was nice to have a convention in our home state once again. Over the next fifteen years, the shows continued on, and so did the memories, meeting a lot of cool celebrities over that time.

At the 2004 show, our table was right next to Clayton Hill and Sharon Ceccatti, who were zombie extras in Romero's *Dawn of the Dead*. Clayton is known as the "Sweater Zombie" or "Elevator Zombie" and Sharon was the "Nurse Zombie." During the weekend, we got to chat with these two quite a bit and became friends. They were one of the nicest and friendliest couples you could ever meet. Clayton had so many great stories about his life, from the film business to all the other crazy jobs he had over the years. His wife Sharon kept right up with him with some of her tales of working with magician David Copperfield. They were so down to earth and genuinely nice people that each time I would see them at another show, it was like a mini-reunion. When Clayton passed away in 2009, it was like I lost a great uncle. Thankfully, I was lucky enough to meet this man, even for a short time, and hear such wonderful stories from him. I truly feel honored for that.

It really does make one take pause at times like that. We go to these shows, meet some of the guests, with some of them becoming friends. But you just never know when the next time will be when you might see them again, even if you're just going up to their table to shake their hand or get an autograph. At the 2005 Flashback, they were doing a *Devil's Rejects* cast appearance, with Sid Haig, Bill Moseley, and some of the other cast members. One of them was Matthew McGrory, who played Tiny in both *Rejects* and *House of 1000 Corpses*. They had a great Q&A panel with plenty of entertaining stories. Then, within two weeks of that show, the sad news came out that McGrory had passed away. Once again, it makes you think about all of the people in our lives, the famous people we meet and the friends we make at these shows. It makes you realize how special these times can be, and how we really should make the most of it, share stories, make memories, and never forget.

It was at these Flashback shows that my son Nick got to meet two of his idols. The first one was Bruce Campbell. Being a huge fan of the *Evil Dead* series, Campbell was pretty high up on Nick's list. The second was George Romero. With *Dawn of the Dead* being one of Nick's all-time favorite films, it was pretty important for him to meet the guy that started it all. When he met them both, it was like I was able to meet them again for the first time, through his eyes. To see Nick's eyes light up and have that same feeling of "I can't believe I'm sitting next to this guy," that I had many years ago, it really took me back.

But the sad part is that our outlook, or at least mine, has changed over the years. I had met both of Campbell and Romero before. Several times before. In fact, I had seen Romero so many times at different shows and events over the years that, sad to say, he had lost the iconic stature that he once held for me. Before it was "Holy Shit! It's George-Fucking-Romero!" Now, it was more like, "Oh great... Romero's going to be there... again." The same went for Bruce Campbell, although there were other reasons for him losing favor with me.

Maybe it is just one of the casualties of being in the convention business, that when you see some of the same celebrities several times a year, year after year, that it's hard to keep them up on that pedestal that we once did. It can start to wear thin. The real sad part is ... it shouldn't. Truth be told, I'm angry at myself for ever thinking that way, because when it comes to a lot of these "convention regulars," no matter how many shows they do, it doesn't take away from their work. I mean, let's face it... I haven't really liked a Romero film since *The Dark Half* in 1993. In fact, I *really* didn't like his last four zombie films. But no matter how I feel about them, it doesn't take away from what he *did* make. The man *invented* a freaking subgenre of films! If I had a Top 25 Films list, guaranteed at least two of them would be from Romero. I have to remind the little devil on my shoulder to ease up a bit when it comes to discussing his career, as well as some others. We, as fans, should never diminish or forget the accomplishments and impact that these filmmakers have made on the genre and in our lives.

It isn't just the celebrity encounters that make this particular show stand out in my memories. I have met some incredible people that I now consider my closest friends. At the 2005 show, I was behind my table as usual when this guy comes up wearing a very cool Godzilla shirt, which had Big G on the front and then sort of a Hollywood Squares design on the back with nine other famous Kaiju monsters. I complimented him on the shirt and inquired where he got it, telling him my son would love one. So we started chatting. He had stopped at the table because of all the reference books I was selling. Turns out he was in the beginning stages of writing his own book. I offered up my services, telling him if he was looking for any film in particular that I might be able to help him out, as well as being willing to lend an ear to listen about his book endeavor. We exchanged cards and he walked away. Little did I realize how much this guy Aaron Christensen was going to change my life.

A short time later, Aaron contacted me and said he'd like to come out, chat horror, and discuss his book project with me. One Saturday, he took the train out to Aurora, where I gave him a tour of the Krypt. The real surprise to him was when we went into the basement and he saw the walls and walls of video shelves. At the time, I had four video shelving units that I bought from a video store going out of business. Each shelf was 7 ft tall and 4 ft across, and they were pretty much filled with DVDs and VHS tapes. One of his reasons for coming out was to try and narrow down his list of movie titles that he was going to cover for his book. But as we started going through the different titles, I'd ask him if he'd seen a particular film as I pulled it out.

"No... Never seen that one."

"Oh, man," I quickly replied. "This needs to be in your list. How about this one?"

"Uh... Never heard of that one."

"Seriously? This needs to be in there too."

This went on for a few minutes before Aaron realized that his list, instead of getting smaller, was instead quickly moving in the opposite direction. After more discussions and some re-thinking on Aaron's part, he decided to change the format of the book, which eventually became *Horror 101: The A-List of Horror Films and Monster Movies* (Midnight Marquee, 2007). The new concept was that this book would be an introduction of sorts to horror fans. If you were new to the genre, by watching all the films covered in this book, you'd have a pretty good foundation to build from, since the volume covered everything from classics to modern-day titles, hitting important features from Italy, Japan, and other countries besides the U.S. I was honored when Aaron asked me if I'd be interested in writing a couple of essays for the book. It turned out to be my first professional published work and I was damn proud of it.

Our friendship grew from there. Over the years, we have had some serious (and some not so serious) discussions on film, life, conventions, celebrities, and so much more. My writing skills have improved considerably over the years thanks to his guidance and attention to grammar and style. He introduced me to the joys of self-editing and making sure not to use the same word over and over again. For example, as a film fan writing about film, you don't want to repeatedly use the word "film" when discussing a particular film or other films that the film's director has filmed and other films that film has influenced. I was amazed at how many different words one can come up with (movie, picture, feature, flick, etc.) instead of... uh... film.

Along the way, Aaron also taught me how to be a different kind of horror fan. In my early days, when I was full of piss and vinegar, if someone didn't agree with me, I would call them out, being much more argumentative (aka... a dick). Hanging around Aaron at a few shows, I realized that kind of attitude potentially alienated younger, less-experienced fans... the very people I was hoping to reach! The chance I might have had to introduce someone to a particular film might have just disappeared because I called him/her an idiot for not knowing something. By taking a much more open, inviting approach, I not only could understand their point of view, but also had a better chance of getting them to understand mine. It's much harder to do that when the conversation starts with, "Dude... that movie sucks... You don't know shit!"

Granted, that still comes out every now and then, but it is a learning process!

Now, almost 15 years later, Aaron has become not only one of my best friends, but a mentor, teacher, and Turkey Day Co-Pilot. Strange how just a chance meeting at a show can guide the path of one's life.

A couple of years later, at Flashback once again, Aaron was helping me out at my table, talking to another guy, when I heard him suddenly say, "Oh my god! You need to tell Jon that!" The look on this poor man's face was as if he'd been caught passing notes in class. This guy sheepishly looks at me and almost quietly says, "I like Larry Buchanan movies." I quickly throw my hands up and cheer! I come out from behind the table and say, "I've got to shake your hand!" I'm always thrilled to meet another fan of Buchanan's work. His name was Alan Tromp and we quickly learned that he was no slouch when it came to the genre. He was at the show by himself, driving up from the St. Louis area. He immediately became one of our convention family and we now see him frequently at other shows. Once again, just a random chance meeting at a show, and now I've got another person in my life that I consider a great friend.

Around that same time at a Flashback show, there was a slight break in the action so I wandered around the dealer's room, checking out other vendors. I came across this kid (okay... maybe in his early 20s) sitting by himself at his table. Hanging in front was a piece of art that mainly featured the turkey-headed monster from *Blood Freak*. Not only was the artwork just amazing, I couldn't figure out why this kid would have art from this rare title.

I walked up to him and asked him about the *Blood Freak* piece. Turns out it was from an album cover for a death metal band named after the cult film. Looking at the other pieces on his table, I was blown away how detailed his work was, immediately reminding me of Bernie Wrightson. As we started talking, I was shocked by the number of movie titles this "kid" not only knew about, but knew well. I could throw out the most obscure shot-on-video movie from the 1980s and he had seen it. His name was Matt Carr, who goes by his artist name of Putrid. We talked movies several times over that weekend, and soon became good friends as well. (I could probably write a separate volume of Putrid stories that I've personally witnessed, but I've got to save something for volume two!) Over a decade later, Matt is still a great friend, whose incredible talent still blows me away each and every time I see a new piece. The detail he achieves in his work is simply staggering.

At the 2015 Flashback show, during the after-hours gatherings where we discuss movies with the usual members of our convention family, we had this strange guy in a kilt walk up to the group and simply ask, "Are you guys talking about horror movies?" followed quickly with, "Can I join you?" It didn't take long before we realized this guy not only was well-versed in the genre, but he *really* knew his shit. His name was Scott Bradley.

Any theoretical question I threw at him not only came back with an answer, but an answer that sometimes had me thinking "Shit. I never thought about it that way!" Once again, he was quickly absorbed into our convention family. The funny thing was that he came to this show on a whim, in hopes to meet some other like-minded horror fans. He had read Adam Rockoff's *The Horror of It All*, and noticed he was from the Chicago area, so Scott came to Chicago hoping that Adam might just be at this particular show as well. The ironic thing was that while Adam wasn't, two of the people he wrote about in that particular book, Putrid and me, were not only at the show, but were sitting in the lobby when Scott first walked up and asked to join! Talk about a small world.

We encouraged Scott to venture to Ohio for the next Cinema Wasteland show to meet even more horror-fiends, which he did, and has continued to since then. A short time later, Scott started his own podcast, *Hellbent for Horror*, where he does just what he did that first night with us, discussing fright films and what they mean to him. His podcasts are extremely well thought-out, showcasing Scott's knowledge, analysis and appreciation of the genre, making for a highly entertaining listen. In 2018, he published his first book, *Screaming for Pleasure: How Horror Can Make You Happy and Healthy*, which is a great introduction to his amazing knowledge and insight. I'm thrilled to know him and proud to call him a friend and fellow fiend.

It's one of those things that make these shows so special to me. These random chance encounters with different people throughout the years that not only bring about great conversations and discussions, but create lifelong bonds as well. For some strange reason, these connections seem to happen more at Flashback Weekend than at any other show. Not sure why, but I hope that Mike and Mia Kerz continue these shows for years to come!

HorrorHound

HorrorHound Weekend is now one of the largest horror/pop culture shows around and we've been to almost all of these events and have always had a great time. There are many stories I could tell from late night shenanigans at these shows, but it would be very hard to repeat some of them here, for fear of legal retribution! But next time you see me at a show, ask me about the late-night karaoke in the lobby and someone singing "Yesterday" by the Beatles.

The very first HorrorHound show took place in Indianapolis, IN, July 6th-8th, 2007. Right underneath HorrorHound Weekend on the Welcome sign in the hotel lobby, there was also a sign welcoming the Jesus Christ Assembly. So we knew there was going to be some fun after hours! Over the next few years, there always seemed to have a strange companion event to the HorrorHound shows, whether it was a karate tournament or a Christian Pajama Party, there was never a shortage of entertainment, that is for sure.

Over a decade later, these shows are bigger than ever. During that time, I've had more than a few special moments, such as getting to meet genre icons like John Landis, Richard Lynch, Christopher Young, Pam Grier, and even Barbara Steele! I got to help run a Q&A for some stuntmen from different horror films, which was a lot of fun, offering my own questions when the audience froze up. At one show, I was sitting behind my table with my camera out. I was looking down but could tell there were some people at the table looking at the books I had for sale, so I raised the camera up and took a quick picture without looking or aiming. I brought the camera back down and looked at it to see the picture. I'm looking at the little screen on the back of the camera and thought, "Hmmm... That looks like Doug Bradley." I look up and sure enough it was. We had a great conversation about Boris Karloff as he paged through different titles before he ended up buying a few of them.

In March of 2011, HorrorHound had a reunion for Lucio Fulci's *The House by the Cemetery* with actors Catriona MacColl, Giovanni Frezza, Silvia Collatina, Dagmar Lassander, and Carlo De Mejo all attending. I'm a huge fan of this flick, no matter that (or maybe because) it is crazy as hell. The issue of *HorrorHound* that was coming out at that show was going to have a retrospective about *House* and I had the honor of writing it. During the show, as I met the different cast members, I had them sign my issue of the magazine, letting them know I was the one that wrote the retrospective.

All of them thanked me for the kind words and said they really enjoyed it. But when I got up to Carlo De Mejo, I was shaking his hand when I told him and he held onto my hand, leaned towards me and gave me the most sincere "Thank you" that I've ever gotten. He said for fans to remember what they did on a movie 30 years ago, and still loved and admired it, just made his day. He was so gracious and so thrilled to be there and meet these fans. It was one of those times that I actually felt proud of what I had written after he told me that.

Now, travel problems weren't only for the Fango shows. Not even close. In March of 2013, we headed to Cincinnati for HorrorHound's first show after they moved it to the Sharonville Convention Center, right across the street from the hotel where these shows had been held but had now outgrown. The Convention Center was huge and at the time seemed like it was too big, until the lines started forming early Friday. Now, this particular show, John Carpenter was one of the guests. But they were also having a big *Walking Dead* lineup, including Norman Reedus, who was probably one of the top draws at any convention at the time. There were so many people coming to that show, it was taking 3-4 hours just for fans to get in the door on Friday. It was just plain crazy. They had the dealer room stay open an hour longer to give the fans coming in late a chance to shop around before the day was over. By Saturday, HorrorHound's staff had come up with a better plan to get people in quicker. But it was still a crazy weekend.

When Sunday came around, there were rumblings about the weather. Snow was coming. Yeah, but how bad could it be? I mean, it's not like Pennsylvania, right? My fellow passengers included my wife Dawn, my son Nick, and Aaron Christensen. Once we got packed up and hit the road, it was probably about 6pm. Cincinnati is a couple of hours from Indianapolis, but the snow was coming down so hard and fast, that it took us more than five hours just to get north of Indy. The state of Indiana doesn't seem to feel the need to plow their roads while it is still snowing. We never saw one snow plow on the roads. Traffic was moving like a slow wagon train through the great west, except it was covered in snow. We were averaging about 10-15 miles an hour, but I was determined to get home, figuring if I just took it easy and moved ahead nice and slow, eventually we'd make it. But even moving that slow, there were times when the van would start to slide around and I'd have to quickly regain control. Finally, at one point, following an encounter with a particularly slippery patch of road, Aaron quietly asked the question that everyone else was already thinking, "Uh... is there a reason we HAVE to get back home tonight?"

Deep down, I knew they were right. All it would take is some idiot to come flying by and we could end up in a ditch. So we got off at an exit where a couple of hotels were supposed to be, only to find them either closed or filled. The next exit we hit didn't have any either, but there was a 24-hour oasis that had an Iron Skillet connected to the gas station. We went inside to grab some shelter and all-you-can-eat buffet action (much to Aaron's delight). While we were eating, we overheard a state trooper telling someone that the smartest thing he could do is stay off the road until the morning. So that is what we did. I'm not sure I got that much sleep in the van, but by the time the sun was out, the roads were a lot clearer and we were able to make our way back without any issue. I hated having to take another vacation day, but I realized that sometimes I need to listen to the concerns of my family and friends more than my own stubbornness.

The following year, back in Cincinnati, we had the official debut of *Hidden Horror*, Aaron's second book, this time with Kitley's Krypt serving as the publisher! About a dozen of the 100 horror fans who had written essays for the book were actually at that show. Aaron had gotten a separate table, specifically for the book, right next to mine, with several of the contributors on hand helping out. Each time we sold a copy, it would make the rounds to all the writers standing around there to sign it. It was so much fun. Not only because the book did really well, but also to be able to hang out with so many of these great people that contributed to the book. *Hidden Horror* went on to win the Rondo Award for Best Book of 2014 (the same year Kitley's Krypt won for Best Column), something I will never forget and always be proud of.

It was at this particular show where we met another Chicago-area fan that had made the trip. His name was Bryan "Kevin" Martinez. We were introduced to him by a mutual friend, Wisconsin filmmaker John Pata, the Saturday night of the show, and we started talking. And talking. By the time we decided we should head back to our hotel rooms, it was around 4am. There is something about having a conversation with someone when everything just clicks. It doesn't mean you agree on everything but you have some sort of connection. It was like that with Bryan. A short time later, he started his web series *The Giallo Room*, an awesome tribute to that wonderfully sleazy Italian subgenre. If you want to know anything about giallo, this is your guy.

For some reason, a lot of these convention stories seem to revolve around food and the restaurants that we gather at in the evening. There was the time that we were driving around in Cincinnati with J.D. Feigelson, screenwriter of the amazing 1981 TV-movie *Dark Night of the Scarecrow*, who was guiding us to this amazing BBQ place he just loved, telling us stories about how Frank Sinatra would go to this place every time he was in town. The closer we got, the more we were drooling. But as we drove into what we thought was the parking lot, we couldn't see any lights from a restaurant or anything like that. J.D. was questioning my driving skills and thinking we went to the wrong place. As it turns out, we were at the right establishment... except it had been closed and boarded up for quite some time! I never let J.D. off the hook on that one, and each time I see him at a show, I ask him if he knows of any good BBQ places!

Then there was the infamous El Dorado, a Mexican place in Indianapolis, right down the street from the hotel, so one would think it was the perfect place. There were probably about fifteen of us in our group one night as we piled into the place. Now, I'm not sure if they just had an off night, or maybe some of the staff had called off, but I have never had such bad service. We all ordered and had plenty of conversations going throughout our crowd, so maybe we really weren't paying attention to the time at first, but we eventually realized that it had been some time since we had ordered with no sign of our food in sight. Finally, our orders started coming out... sort of. Our friend Nicole, who is vegetarian, had ordered a bean burrito. She got a beef one and had to send it back. Then it came back as a chicken burrito. I had ordered a burrito dinner, which came with rice and beans. When I got my plate, I told my waitress I needed silverware. Twenty minutes later, after asking a second time, I finally got some. At one point, our waitress came back out to hear more complaints, and she was actually crying, even before we started to complain!

I think we were there probably close to two hours, waiting on different things, or for them to fix incorrect orders. Of course, alcohol was flowing pretty freely so some members of our group were getting a little loud. In fact, our buddy Bob was convinced that his fajita was made from raccoon. We finally asked for the check, but another twenty minutes or so went by and we hadn't seen our waitress. So we flagged down the manager to complain about the whole affair, stating that with all the mistakes, the waiting, and all the other issues, like the fact that we still hadn't seen our waitress or check, that there should be some sort of reduction on the bill. He agreed and said he'd get the bill for us. After waiting another thirty minutes without seeing anybody, let alone our bill, we all just got up and left.

Oddly enough, the next time we were in town for the next HorrorHound show, we were shocked to see the place was boarded up. So I guess it really wasn't just a single bad night of service.

Another place that we would usually go to on Friday nights in Indianapolis was the Texas Roadhouse. That is until one year when we were all set to go only to find out the place had literally burnt down to the ground! Were these restaurants cursed or were we? As we were trying to figure out another option, our buddy Ken Johnson, a resident of the fine city of Indianapolis, suggested a pizza place called Jockamos that was pretty close by, so off we went. While driving there, I asked Ken if it was a pretty good place. He replied nervously, "Uh... I've never been there before." I informed him that I hoped he realized that if this place sucked, he would be riding on top of the van back to the show afterwards. We all laughed... though I think Ken wasn't sure if I was really joking or not.

As it turns out, Jockamos isn't a good pizza place; it's an AMAZING pizza place. In fact, every single time we are in Indianapolis, we make sure we go there. They have a wide variety of pizzas, a great and friendly staff that is always willing and able to accommodate a large group of crazy horror fans at any time. After our first stop there, I think I might have scared the manager a bit when I told him that we kind of have a history of closing down restaurants here in town, so they may want to make sure their fire alarms were working.

Yes, believe it or not, food is a very important part of our convention experiences, as is the company. Getting together and sharing a meal with our convention family is one of the best parts of these weekends. As I've mentioned before, they really are like mini-family reunions and are always so much fun.

The Bash

Another show that I wish we had started doing years ago is Ron Adams' Monster Bash, held in Mars, Pennsylvania. This show started back in 1997, though I'm not sure when I actually first became aware of it. Once I had learned about it, there were more than a few times that I thought about getting a dealer table there, but it was around two hours past Cleveland where we do Cinema Wasteland, and I figured it was just too far away to be financially viable. By 2015, I was getting more and more disillusioned with some of the other shows we were doing, since they were more and more about the autographs and less about the movies, so I decided to get a table for the next show.

Much like Cinema Wasteland, Monster Bash is for serious fans. It's also about having fun. This isn't a huge show that brings in crowds by the thousands. But the ones that do come tend to be dedicated fans, usually of the older and classic monster films, and they know their horror history. There are so many activities to do at this show, with movie screenings from the early hours of the morning until the wee hours of the *next* morning. The dealer room is one of the best around and I'm always finding great stuff to bring home. That doesn't happen too often at other shows these days. Just wandering around the vendor's room, you can see so much cool stuff, even if you're not planning on buying it, because of the selection of older material, posters, toys, books, or whatever, it's almost like stepping back in time. For an older fan like myself, walking through a vendor room and not seeing every other table selling *Walking Dead* merch, or countless images of Freddy, Jason, and Michael Myers is a nice change of pace.

At the 2017 show, a dealer was set up across from me a little further down the aisle. I saw a bunch of wood plaques with different monster faces burnt into them, including a Naschy one, so it immediately got my attention. When I went over to get a closer look, there was also a mini-Naschy figure in a little shadow box. Okay, so the guy actually knew what the hell he was doing and had plenty of items from films that were not the same run-of-the-mill titles you're likely to see at a bigger show. Then I saw a little poster for Al Adamson's *Dracula vs. Frankenstein*. As I looked closer, there was also a replica made of the ring Dracula wore in the movie. The madman behind all of this was Rob Floyd, who actually sculpted the ring and made castings of it. My first thought was how crazy was this guy that he would make a replica of a ring from a film that not too many people knew about, let alone try to sell one! My second thought was how much did it cost, because I was going to have to get one for my collection! *Dracula vs. Frankenstein* is a train wreck, but damn if I don't just love it. Now, over the last couple of years, we have become friends with Rob and his lovely wife Phyllis and look forward to seeing them every year.

Another vendor that is usually set up is the uber-talented artist, Mark Maddox. I had become aware of Mark's work from all the magazine covers that he's done over the years. When I wrote the retrospective for John Carpenter's *The Thing* for *HorrorHound*, Mark did the cover. At our first Monster Bash show, when I went up to him and mentioned that I was the one who wrote the piece, he replied in a booming voice, "Hey! We're collaborators!" We became friends from then on! I have several prints of Mark's work hanging in the Krypt and they are always just amazing. Whether he is doing classic horror figures, Godzilla battles (which are just incredible), Dr. Who, or any number of Hammer characters, his portraits are just dead on.

The Bash doesn't have a big number of guests, and the ones they do have are geared more towards the older films, which is fine with me since they aren't the same ones that you'd see at just about every other show. If you would have asked me if I was ever going to have the chance to meet two members of the cast of *Robot Monster*, I would have thought you were nuts. Because of the Bash, I able to meet stars Claudia Barrett and Gregory Moffett and had a great conversation with both of them. I know at most shows, guests like these wouldn't draw too many fans, but that is very different at Monster Bash.

Another great thing about the Bash is that they usually have a few authors there as well. Not fiction, but non-fiction, such as the illustrious Tom Weaver and Gregory Mank. I think between the first couple of shows they were at,

I must have had them sign a couple dozen books, and they never charged me a dime. They seemed to be content with the fact that I'd already paid for the books and were just thrilled that I had enjoyed their work. Shame it can't be like that with more guests at other shows.

In all the years I've been going to shows, I've never had car trouble. No flat tires or breakdowns or anything like that. I would even brag about such luck. All of that ended when we were heading off to the Monster Bash in 2016. We had left for the show Thursday night, planning to stop once we got to the east side of Ohio for a few hours of sleep before finishing the rest of the trip on Friday morning. The "We" this time was my wife Dawn and Bryan Martinez. We hadn't gotten that far into Indiana, maybe close to South Bend, when we stopped for gas. Once we got back in the van and I started it, the engine light came on. We still had several hundred miles to go, and needless to say, my mood dropped pretty fast. Since none of us really know squat about cars, after a little Googling, we found that an engine light could mean a few different things. Possibly the battery is going bad, or the alternator is. If it is the alternator, the battery would die soon because it is not being charged. We were told to let the car run for 20-30 minutes, and if the lights start to dim, it is probably the alternator. So we sat there in the parking lot of the gas station and waited for about a half an hour, all the while thinking of different plans of attack. There were several service stations around us, but it was 10:30pm and none of them opened up before 7am. We were also near a rental car place at the airport which was still open; we could potentially rent a van, pack everything into the rental, and Dawn and Bryan could head off to the show, so they could at least make it there. Then I would stay and wait for the garage to open the next morning, hoping they could quickly fix the car that same day. But after sitting in the van for that time, the lights never dimmed and the engine light never came back on, so we decided to take the chance and try and drive straight through to the show without stopping for sleep.

I have to say it was a very nerve-wracking trip, with me probably looking at the dashboard waiting for that engine light to come back on more than paying attention to the actual road. At one point, Dawn unfastened her seat belt to move to get something and the car made that "ding" sound. My heart nearly stopped because I thought it was the engine light coming back on. Somehow, we were able to make it to the Bash hotel around 6am. Being that our reservations weren't technically until tomorrow, I checked with the front desk to see if we could get a room for an extra day. They were gracious enough to let us check in early and not charge us anything extra. Another good sign for a very shaky start. We all went up to the room and crashed.

Of course, knowing there was still a lot of work to do, and the show lets dealers into the room to set up at 8am, I set my alarm for then, which gave me about an hour and a half of sleep before I had to be back up. I moved the van to the dealer load-in area, unloaded, and brought everything into the vendor's room to our table. I then took the van to an AutoZone right by the hotel to have them check out the alternator. My fear was confirmed that it was going bad. How we made it all that way is beyond me but I'm forever thankful. I drove it to an auto shop about a mile away that had just opened. I explained my problem and that I was at a convention down the street for the weekend. They said they could get the van in and take a look at it and call me with an estimate. They gave me a ride back to the hotel, which was really nice. I then went back into the dealer room and set up our table. Once that was done, maybe close to 11am, I went back up to the hotel room to shower and wake up the two sleeping beauties that were still deep in la-la land.

A couple of hours later, I heard back from the auto shop. It was indeed the alternator, and the serpentine belt needed replacing as well. They could fix it that day and it would run me about $800. So much for having any spending money this weekend! But we actually did really well at the show, more than enough to pay for the repairs, so at the end of the whole weekend, I considered myself extremely lucky on how it all worked out. Yeah, sometimes it's hard to see that when you're in the thick of it. Lucky for me, I had two traveling companions that were much calmer than I was, which really helped. Not sure what I would have done had I been by myself. So thanks to Dawn and Bryan for keeping my head straight, and to karma for not totally putting the thumbscrews on!

Thankfully that has been the only car issue to date (knock on fiberglass), but we've been back to the Bash ever since our first show in 2015 and now it is one of our favorite stops on our Kryptic World Tour that we look forward to each and every year. Maybe one day we'll see you there.

Old School Collecting at Cinevent

A very different kind of show, one that seems to be stuck in a decades-ago time zone, is the Cinevent Classic Film Convention, held every year in Columbus, Ohio. Out of all the shows that I know about, I believe this is the oldest one around, going on fifty years now. One of the originators of the show has since passed away and now his son is continuing to carry the torch. It's not a horror-themed show but a movie memorabilia show, where you can find merchandise from about every genre out there: posters, stills, lobby cards, animation cels, etc. Cinevent still has that same feel as the shows that I first used to attend those many years ago.

Somewhere in the mid-'90s, my buddy Jon Stone told me about this show, saying that he had set up there the year before and had a good time.

So I decided I'd get a table at the next show and do it with him. At the time, I was selling pre-recorded VHS tapes, when you could only get $5 or $6 a title. Not like now with some of these crazy VHS collectors out there. Man, if I'd only saved those for about a decade, I could have retired!

One strange thing about this show is that not only does it go from Thursday to Sunday, but the hours are from 9am to 11pm each day! I asked the promoter if you're actually expected to stay at your table the whole time and what were you supposed to do for lunch and dinner. He said you just cover your table up and leave. Huh? I never understood that since if someone was walking around the dealer room looking to spend money and comes to your table that is covered up, he might just go to the next table and find something else to buy. So we struggled to stay most of the day, but ended up leaving for the night around 9pm, so starved that at the very first restaurant that we could find open, we devoured our food as soon as it hit the table.

This dealer room was jam-packed with dealers too! Normally, you have about four feet behind your table, to store your other merchandise, or just to have room to move around. But here, the distance between your table and the guy behind you was about 3 feet total! Needless to say, it was a little cramped in there.

We did okay and loved digging through the different vendor tables, looking at lobby cards, posters, stills and other good old-fashioned movie memorabilia. But at the end of the long weekend, I decided it was just a bit too much to return the next year. I think Jon did it for a couple more years, and then stopped. Granted, he was coming from Dayton, so it was a lot closer for him.

Well, over a decade later, I decided to give it another try. As with Monster Bash, I wanted to try a show that was different than the same old over-priced autograph shows. An old movie memorabilia show, like the ones I used to go to years before being a dealer, sounded like fun or at least a nice change of pace. I also hoped that since it was an older crowd, maybe some of them would be book buyers!

In 2016, Dawn and I, in our van loaded with goodies, headed off to Columbus. Because of work, I couldn't get Thursday off so we were going to miss the first day, which is when set-up was, with the dealer room opening around 1pm. But Michael, the guy in charge, was nice enough to come down early Friday morning and let us bring our stuff in so we could set up before the show opened. It was a pretty big dealer room so we were very hopeful the weekend would go well as we got ready for the show.

When the show opened, instead of the onslaught of eager buyers piling in, there more like a small handful wandering in. I immediately wondered if this whole thing was a mistake. People slowly crept in throughout the day, but I don't think there were ever more than thirty or forty people in the room at any given time. I could be wrong since I've always been terrible at counting crowds, but due to the long hours, it really did make the day drag at times. There could easily be two or three hours between sales.

The funny thing was, by the end of the weekend, we still ended up having a good time. We did pretty decent sales-wise and I found a few more things for my collection. I think what was most enjoyable was looking through all the merch at the other tables, digging through piles and piles of posters and stills, hoping to find that little piece of gold. It was also fun talking to the variety of people that came up to our table.

While this wasn't a horror show, there were a lot of posters and memorabilia from the classic age of the genre and the prices showed it too. When you see a single lobby card go for $650, it quickly makes you realize you are not at that level of collector. It is cool to see these original pieces and how much they go for. We always manage to find a few items to add to our own collection while we're there. Sure, some things you have to dig for, but that is part of the fun.

Just like any other show that we travel to, we are always on the lookout for interesting places to eat. Hitting chain restaurants is something that we really try to avoid. Even though we'd already been there a couple of times, we discovered a hot dog place in 2018 that was very close by that made that weekend even better. Now, I really don't care what is actually in a hot dog. I know they're not good for me, but I still love them. So when you discover a place that takes this form of cuisine to a whole new level, you have to give them credit. This place is called Dirty Frank's Hot Dog Palace. You can buy T-shirts with different sayings like, "Stuffing Wieners in Faces Since 2009," or "Ask Me About My Wiener." Looking at their menu will blow your mind. They have over 40 different kinds of styles for the dogs, with strange and unusual combinations. You can get "Satanically Spicy Giardiniera," cabbage & carrot mustard slaw, baked beans, Sriracha slaw, sauerkraut, bacon-wrapped dogs, spicy corn relish, and so much more. I'm sure everyone can find something that will satisfy their hot dog cravings here. We ended up there twice over the weekend, each of us ordering four different hot dogs each time, then splitting them with each other. So by the time we were done, we had tried 16 of their different items. Not to mention some of their appetizers like the spicy cauliflower! The best part is that they are open until 1:45am every single day! So no matter what time we get out of the show, they are going to be open! Needless to say, that won't be the last time we visit Dirty Franks.

Even though Cinevent tends to be a bit slow at times, it is still a lot of fun overall. One of those reasons for that is the people. The folks coming through the door are die-hard movie fans, some in their 80s, making their way to this movie memorabilia Mecca. It doesn't matter if they're not horror fans, it's just so cool to see them loving what they do as much as they do. I've had great conversations with people here and just love hearing the same enthusiasm coming from them. I do feel that having a deep passion for something (like movies) can keep your mind active and alive. And they said that watching TV is bad for you!

Like Monster Bash, this has become a regular stop on our Kryptic World Tour.

The Wasteland

There are horror conventions… and then there is Cinema Wasteland. As I mentioned earlier, Ken and Pam Kish have been staples at horror conventions as long as I can remember going to them, especially in the Midwest and East Coast shows. They were always there. After our little debacle getting snowed in on our way home from the Fulci/Fango show, I started to get to know Ken, the mastermind behind Video Wasteland. Simply put, this man knew his stuff. There weren't too many titles from the drive-in era that you could whip out that Ken didn't just know about, but knew well. For years, usually preceded by him bitching about whatever one we were at, usually the Fangoria conventions, he would always tell us, "One day I'm going to put on my own show!" We'd all laugh until the next time we'd see him, where we'd get the same story again. This seemed to go on for a few years. The thing is most of the complaints that Ken had about these shows were dead-on. Being a vendor and a fan himself, he had seen enough mistakes and enough poorly run shows that he figured he knew what would be the best way to make a show worthwhile for both the people paying as attendees as well as ones paying to be vendors.

Now let's be honest here. Ken is not one to hold back his thoughts on the world of movie conventions, celebrities, or life in general. Some of those thoughts are a little exaggerated, but for the most part, he's usually correct and that's part of his charm.

Then it happened. At the Wizard World show in the fall of 1999, after we had gotten our own booth set up, we were walking about the vendor area and came up to Ken's table, where he promptly held out a flyer. It was for his show, Cinema Wasteland, which was going to be held the following year. Holy Shit! He really was going to put on his own show!

Since their first convention in September of 2000, Cinema Wasteland has been going strong, always in the very same hotel in Strongsville, OH, which is some kind of achievement. I can't name another show that has done that. Sure, some cons get bigger and need to move to a bigger venue. By keeping his show small and at the same place, Ken has never lost the feel or the meaning behind it. And that meaning was simple: Creating a weekend of fun for people coming through the door, both customers and vendors alike. In all my years of going to shows, if there was ever a convention that I will continue to attend if I ever stopped being a dealer, it would be this one. There is always so much stuff going on, including movies playing in two different rooms pretty much non-stop from 10am to the early morning hours.

At the very first Wasteland, we were set up right beside cult filmmaker Ted V. Mikels, creator of such classic films as *The Astro-Zombies* and *The Corpse Grinders*. I say "creator" because Mikels would usually be the director, writer, editor, producer, sometimes actor, and whatever else needed to be done to get his films made. While his films may not be considered "high quality," they are still damn entertaining. Meeting Mikels for the first time, seeing and hearing how he interacted with fans, standing up each time someone came to his table to shake their hands, showed me that he was a hell of a nice guy and very appreciative of his fans.

Set up right across from us was a woman selling T-shirts, Jill Van Voorst, and her business was called Lix. I've known Jill now for close to 20 years. We see her at just about every show and I can honestly say that I've never met anyone like her. In all of that time, I've never known someone that is always so happy and chipper, no matter how little sleep she may have gotten at the show! She has gone from selling t-shirts that she has designed featuring amazing artwork (for films that you wouldn't normally see on shirts) to even more creative items like hoodies and work shirts, many of which I still own and wear. When she partnered with Gregg Olheiser (both in business and in life), this pair became an unstoppable force for good at the shows. Always having delicious cookies to pass out, not to mention plenty of great conversations over the years, these two are some of the best people on the planet, which you can tell right away by their loyal following of fans and customers. If you've been to a horror convention in the States over the last twenty years, most likely Jill and Gregg were there. They definitely are two that I am lucky and honored to include in my convention family.

Over the years, I've been able to meet some incredible legends in the genre, many of which I know I never would have seen at other shows because they just aren't big names. People like Gary Kent, Bud Cardos, Greydon Clark, and Charles B. Griffth, some of whom I've had the opportunity to actually interview! Reb Brown was a guest at one of the shows, and my son Nick was a huge fan, especially of the cheap Italian action pictures Brown made like 1983's *Yor: Hunter from the Future*. So seeing Nick's face light up with excitement as he went up to meet Reb, who couldn't have been a nicer guy, was so much fun. Having seen so many celebrities over the years, I've kind of lost some of that excitement, so being able to relive that feeling with Nick at that moment was a wonderful reminder.

In 2004, at their first Wasteland Spring show, they had a *Texas Chain Saw* reunion, with guests from the first three films, including most of the remaining cast members from the 1974 original. To be able to hear these actors discuss what it was like making this seminal shocker back in the day made for a truly memorable show.

Two of my all-time favorite films are Robert Wise's *The Haunting* and Lucio Fulci's *Zombie*, both starring Richard Johnson. When Ken announced that for the April show in 2010, they were going to have a *Zombie* reunion with Ian McCulloch, Al Cliver, Ottaviano Dell'Acqua (who played the zombie on the poster art), AND Richard Johnson, I was more than a little excited. Not only was I going to see a cast reunion of one of my favorite flicks, but getting to meet Johnson was just icing on the cake! It just boggles the mind when you look back at those times when you're watching one of your favorite films, seeing an actor on screen over and over again throughout the years, only to later be able to meet them, shake their hand, and even get a photo with them. I can't thank Ken enough for that.

Ken set out to make a show like no other, and he did, and continues to do so. He keeps threatening to stop doing them, before they start to become stale, retreading the same old things. I hope this never happens because Wasteland really is "a show like no other" and one of my favorite times twice a year.

A Kiss from Ingrid

In June of 2002, there was a small movie fest called the Chicago Fantastic Film Festival which was going to be held at the Gateway Theatre, originally built in 1930 and located in the Polish part of Chicago. For this event, they had a few guests scheduled to attend, such as Stuart Gordon, Joanna Cassidy, Billy Gray, Basil Gogos, and Ingrid Pitt. It had been eight years since I had last seen Ms. Pitt at my first Fanex show. Since that time, while I still loved her films, I had gotten a little tired of just how full of herself she seemed to be during interviews and appearances, always bragging how gorgeous she was back then. Plus, I think I was starting to show the first signs of GOMS (Grumpy Old Man Syndrome). Since this was being held in a theater, they were also going to be screening several films throughout the weekend, including *The Day the Earth Stood Still* and *Who Framed Roger Rabbit*.

There were two titles that I was most excited about, the first being Gordon's latest effort, *Dagon*. I've always loved anything that Gordon has done, especially when his projects had any connection with Lovecraft. When he got up to do the intro, he thanked the promoters. As a boy, he had come to this very same theater and watched movies on the same screen where now one of his own pictures was going to be shown. So it was a special moment for him, and I'm glad I could be there to see it as well. I really enjoyed the film and still think it is one of Gordon's best. Before the screening, he was sitting out in the lobby at a table, signing free *Dagon* mini-posters. For free. Unfortunately, he was the only one signing for free.

The other title that I was excited to see was a reportedly uncut version of 1970's *The Vampire Lovers*, from a 35mm print. This was years before an uncut version was available in any format, so getting to see one of my favorites from Hammer Studios, with extra gore and more of Ms. Pitt's naughty bits, was a pretty big deal for me.

Because the dealer tables were more than reasonable, and I figured I was going to be there anyway, my buddy Jon Stone and I decided to get a couple of tables and see how the event went. Since they had a decent guest list, we figured it definitely would be worth it. The dealer's area was a little room off to the side of the lobby with only maybe six or seven dealers total, which was all that could fit. Now, at first that made me kind of worried, but then sometimes, with a good crowd, the smaller number of dealers means the better percentage you have getting some sales.

At that time, I was still mainly selling pre-recorded VHS tapes (years before the big collecting boom) and DVDs were the new thing. In fact, the VHS tapes were hard to give away, since everybody wanted their movies on this fancy new format. But since they had some decent guests and some great movies playing, I was expecting a decent size crowd for the weekend. Not thousands, but hopefully at least several hundred to fill out the place and keep things busy. Key word here was "hopefully."

Not sure where the ball was dropped, but I think it was whoever was in charge of advertising. Or maybe they didn't have anybody in charge because there certainly didn't seem to have been ANY advertising whatsoever. I knew several Chicago area friends that didn't even know this was going on. I have no clue just how many people came through those doors that weekend, but if I would have to make a guess, it was way less than a hundred. I've been at some shows where the turnout can be this bad, but sometimes something happens to make it more than worth it. This just happened to be one of those shows.

Since Ms. Pitt was going to be there, I had brought along my copy of her autobiography to possibly get it signed, depending on how much she was charging. I had already gotten her autograph for free at Fanex, so I really didn't need another one, but the signed book would be nice for the library. On Friday, after we had gotten our tables set up but before we opened to the public, Ms. Pitt came into the little dealer room, looking at the tables and the different items being sold. As she came over to my table, she noticed some Hammer VHS tapes there and asked if I had "this new DVD that had come out that just featured Hammer trailers." The disc she was referring to had recently been released by All Day Entertainment and was a collection of trailers from different Hammer films. I explained to her that I had the DVD in question in my collection at home, but I didn't have a copy with me for sale.

"Could you bring it tomorrow for me?" she asked excitedly.

"Uh... yeah... I guess I could," I stammered. I mean, this was Ingrid Pitt. How could I refuse?

Now here's my dilemma. If I brought the disc to her and she expected for me to just give it to her, because of who she was, it would have really irritated me. I hate it when it feels like they (celebrities) think they are so much more important than us "regular" fans. But that night, once I got home, I grabbed the DVD and put it in my briefcase to take back to the show the next day. I wasn't sure what I was going to do just yet. I could charge her a price equal to what I had paid for the disc, or maybe a little more, since I wasn't sure if I could even get another copy. Fandom or finances. What should I do?

By the time the next morning arrived and we were uncovering our tables getting ready for the Saturday crowd, I looked up just in time to see Ingrid come into the dealer room and make a beeline straight to my table.

"Did you bring it?" she asks anxiously.

I give her a positive nod as I reach behind my table and hand it to her. In my heart, I knew there was no way I was *not* going to just give it her. I mean, it was Ingrid Pitt, for god's sake! Just when I expected to be disappointed by her response, she looked up and asked, "How much is it?"

That was all I needed to hear. The fact that she wasn't just expecting it to be a gift made me feel a thousand times better. I shook my head and told her, "No charge. It's yours."

Before I could get anything else out, she lunged forward and wrapped her arms around me giving a huge bear hug, saying, "Thank you so much!" and then planting a huge wet kiss on my cheek.

I think I started to go into shock at that point. A little more than a decade or so ago, I was entranced by this woman's performance (among other things) in *The Vampire Lovers*, drooling over her body and that beautiful face and alluring eyes. And here I am, years later, close to being mauled by her. I was able to get a few words out, thanking her for all the hours of entertainment she had given me, and that was payment enough. I asked if she would sign my copy of her book, which she gladly did. She then told me to make sure I stopped by her table to get a photo or two that she would also sign for me. Then she walked back out of the dealer room to get to her table before the show opened for the public.

I looked over at Stone, who for some reason had a huge smile on his face. I'm sure he could see the same smile on my face and with the puzzled look in my eyes, as if to say, "Did that really just happen?" But the smile on his face also could have been because I still had lipstick on my face, which he never bothered to tell me about. So for the next couple of hours, I was working my table with Ingrid's lip prints on my cheek!

Later on, every time I walked past her table, Ingrid would call out my name, waving to me. Even when she was posing for some photos alongside Joanna Cassidy and I was standing there getting some photos, she looked right at me, called my name out again and waved. I can't say how much that weekend meant for me. The negative thoughts that had been building up around her for some silly reason were completely gone and I fell in love with her all over again. Her generosity and warmth towards her fans was not only genuine, but something she really seemed to enjoy.

That evening after the dealer room closed, we got to watch the uncut version of *The Vampire Lovers* on the Gateway's huge movie screen, another highly memorable screening for me. Not only was it one of my favorite titles I was getting to see uncut from a 35mm film print, but that it was introduced by Carmilla herself, the one and only Ingrid Pitt. What more could a Hammer horror fan ask for in this life?

After the movie was over, Stone and I walked down the street a bit and found a little Polish restaurant to have dinner in. I think we were the only people English speaking there, but had some amazing sauerkraut (which I normally hate), some potato pancakes, and, of course, some sausages. Such great food to cap off an incredible experience I will never forget. Especially now that I've written it down here, I can go back and remind myself once the mind starts to go!

Bill Rebane Film Festival

Back in the early spring of 2005, I was sitting at my computer, browsing different horror websites, trying to keep up what's going on in the world of horror when I came across a news posting about an upcoming film fest that made my jaw drop. On May 7th & 8th, there was going to be a Bill Rebane Film Festival, held in Madison, Wisconsin, and Rebane was going to be in attendance!

Okay, so let's back up a bit here and give you some background if you're not sure who I'm talking about. Bill Rebane is the illustrious director of 1975's *The Giant Spider Invasion*, a favorite of *Mystery Science Theater 3000*. He also directed several other features including *Invaders from Inner Earth* (1974), *Rana: The Legend of Shadow Lake* (1981), *Demons of Ludlow* (1983), and even a slasher movie starring Tiny Tim as a clown in *Blood Harvest* (1987). Most of these films were shot in and around his home in Wisconsin, where he had built his own movie studio in the late '60s near Gleason, which he called The Shooting Ranch. There, besides all of these feature films, he created industrial films, films for corporations, and a ton of commercials.

Besides *Giant Spider*, which did fairly good business, the rest of these titles didn't fare too well at the box office. It might have been because the quality of these films was, shall we say, less than stellar? Now, don't get me wrong. I actually am a huge fan of most of Rebane's work and enjoy the hell out of his pictures. Most of them are all great candidates for any Turkey Day Marathon. (Though, just a warning, trying to watch *Inner Earth* is like watching paint dry... in slow motion.) Another one of his more famous Turkey titles is *Monster A Go-Go*, which was eventually released in 1965. It had started back in 1961 as *Terror at Halfday*, but the production eventually ran out of money. H.G. Lewis, another independent filmmaker, was looking for a second feature to run with one of his own and, as Lewis explains, "Rebane had exposed an incredible amount of film on this thing – almost 80,000 feet. That is ten times the amount of raw stock we bought when we made *Lucky Pierre* (1961). I felt that, with 80,000 feet of film to work with, there had to be a movie in there somewhere. I was wrong." Lewis added some footage, came up with a narration over some of the stock, and released it under the *Monster A Go-Go* title. The rest is cinematic history!

Rebane is a unique character. He is one of those guys that worked his ass off making these features and really does think they were, and still are, quality productions. While I'm not sure we agree on the reason that they are entertaining, I give him a hell of a lot of credit for doing what he did all those years, all in Wisconsin. In 1979 and 2002, he even ran for Governor!

My good friend Eric Ott is a huge fan of Rebane and his work, even owning 16mm prints of a couple of his films that he would proudly run at the Cinema Wasteland conventions. So when I found out about this upcoming film fest, I immediately called him.

"Eric... what are you doing May 7th?" I said on the phone. "Wait. Let me correct that. Whatever you might have planned for that day, cancel it, because we're going to Madison."

"What are you talking about?" he quickly answered back. "What the hell is going on in Madison?"

"A Bill Rebane Film Festival. And he's going to be here."

"Oh my god! Are you serious?"

So, of course, the trip was a done deal. There was no way I was going to miss this. Plus, I had a poster from *Giant Spider*, as well as a still from the film, that I would love to have signed. We found out that Kevin Murphy and Mike Nelson from *MST3K* were also going to be there hosting the event.

Another good friend, Dave Kosanke, lived in Wisconsin and we would be going close by him on our way to Madison. Dave has been putting out his fanzine *Liquid Cheese* since 1993. It's very old school, packed full of thoughts, facts, and opinions about horror, cult and exploitation flicks, and anything else Dave wants to rant and ramble on about. That's the beauty of what he's doing. It was all coming from him and his passion. He wasn't doing it for fame and fortune, but because of his love of it all. Plus the fact that Dave has pretty much an encyclopedic knowledge of the horror genre, whipping out trivia and facts that amaze even me. Dave started coming to these shows as a fan and eventually started setting up there as well. We became great friends over the years, traveling to many Cinema Wasteland shows together. So I reached out to him to see if he'd be interested in going to see Rebane as well. Of course, he jumped at the chance!

This was a two-day event and was being held at the beautiful Orpheum Theatre. This place was huge! It could seat about 1700 people, had two balconies, and even had a restaurant inside the lobby! It is one of those old theaters that you don't see around as much these days, which is a real shame. These palaces are just glorious to walk through and so much more of an experience than one of these modern-day, "get them in, get them out" multiplexes. As much as I really wanted to make it to both days of the festival, we just weren't sure if we'd be able to. We'd have to figure out where to stay overnight and all that fun stuff. But if we made it through the first day, that just might be enough. We rolled up into Madison and found the theater, early enough to make sure we'd be able to get in, hoping there wasn't too big of a line. Instead of having to fight our way through a massive crowd of fans converging on the theater… we walked right up and bought our tickets and went inside. Granted, we still had some time before the event started, so maybe the rest of the Rebane fans were just running late?

To this day, Eric still claims attendance was good. At best, there were probably no more than 50, maybe 75 people. Total. In this ENORMOUS theater. The saddest part was that most of them were there to meet Murphy and Nelson, not Rebane. As we walked into the theater lobby, there were a couple of tables set up selling different Rebane and *MST3K* merchandise. Inside the theater, in front of the stage, Nelson, Murphy, and Rebane were sitting at a couple of tables, signing items for the few people that were there. Again, most of the people in line were for the *MST3K* guys. We quickly went over to Rebane and started busting out our posters and stuff for him to sign. He just loved seeing this stuff and gladly signed whatever we put in front of him. For free, of course.

Once that was done, we settled in our seats and waited for the films to start. The first one, *Wisconsin Movie Scrapbook*, was a documentary on Rebane and his work, which seemed a bit long and even a little self-indulgent. But it did at least give a good insight into Rebane, his passions, and how he has worked in the film industry for all of these years. One of the best parts of the documentary was that it featured a clip from a TV pilot that he did that for some reason never got picked up. It was called *Grin and Bear It*, and was about a detective named Fritz Schlitz, who kind of looked like Charles Bronson, and his partner who was... Yep. A bear. Not a real bear, but a guy in a bear suit that was supposed to be a real bear. That talked. And dressed in a suit. It really has to be seen to be believed. You might still be able to find it on Youtube. It only had a few minutes of the show, but wow. Just wow. For some reason, this documentary has never gotten an actual release, and doesn't even show up on Rebane's IMDb page.

The Giant Spider Invasion showed next and no matter how many times I watch it, it is still a fun watch. It looked like it was being projected from a DVD, so the quality was a bit fuzzy once it hit the giant screen, but it was still great getting the opportunity to see a film like this in this atmosphere. If you haven't experienced any of Rebane's work, *Giant Spider* would be your best place to start.

The last feature of the day was called *Nightmare*, which is actually the 1987 film *Blood Harvest*, now re-titled and promoted as a "director's cut." I had heard rumors that this was due to a legal issue over who actually owned the rights to *Blood Harvest*, but I'm not really sure. The important thing is for you to find a copy and give it a watch. It is more of a modern-day slasher flick, but is mostly known for its star being the utterly bizarre Tiny Tim. He appears as an ex-clown, in clown-face makeup for pretty much the whole movie, and is, well... he's Tiny Tim. So to say it is a very strange performance would imply that he's acting.

In between each of the features, there were little Q&A sessions with Rebane, as well as with some actors that appeared in some of the films, such as Paul Bentzen from *Giant Spider*, Jim Iaquinta from *Rana*, and Lori Minnetti from *Nightmare*. They all had plenty of great stories of working with Rebane, as well as working on these low-budget features, especially Minnetti who had some creepy stories of working with Tiny Tim.

We decided to call it a day and made our way home. As much as we would have like to see the films they were screening on Saturday, including *Rana*, it would be just too much Rebane for one weekend! It still amazes me that this event was actually put on and there were some fans like us crazy enough to show up for it. It really was great to be able to meet Rebane and learn more about his film career. While it doesn't make his films any better, it does give one a little more appreciation for what he has done. And at the end of the day, isn't that what is important?

Driving Freddy Krueger

Fangoria had been putting on their Weekend of Horrors conventions in Chicago for a couple of years when, in 2008, I was given the opportunity of the lifetime. Guests at this show included Robert Englund and a cast reunion of the original *Friday the 13th*, including Betsy Palmer, Adrienne King, Ari Lehman, and composer Harry Manfredini. I was setting up again as a vendor, with Aaron Christensen helping out as he had for the past two shows. Now, as part of Fango's weekend activities, they were screening *Friday the 13th* that Friday night at the Music Box Theatre with a Q&A featuring the cast following the film. A mutual friend approached Aaron and me, asking if we would be willing to drive the guests to and from the theater for the event. How could we refuse? We were told to get in contact with Adam Rockoff at some point on Friday to sort out the details. Now, being a crazy book collector, I knew Rockoff had written *Going to Pieces: The Rise and Fall of the Slasher Film, 1978-1986* which was later made into a documentary under the same name. The problem was that we really had no idea who he was or what he looked like.

During the show that night, a guy came up to our table and started looking over the reference books we were selling. We started talking, discussing different books and movies. I introduce myself and he says, "I'm Adam Rockoff." I guess we didn't have to worry about finding him any longer! Since that show, we've become great friends with Adam, meeting up with him at many events in the Chicago area. In 2015, Adam wrote his second book, *The Horror of It All*, where he wrote about growing up with horror movies. We have had some pretty heated arguments on different films, such as Jorge Grau's 1974 classic *Let Sleeping Corpses Lie*, but I won't hold that against him.

So, later that night, I was sitting in my van in front of the hotel with Mrs. Voorhees herself, Betsy Palmer, sitting next to me in the passenger seat. Adrienne King and Harry Manfredini were also in the van, but Aaron had to go find Lehman, who was apparently the diva. Go figure. While we were waiting though, I did get to hear some interesting stories about him from Ms. Palmer. Once Aaron showed up with Lehman in tow, we drove everyone out to the theater, dropped them off, found parking, and got into the theater in time for the Q&A. There were some great stories told that evening, many at the expense of Lehman, which made it even funnier. Then we piled everyone back into the van and made it back safe and sound to the hotel.

The next night, they were doing the same thing, except they were going to be screening two of Wes Craven's films, *A Nightmare on Elm Street* and *Swamp Thing*. So that meant that Freddy Krueger himself, Robert Englund, would be sitting in my van, along with actor Ray Wise. Surreal doesn't even begin to explain this experience. Here I am, driving into Chicago on a busy

Saturday night, with Robert Englund sitting right across from me in the passenger seat, pretty much talking non-stop the whole trip. I was amazed at the knowledge this man has about his fellow actors. He watches a ton of movies, knows who's been recently nominated for Oscars, and goes back and not only watches the nominated films, but anything that actor/actress has ever been in! You could tell how much Englund loves the craft of acting, not just on screen but on the stage as well, telling us stories of seeing different actors in live theater performances. And here I am driving, trying not to look over and stare at him, thinking that I don't want to be the guy who gets in a car accident and kills Freddy Krueger!

Once again, we made it to the theater without any issues. Director Gary Sherman, who had worked with Englund on his 1981 film *Dead & Buried*, was there running the Q&A. It was great to see these two guys together reminiscing about the movies.

The drive back was just like the way out there, with Englund talking the whole way. I successfully made it back without killing anyone, so I have to say that was a pretty big win on my part. It really was such a thrill to hear the passion from Englund about his fellow tradesmen. He really knows what he's talking about and I will always be impressed by that.

The Bowling Show

Now a show doesn't have to be huge or even crowded to be a good show. There was a little collector's show that we used to set up at in West Allis, Wisconsin, at a bowling alley called the Burham Bowl. The bowling alley only had maybe ten or fifteen lanes, and a full bar (I mean, this IS Wisconsin), but also had a side room or banquet hall to the side of the bowling alley. We had a blast every time we were there for one of these shows. Now, it's probably been over ten years since I've set up at this one, but back when we did, the vendor tables were around $35 each. Most regular cons at the time, tables would run you anywhere from $200 to $300 or higher per table, so it was very cheap to do. Granted, it was about a two-hour drive, but I would pick up my buddy Eric Ott, who lived on the Illinois/Wisconsin border, and we'd throw his stuff in my van and make our way up to the show.

I think on average they would get maybe 50 people through the door. I'd always sell more than enough to cover the table and our expenses, not that there was that much. The best part of this show, what kept us coming back, were the other dealers and what they were selling, and most importantly, the prices they had! I think the average age of these dealers was maybe the upper 60s with some even into their 70s. I don't think they knew sometimes the value of what they were selling. I would be amazed at some of the items for sale and even more so at the prices. Here are some examples of the treasures that I would find there over the years: novelizations of the two *Dr. Phibes* movies ($5 for both), a German one-sheet for Joe D'Amato's *Le notti erotiche dei morti viventi*, known here in the States as *Erotic Nights of the Living Dead*, ($10), an American one-sheet of Bill Rebane's *Giant Spider Invasion* ($10), and a stack of the wax barf bag promo items from one of the re-releases of 1970's *Mark of the Devil* ($.25 each). I think I still have a few of those barf bags around here somewhere....

These shows were always a lot of fun, from the great finds, to the interesting characters that came there to shop. Yeah, it was a bit of a drive, but when you can find some great deals, chat with your friends and different customers, it always made the trip worthwhile.

Movie Marathons

The Music Box Theatre, located on Chicago's north side, is a theater that I have been going to for close to 25 years. I'm not exactly sure when my first trip there was, but it was probably for one of the endless midnight screenings that they hold every weekend. The Music Box first opened back in 1929 and has gone through quite a few changes over the years, even screening adult films at one point. A relatively small theater by "classic movie palace" standards, with only 800 seats in the big theatre and 70 in the smaller one, it still has the look and feel of one of those grand old theaters from an age gone by. I look on in wonder every single time I walk into the beautiful lobby and am so thankful that these kinds of theaters still exist in today's multiplex market.

In my early days, I would make trips out there on the weekend to see midnight screenings of films like Fulci's *The Beyond* (way before the Grindhouse release), Shinya Tsukamoto's bizarre *Tetsuo: The Iron Man*, Toshiharu Ikeda's *Evil Dead Trap*, a variety of Universal and other black-and-white classics, and so many more amazing cinematic experiences. Movies are always better on the big screen, a grand experience, with visuals and sound bursting into your consciousness. Yes... even something like *Friday the 13th: The Final Chapter*. Trust me.

In October of 2005, the Music Box held their first 24-hour horror movie marathon, called The Music Box Massacre. I had always loved seeing newspaper ads for all-night horror marathons in the '60s and '70s, usually held at drive-in theaters, when I was a kid. But getting to watch horror movies for a whole 24 hours straight?!?!? Pure heaven, or insanity, or both. Of course, I was going to be there. My buddy Jon Stone was making the trip all the way from Dayton, Ohio, for the event as well!

Now before we get to the actual event, let us give some thought to why movie fans, even the most die-hard fanatics, would put themselves through this kind of 24-hour ordeal. Remember, old-fashioned theater seats were never designed to be parked in for more than two hours at best. Sure, you can get up and stretch, walk around a bit, and even take a break here and there. But it is still a very long time to be sitting there. It is not for the weak of mind, body, or spirit. Your spine becomes a crooked piece of spaghetti and your mind is the pasta sauce! Even the biggest horror fans might have trouble putting themselves through this kind of an endurance test. And that is exactly what it is... a test.

So why do fans line up every year to put themselves through it? Sheer blind dedication to the genre. At least, that is my guess. A lot of the titles screened at these marathons may never have been seen by fans on the big screen. Now they have the chance to change that, not to mention getting to see some classic titles that they had missed so far in their path as a horror fan. It also shows their dedication to support these types of events. If nobody showed up, the theater would stop doing them. It also is a place to wear your horror fandom proudly. Just like at a horror convention, you can be at this theater and stand proud with your fellow horror brethren. Strike up a conversation with a total stranger, and know you have that same connection. This is what makes the horror community so great and makes me so proud to be part of.

Back to this first marathon. The beauty of this one was the lineup of films they were screening. They started off with the silent version of *Nosferatu* (1922) with a live organ accompaniment. How freaking cool is that? Later on in the program, they screened *Creature from the Black Lagoon* (1954), which I still feel is one of the best 3-D movies ever made, projected in its original 3-D format (complete with the cardboard glasses). As the marathon continued, they screened other classics like George Romero's *The Crazies* (1973), Nacho Cerdà's 1994 short film *Aftermath* (a brutally realistic tale of necrophilia), as well as Cronenberg's *Scanners* (1981), *Return of the Living Dead* (1985), *Demons* (1985), H.G. Lewis' *Two Thousand Maniacs* (1964), *The Howling* (1981), and *Near Dark* (1987). They also screened Gary Sherman's 1972 feature debut, *Death Line* (aka *Raw Meat*, a title that he hates!), with Mr. Sherman there to introduce the film and do a Q&A afterwards. This was the first of many times I would meet Mr. Sherman at this theater over the years, and it has always been a pleasure chatting with this underrated talent. At one of these events, I gave him a large 40x60 foreign poster for his 1981 film *Dead & Buried*, which he later got refurbished and framed (jokingly blaming me for the expenses) and hanging it in a place of honor in his office.

The first Massacre also had a couple of dealers set up in the lobby, which made the marathon more like an event than just a bunch of movies, which was very cool. One of the vendors was our good friend Jill from Lix, selling her usual awesome t-shirts and merchandise. It was nice to be able to go out and chat with her and her helper Andrew in between the movies, trying to stay awake and keep blood flowing in our legs.

We were having a blast at the show and loving all the different films being screened. Then something happened, around 2am, when they were screening Lamberto Bava's *Demons*, which I just love. The film started, with the famous music from Claudio Simonetti pounding from the speakers during the opening credits. Then, for some reason, it jumped right to the end credits! What the hell? I started to look around at the audience to see if anybody else noticed this, but nobody was making a sound other than a few cheers. Then it hit me. I had fallen asleep just as the movie started, slept through the entire thing, and then came out of my little coma when the ending credits music started. I had no clue that I had even passed out! I think that was a sign of just how tired I was. But we still had about 8 hours or so to go!

I headed out into the lobby to try and wake up and to find Mr. Stone, who I seemed to have lost by then. When I did find him, we stayed out in the lobby for a while, chatting with Jill, popping back in the theater every now and then to catch a peek at *Two Thousand Maniacs*, or going outside to let the cold Chicago night air help wake us up. As we were talking outside, the sun was just starting to come up. As much as we both wanted to watch the last few films, I figured that I was awake enough to make the 45-minute drive home now. But if I was to stay any longer, it would definitely be tough. Stone felt the same way. So as much as we hated leaving, we said our goodbyes to Jill and staggered out of the theater into the brisk Chicago morning, with the sun blazing down in our eyes, surely a reprimand for staying awake as long as we did!

Every time I've had to drive home from one of these marathons, it's been brutal. Getting out of the city is easy. But once I get out on I-88 which takes me back to Aurora, it is all just straight highway, plain with little to no scenery to speak of, which has a tendency to lull me to sleep. Thankfully, I've never fallen asleep yet on the way home, but have come close a couple of times. It is usually at this time when I declare that I'm too old for this shit and I'm never doing it again. At least until next year comes around.

I was there once again for the second Massacre. But instead of being a fan coming through the door to watch movies, I decided to get a vendor table and set up shop. It was a tough decision because I still wanted to be able to sit and watch some of the great lineup they had scheduled. But I figured it would be a good way to make a few dollars and also do a little promotion for the website. Being behind the table was very different this time around. Yes, we did get to sell some books and other merch that we had, but we were stuck behind the table for the most part.

Once again, they had an incredible lineup of films, as well as directors Joe Dante and John Hancock as guests. They were screening Dante's *Piranha* (1978) and Hancock's much underrated *Let's Scare Jessica to Death* (1971), as well as many others. Rusty Nails, the promoter, always insisted back then that any autographs would be free, which I always gave him credit for.

It really is a double-edged sword at these events. It is always great to be able to sit in the theater and watch these great classic pieces of genre cinema on the big screen, but after four or five titles, it can get a bit exhausting. Being out in lobby behind our tables, it gave us a chance to chat with a bunch of different friends and fans as they were coming in and out of the theater, which is always a lot of fun. The problem is that after about 9pm, the only time people are really out in the lobby is in between the features. So there would be a mad rush for about five or ten minutes, until the next movie started and then everyone would be back inside. So it can be quite slow and tiresome out there. But that is the choice we made, for better or worse.

For the next four years, we set up at the Massacre, popping in to watch a few movies here and there. But the fun and excitement of being a vendor at these marathons was starting to wear thin. We were set up right outside the theater doors, so once the films let out, there would be a massive amount of people trying to get out of the theater, either going to the bathrooms, down to the lobby and concession area, or just somewhere to stretch their legs. This made it kind of tough for people to even get to our table, let alone buy anything. So in 2011, we decided to go back to being fans again and just come out to watch the movies. We did this for the next couple of years and always had a great time, and it was kind of nice not to have to worry about watching our table. Deep down though... I missed it. A lot.

In 2012, something else happened. Rusty parted ways with the Music Box and started his own 24-hour marathon at a different theater, calling it just The Massacre, and the Music Box Massacre became The Music Box of Horrors. Some things were a little different but it was still a great time with an amazing lineup of films with Rusty's Massacre usually held a week before or after The Music Box of Horrors. I have to say it is kind of nice to have not one, but now two 24-hour marathons. Granted, it would be nicer if they were maybe a few months apart instead of a week... Whoops, there's my Grumpy Old Man Syndrome flaring up again.

By 2014, I decided it was time once again to set up as a vendor at the Music Box and had a great time doing so. We were the only dealers there, since the theater was in the middle of building a new lounge area, incorporating the building next door. This eventually changed the whole layout of the main lobby, allowing for more vendor space. We've been setting up there ever since in the new lounge area, which has just been great. I think the first year we were there, people were still getting used to the fact that there was another room, so it didn't feel like we were getting as much traffic, but over time people have gotten used to it, especially when guests come into the lounge to sign autographs.

As of this writing, the Music Box is approaching its 15th year of their movie marathons, and I'm thrilled they continue to support to the Chicago horror community by holding these events. Over the years, I've had the opportunity to experience some of the best of the genre, films like *Burn Witch Burn* (1962), Tod Browning's *Freaks* (1932), Michael Powell's *Peeping Tom* (1960), *Eyes Without a Face* (1959), *Isle of the Dead* (1945), *Pontypool* (2008), *Dark Night of the Scarecrow* (1981), *Theater of Blood* (1973), Hammer's *Vampire Lovers* (1970) and so many more. I've also had the chance to meet some of the people behind these movies, people like directors Clive Barker, Mariano Baino, and Joe Zito. Just as important, I've got to meet and make so many new friends and have countless conversations about these movies that we all love so much. I will be forever grateful to the Ryan Oestreich, the General Manager of the Music Box, and Will Morris, who programs the marathons now, as well as all the people working at the Music Box. Here's hoping this tradition continues for many years to come.

As you can tell, over the last three decades, I've had the joy of meeting a lot of wonderful people at these events. Through all the late-night debates, movie recommendations, meals both lousy and amazing, horrible weather, inept event organization, long road trips, and sleepless nights, conventions are places to meet other like-minded folks, share a common bond, and make connections. Movie screenings come and go. Posters and other collectibles are added to collections, only to be traded or sold later on. But the friends you make in life can last forever. That is the reason why I keep coming back to these shows. I'm sure there will always be something for me to complain about. Sometimes it's easy to get frustrated with the changes that come to something you feel so passionate about. But, at their heart, conventions are special places for fans like us to come together, to celebrate what we love with those we're lucky enough to share it all with. I hope you'll take the opportunity to go to a convention, a memorabilia show, or movie marathon and create your own adventures, forge your own friendships, and make your own memories sharing your love of the horror genre with others. That, at its core, is what fandom, and life, is all about.

25

Epilogue... Now What?

"I wasted my time 'til time wasted me."

"When the Crowds Are Gone," Savatage

Hold on there... I'm not quite finished just yet.

You're obviously a fan of the genre and want to help keep it alive and going, right? So the question now comes to what are *YOU* going to do to "Discover the Horror?" Will you start to dig deeper into our Horror History, learning about those who came before, the ones responsible for working in horror cinema for the last hundred years? Will you seek out some of the many classics that you haven't gotten around to yet? Will you reach outside of your comfort zone and experiment with different subgenres to expand your interests, even if it is something as simple as watching a film with subtitles? Be creative with it. Decide that you're going to watch 20 Boris Karloff movies you've never seen before over the course of the year... or in a single month! Or find and watch and re-watch all the versions of Dracula you can find. Dig deeper.

It doesn't stop there though. Pay it forward! Spread the word! If you take on one of these challenges, or you've just seen a movie you like, old or new, let people know. Start a blog. A podcast. Or even something as simple as posting reviews on Amazon or IMDB. Also, with those reviews, try and stay positive and constructive. That doesn't mean you have to love everything. There will be times when you won't, but be specific and intelligent in your criticism, rather than dropping an unhelpful "Dude... that sucked." Let's continue to show that horror fans are not the death-obsessed, drugged-out, psychotic cretin stereotypes that "normal" people try to make us out to be. I mean, sure I like death and all, but I wouldn't say I'm really obsessed with it....

Build your community. Start a movie night at your house. Invite a few friends over and have a theme-based viewing party. Maybe a few Hammer films. Or some giant monster movies from the '50s. Try to show films that your fellow fiends haven't seen before, introducing them to something new. Maybe take turns bringing the flicks. And try to make it a continuing event.

Plus, you can also start your own Turkey Day! I have a dream that at some point in the future, there will be Turkey Day events being held across the world on the Black Friday after Thanksgiving, with everyone reporting in throughout the day what they are watching. How cool would that be?!?! The whole point is to celebrate the genre and what better way to do that than amongst friends.

The most important part is to have fun and always feed your passion.

The main narrative of *Frankenstein* follows a man who creates something and then abandons it, not wanting or caring to know what happened to it. As much as Shelley's story and all the film versions over the years have been a big part of my life, it's ironic then that the book you hold in your hands is the complete opposite. I am proud of what I've accomplished here and hope to see it move into the world making a positive mark, no matter how big or small. If it helps one horror film fan realize that they are not alone and helps them find the means by which to feed their passion, then I've succeeded. Plus, I'm at the point that I really don't care what normal society thinks of us horror fans. I know that we are some of the kindest, nicest, creative, and intelligent people out there.

This book has been a very long journey for me. I honestly can't remember when the idea for writing it formed in my head. As personal as some of these stories are, it has been great to revisit these old memories. Writing them down, I've had a lot of smiles and even laughed out loud a few times over moments I had almost forgotten, remembering and appreciating the fellow fiends who have made the past few decades so enjoyable.

So until the next movie marathon, convention, or Turkey Day, just remember this life is way too short not to enjoy yourself. Always remember to have fun, feed your passion, and to Discover the Horror!

About The Author

While Jon Kitley continues to be a Cinematic Archeologist, he is also a staff writer for *HorrorHound* magazine, where you can find his Rondo Award-winning column, They Came from the Krypt. His work has also appeared in *Evilspeak* magazine, as well as in the books *Horror 101: The A-List of Horror Films and Monster Movies*, *Hidden Horror*, *When Animals Attack*, and *Strange Blood*. He has also appeared in several documentaries, such as *Monster Madness: The Golden Age of the Horror Film*, *Monster Madness: The Gothic Revival of Horror*, and *Fanex Files: Hammer Films*, as well as in Shout Factory's *Horror Hunters*! When not attending multiple horror conventions, 24-hour movie marathons, and hitting the drive-ins, he is hard at work on his website Kitley's Krypt, which has been helping fans Discover the Horror since 1998.

Kitley's Krypt
P.O. Box 2921
Aurora, IL 60507

www.kitleyskrypt.com

jon@kitleyskrypt.com

Facebook: Kitley's Krypt
Twitter: @kitleyskrypt
Instagram: @jonkitley

www.ingramcontent.com/pod-product-compliance
Lightning Source LLC
Chambersburg PA
CBHW051041160426
43193CB00010B/1027